MICHAEL DAVIE

TITANIC

Michael Davie was a leading British journalist. He was a reporter, columnist, and editor for the London *Observer* and the Melbourne (Australia) *Age*, and wrote books on topics as varied as Lyndon B. Johnson, California, and cricket. He died in 2005.

Dave Gittins lives in Adelaide, South Australia. He is the author of *Titanic: Monument and Warning* and coauthor of *Report into the Loss of the SS Titanic: A Centennial Reappraisal*.

TITANIC

TITANIC

THE DEATH AND LIFE OF A LEGEND

MICHAEL DAVIE

UPDATED AND REVISED BY DAVE GITTINS

Vintage Books
A Division of Random House, Inc.
New York

FIRST VINTAGE BOOKS EDITION, APRIL 2012

The poem "Master and Man" by Ben Hecht was originally published in
The Grand Rapids Herald, April 19, 1912.

The Library of Congress has cataloged the Knopf edition as follows:
Davie, Michael.
Titanic : the death and life of a legend.
Bibliography: p.
Includes index.
p. cm.
1. Titanic (steamship). 2. Shipwrecks—North Atlantic Ocean. I. Title.
G530.T6D38 1987
363.1'23'091631 86-46021

Vintage ISBN: 978-0-307-94839-7

www.vintagebooks.com

Printed in the United States of America
10 9 8 7 6 5 4 3 2 1

To Peter

CONTENTS

ILLUSTRATIONS

Colonel and Mrs. J. J. Astor.

Survivors from the *Titanic* approaching the *Carpathia*.

Following page 172

Senator William Alden Smith, chairman of the U.S. Senate inquiry.

J. Bruce Ismay, hand to moustache, giving evidence to the Senate inquiry in the Waldorf-Astoria Hotel, New York.

Lady Duff Gordon.

Captain Lord.

Guglielmo Marconi (*right*) with Godfrey Isaacs.

Harold Bride being carried off the *Carpathia* in New York.

All these Southampton children lost a father, brother, uncle, or cousin on the *Titanic*.

J. Bruce Ismay giving evidence to the British inquiry.

Outside the White Star offices in Southampton; drawn for the *Sphere* by H. M. Paget.

Artist's impression of Quartermaster Hitchins giving evidence to the British inquiry.

Lord Mersey (*right*) and his son, the Hon. Clive Bigham, arriving at the British inquiry.

Embalming a corpse aboard the *Mackay-Bennett*.

Undertakers and coffins on the jetty in Halifax, Nova Scotia, awaiting bodies picked up by the *Mackay-Bennett*.

Dr. Robert Ballard.

Members of the Franco-American team that found the *Titanic*. Standing in front of *Argo* (*from left to right*): Jean-Louis Michel; Lieutenant George Rey, U.S. Navy; Jean Jarry; Dr. Robert Ballard; and Bernard Pillaud.

The research vessel *Knorr* returning to Woods Hole in September 1985.

Two cranes, still locked into position on the deck of the
Titanic on the seabed.

Bottles of wine, including French Bordeaux, scattered over
the ocean floor around the wreck. A photograph taken
by the Woods Hole expedition of 1985.

ACKNOWLEDGMENTS

My thanks are due especially to the following: Anne Chisholm, Archibald Chisholm, Sir Andrew Duff Gordon, John Grigg, Mrs. Dorothy Ismay, Edward S. Kamuda, Russ Lownds, Howard Matson, Viscount Mersey, Edith Newhall, Patrick Stenson, Jesse Stoecker, Robert Straus, John B. Thayer, and members of the Halifax Maritime Museum, the Halifax Public Archives, Harland & Wolff, the International Ice Patrol, the Library of Congress, the Marine Library of the Department of Transport, the New York Public Library, the Philadelphia Maritime Museum, the Public Record Office, the Southampton Public Library, the Ulster Folk and Transport Museum, the Widener Branch of the Free Library of Philadelphia, and the Woods Hole Oceanographic Institution. Most generously, Michael Moss of the University of Glasgow made available before publication his research for the official history of Harland & Wolff.

Copyright photographic material is reproduced by permission of the following: the Ulster Folk and Transport Museum; Harland & Wolff; Radio Times Hulton Picture Library; Beken of Cowes; the *Cork Examiner;* the *Illustrated*

London News; the *Southampton Echo;* the Mercantile Marine Service Association; the Marconi Company; Halifax Public Archives; the Woods Hole Oceanographic Institution; Popperfoto; and Associated Press.

While every effort has been made to trace the correct owners of all copyright material reproduced in this book, the publishers regret any errors of attribution that may have unwittingly occurred and will be happy to make suitable acknowledgment in any future editions.

FOREWORD

During his career as a journalist and newspaper editor in the U.K. and Australia, Michael Davie (1924–2005) wrote on a wide range of topics, including international relations, religion, American politics, cricket, and much in between. Though he would self-deprecatingly call himself a "scribbler," the prose style in his newspaper stories and his several books was of the highest quality, combining, as a former colleague described, "a graceful style with a sharp edge." Many younger journalists, who worked with him at *The Observer*, or during his later time as editor of *The Age* in Melbourne, Australia, remembered him as a well-loved mentor.

Davie brought special qualifications to the story of the *Titanic*. The reporting skills and storytelling ability he'd learned in the newsroom take the book beyond a dry recitation of discovered facts, and his considerable knowledge of English and American politics—displayed in his books on Lord Beaverbrook and President Lyndon Johnson—inform this history of a tragedy that linked these nations. He also had experience at sea. Davie's Oxford education was interrupted when as a member of the Royal Navy Volunteer Reserve he served from 1942 to 1946. Our author thus combined talent at the typewriter with knowledge of the hard realities of the sea.

There was even a tenuous, personal connection to the *Titanic* tragedy. For many years his editor at *The Observer* was David Astor, a member of the wealthy Anglo-American family, whose most famous member, John Jacob Astor IV, was among those lost at sea.

This book was the product of very extensive research. Davie traveled widely, visiting many places associated with *Titanic*. He contacted relatives of those involved in the story and gained insights into their backgrounds. The ship herself is put into the context of her time and its political and financial machinations, and the complexities of the ship's ownership are explained in useful detail. Context was clearly important to Davie. He ties the *Titanic* disaster to more recent large-scale transportation tragedies, such as the *Challenger* disaster, which was still fresh to readers the year this book was first published.

Davie's book is as much a psychological portrait of the protagonists as it is a technical investigation of the mechanics of the sinking, and he gives fascinating portraits of characters such as Bruce Ismay; John Thayer, Jr.; Sir Cosmo Duff Gordon, and others. Lord Mersey is well covered, as is Senator William Smith. Guglielmo Marconi's relationship with the press is examined in considerable detail and the inventor receives less deference than was accorded him in the *Titanic* inquiries of 1912. Sir Rufus Isaacs's involvement with Marconi's shares is examined. Cupboards are shaken and skeletons rattled.

There is very little that is speculative, but Davie allows himself to consider the state of mind of Bruce Ismay, and it is telling that he provides a more objective and sympathetic portrait of the man who would later become the chief villain of the story. This was novel at the time, as other writers had been more concerned with imagining Captain Smith's thinking.

Drawing on foreign office archives, Davie looks at the official British attitude to the American inquiry into the disaster and considers the value of its findings. Lord Mersey's inquiry is examined and the question of whitewash considered. This section is aided by Davie's knowledge of the workings of British politics.

There is room for a little frivolity and Davie enjoys recounting some of the nuttier plans to raise the *Titanic* wreck.

Topics little seen in other books include the foundation of the Titanic Historical Society and the activities of the Woods Hole Oceanographic Institution. There is a subdued final chapter on Halifax, the last resting place of many of *Titanic*'s company.

This is not a book of romance and derring-do but a sober account of the disaster and its aftermath. Davie's achieve ment was to make the saga interesting, richly detailed, and readable. In the long *Titanic* bibliography, it has a high place, regardless of the passing years.

A NOTE ON UPDATES

In the more than two decades that have passed since the publication of *Titanic: The Death and Life of a Legend,* many new technical details have been discovered that shed light on how the ship went down. Indeed, while this book was in preparation, the biggest breakthrough in *Titanic* studies had just occurred, when a joint French/American expedition discovered the wreck of *Titanic* on September 1, 1985. The team was headed by Jean-Louis Michel of IFREMER

(Institut Français de Recherche pour l'Exploitation de la Mer) and Dr. Robert Ballard, of Woods Hole Oceanographic Institution. They discovered the remains on the ocean floor, lying under almost two and a half miles of water. Information about the wreck was released piecemeal and Michael Davie had only incomplete and inaccurate material to work with as his date for publication drew near. Consequently, some of the facts in the book required updating for this reprint. Small amendments have been incorporated into the original text and included as footnotes, and longer discussions of some of the technical details of the sinking are included in the appendix.

—Dave Gittins, November 16, 2011

INTRODUCTION

The keel of the White Star liner *Titanic* was laid down at the Harland & Wolff shipyards, Belfast, in 1909. She was launched on May 31, 1911, and sailed on her maiden voyage from Southampton to New York, via Cherbourg and Queenstown, on April 10, 1912. With a gross tonnage of 46,328 tons, she was the largest ship afloat; 882 feet 9 inches long, 92 feet 6 inches wide, 8 decks rising to the height of an 11-story building. On the fifth day after the voyage began, at 11:40 p.m. on Sunday, April 14, she hit an iceberg and was badly damaged. Two hours and forty minutes later she sank. Of the 2,208 passengers and crew, 712 escaped in sixteen lifeboats and four collapsible boats, two of which were disabled: 1,496 died, by hypothermia or drowning, including her master, Captain Edward Smith.★ At dawn on April 15 the Cunard liner *Carpathia,* having heard the *Titanic*'s distress calls from about fifty miles away, arrived at the scene and began picking up survivors. On her return to New York on the evening of Thursday, April

★These figures are from modern researchers, notably Lester Mitcham of New Zealand.—DG

18, she was met by 30,000 people. Next morning, in the Waldorf-Astoria Hotel, a committee of the United States Senate, chaired by Senator William Alden Smith, started to investigate the disaster; thereafter the committee moved to Washington, where its report was published on May 28. A British government inquiry, conducted by a judge, Lord Mersey, began to sit in London on May 2, heard 94 witnesses, and reported on July 30. Between April 17 and June 8, four ships chartered by the White Star Line recovered 328 bodies from the North Atlantic; of these, 209 were taken to Halifax, Nova Scotia; the rest were buried at sea. These are the basic outlines of the sinking of the *Titanic* seventy-five years ago.

The story has retained a remarkable power; no disaster of modern times, neither the San Francisco earthquake of 1906, nor the Colombian volcano of 1985, nor the *Challenger* space shuttle explosion of 1986, nor any of the jumbo jet airliner crashes, nor even the Chernobyl nuclear accident, has excited quite the same horror and fascination. Some disasters are undeniably acts of God, but the *Titanic* sinking has always seemed ambiguous. Although caused by an iceberg, it was also manmade, the result of the state of mind—grandiose, avaricious, and self-confident—of the British and American magnates and engineers who conceived and built the ship.

A further reason why this particular disaster is of permanent interest is that it happened slowly, unlike a jet airliner crash. Nobody expected it. Everyone on board, whether rich or poor, passenger or crew, was confronted with a sudden test and given time to fumble or meet it.

Over the years, many images from the disaster have proved indelible, and many legends and rumors have circulated. Reinvestigating the story, I have found that for most people the facts and rumors are inextricably entwined.

Most people recall that the ship was traveling too fast: had not the captain been urged to set a record? The band was playing as she went down: was it not a hymn, or was it a jazz tune? And the other liner nearby: was there not a ship whose captain would have gone to the rescue if he had not assumed that the rockets he saw and the music he heard wafting across the water were evidence of revelry? And Captain Smith of the *Titanic:* surely the real reason for the collision was that he was drunk, a fact that subsequent inquiries hushed up under pressure from the Board of Trade and the shipping company?

My main purpose in writing this book has been to re-examine the evidence and tell the story as clearly and comprehensively as possible, trying to sift fact from fiction. Although many books have been written about the *Titanic,* none has told the complete story, from the background of the building of the ship to the aftermath of the disaster. The early accounts, like the one by a fluent British journalist and man of letters, Filson Young, tended to be full of rhetoric but short on facts. Survivors quickly published moving but inevitably incomplete accounts. The United States Senate and the British Board of Trade inquiries produced hundreds of pages of verbatim testimony. Ballads were composed; memorials erected; sermons preached. The early books mostly turned the tragedy into a triumph for Anglo-Saxon phlegm. "Before the doomed ship was engulfed in the devouring waters," wrote Filson Young, "there was a drama upon her decks more wonderful in its dignity and splendor than any that has been invented by the imagination." Such remarks sparked off a vivid exchange as early as May 1912 between two great literary figures of the time, Bernard Shaw and Conan Doyle. Shaw, for the iconoclasts, pointed out the discrepancies between the tales of heroism written up by the press and the grim realities revealed by the inquiries. "The occasion has been disgraced by a callous outbreak of romantic lying," he proclaimed. Conan Doyle, for the conservatives and traditionalists, maintained that the captain, crew, and survivors had indeed behaved in a heroic, exemplary, and quintessentially British manner. No subsequent account has settled the argument conclusively.

The best known book on the *Titanic,* Walter Lord's *A Night to Remember,* published thirty years ago, simply told the powerful story of the disaster itself, blow by blow. Subsequent writers have looked behind the facts but have tended to promote a particular line or theory. Thus Geoffrey Marcus, in *The Maiden Voyage,* published in 1969, states his suspicion of all official inquiries and argues that the British commission under Lord Mersey was a whitewash designed to protect the White Star shipping line and their officers. A book by an American clinical psychologist from Michigan, Wyn Craig Wade, aims to vindicate the senator from Michigan, William Alden Smith, who conducted the U.S. inquiry, and turn him into the hero of the story. In these books one sometimes hears the grinding of an ideological or nationalistic axe.

I have approached the *Titanic* story as a reporter but have also tried to explain its causes and repercussions; to see how the ship symbolized the shift of power across the Atlantic from Europe to the United States, and why this particular disaster has cast such a long shadow down seven decades, becoming a metaphor for the human predicament. I have visited, in North America, Northern Ireland, and England, the main places that feature in the story, including Woods Hole, where most of the scientists who located and inspected the wreck of the *Titanic* in the summers of 1985 and 1986 are based. I have talked to experts and to collectors and to the families and friends of survivors. I have not gone back to the handful of remaining survivors themselves—two or three in Britain, less than two dozen in the United States; they were very young then and are of advanced age now; long ago, they said what they had to say.

The story is not ended yet. The miraculous underwater photographs and film taken by the Woods Hole expeditions have given it a bizarre new perspective. The *Titanic* has reappeared; and the ship herself is set to be the final survivor. The last member of the crew, Sidney Daniels, died in Portsmouth in 1983. But the *Titanic* is still there, in reasonable shape, and one of the first photographs of her showed the crow's nest in which Fred Fleet, the look out man, suddenly yanked his bell-pull three times, telephoned the bridge, and called out, "Iceberg right ahead!" Many years after the sinking, Fred Fleet hanged himself on a clothes post in his brother-in-law's garden, but the telephone is still intact, two and a half miles down, on the bed of the Atlantic. Precisely what else may be down there, perhaps scattered across a mile or more of the ocean floor, will not be known for years yet, if ever. Wild schemes have been published that envisage raising the ship, towing her back to Belfast, where she was built, refitting her, and sailing her off to complete her maiden voyage, on the if-at-first-you-don't-succeed principle. The *Titanic* has always inspired fantasies.

From the world's imagination the *Titanic* never altogether vanished. She has inspired novels, an opera, and poems—latterly of a more sardonic kind than the heroic writings that immediately followed the sinking. The disaster has been seen as a turning point in history, a symbol of the change from a reasonably settled world to much more alarming times: "The event," as John Thayer of Philadelphia wrote twenty-eight years after he was rescued, "which not only made the world rub its eyes and awake, but woke it with a start, keeping it moving at a rapidly accelerating pace ever since, with less and less peace, satisfaction and happiness . . . To my mind, the world of today awoke April 15, 1912." Osbert Sitwell described the sinking as "a symbol of the approaching fate of Western Civilization."

Even at the time, and certainly ever since, the *Titanic* has been seen as a prime example of man tempting fate, or technological hubris, the event that made people wonder for the first time whether man's ingenuity would necessarily produce the beneficent results he hoped and expected it would. Some thought that the disaster, because it was so plainly the result of overweening pride, would teach the world a lesson. As the Bishop of Winchester said, preaching a sermon on the Sunday after the disaster, the iceberg had the right to be there; the *Titanic* did not. But her begetters' spiritual successors, not only in shipbuilding, continued on their merry way. Nevertheless, the *Titanic* is still lodged in people's minds as a warning, even though unheeded, of the dangers of human presumption.

Traveling around, I have been surprised to find how many mysteries still bedevil the event. Did the people who built her really think her unsinkable? How can anyone have thought it safe to belt through a region of ice at high speed? Did the rich really come off best? Should the half-filled lifeboats have tried harder to rescue the drowning? Was Captain Lord of the *Californian,* the ship that failed to go to the *Titanic*'s rescue, rightly condemned? What was the role of the president of the huge international shipping combine that owned the *Titanic*—J. Bruce Ismay—who unlike his skipper did not go down with his ship? What was Marconi up to, and how was the *Titanic* linked to the Marconi scandal? Was Senator Smith as incompetent as the British government privately thought? Was there a Lord Mersey cover-up?

I heard echoes of the *Titanic* story in recent events. The dispute in Whitehall, in 1985–86, about the sale of Westland Helicopters to an American giant closely parallels the concern felt by ministers at the turn of the century over predatory American attitudes to the proud British transatlantic shipping lines. In the gigantic "build-up shop" at Harland & Wolff, I saw posters saying "No" to the 1985 Hillsborough agreement between Britain and the Republic of Ireland—a reminder that the *Titanic* and the Home Rule Bill of 1912 were contemporaneous, and that the "reef" on which the final Home Rule scheme was "shipwrecked" (the words used in the standard constitutional history of modern Britain by D. L. Keir) was the fierce provincial sense of nationality of Ulstermen—especially as represented by the Protestant workers in the Harland & Wolff shipyards who joined Carson's Ulster volunteers to prepare for armed resistance to Home Rule. Again, when part of a British Airways jumbo jet landed in the garden of a house in Boston, late in 1985, the pilots' spokesman who said that aircraft inspection regulations had not kept up with airline developments was echoing the furor which followed the revelation in 1912 that Board of Trade rules about safety at sea had been outdated by advances in shipping technology, also across the Atlantic. When *Challenger* exploded, someone at Cape Canaveral said that such an accident had been thought impossible. The Chernobyl fireball provoked exactly the same alarm about man tempting fate that had first been heard seven decades earlier. But the loudest echo is still of the faint sound, described by a fireman, Jack Podesta, as "like tearing a piece of calico, nothing more," that the iceberg made as it pierced the hull of the *Titanic*.

TITANIC

I

THE EVIL DREAM

In the 1860s, British industry was entering the most expan-
sive and prosperous era it has ever known or is ever likely
to know. In particular, shipbuilding and transatlantic traffic were growing in volume year by year. It is impossible
to understand the genesis of the *Titanic* without looking
at the men who conceived the idea of a giant ship; and
impossible to understand them, and the reasons why they
ever imagined such an extraordinary vessel, without some
notion of the tortuous and ruthlessly competitive international shipping business—British, German, American—of
which they were part.

The man behind the *Titanic,* as it happens, was Canadian. He was born in Quebec in 1847 as William James
Pirrie, the son of A. J. Pirrie, an Ulsterman of Scottish
descent. His mother was also from Ulster, a member of
the Montgomery family. After the father died, mother and
son returned to Ireland, where the boy was apprenticed at
the age of fifteen to the shipbuilding and engineering firm
of Harland & Wolff. Pirrie was a partner in Harland &
Wolff by the time he was twenty-seven. During the next
half century, largely thanks to his leadership, it became the

greatest shipyard in the world and the birthplace of the
Titanic.

People these days are inclined to think that the *Titanic* was
a freak, a huge ship of unique size and luxury. This misun-
derstanding underrates the scale of the enterprise. Pirrie's
idea, conceived in 1907, was that his firm, in partnership
with the White Star Line, would build not one but three
monster transatlantic liners. They would sweep the opposition off the seas. The first would be named the *Olympic;* the
second the *Titanic;* and the third—the *Britannic.*

All three were built. The *Olympic* had an illustrious
career, carrying more troops than any other vessel in World
War I. The *Britannic* was sunk by a German mine in 1916
while serving as a hospital ship. Nowadays, nobody outside the passionate fraternity of lovers of old ships remem-
bers this useful pair. But the *Titanic* became, as she has
remained, the best known of all ships to the man in the
street, her name springing to mind more readily than the
Golden Hind, the USS *Arizona,* or HMS *Victory.*

It is odd that Pirrie, the bold prime mover, has disappeared so completely from the story. Had he sailed in the
Titanic on her maiden voyage, as he fully intended, he would
have been better known. He would either have drowned,
in which case he would have been as closely associated
with the ship as her skipper, Captain Smith, and her richest
passenger, Colonel J. J. Astor; or he would have escaped,
in which case he would have been as universally reviled as
the chairman of White Star who got away in one of the
last lifeboats, J. Bruce Ismay. As it was, his doctor forbade
Pirrie to take the trip because of prostate trouble; he did
not testify in the much-publicized official inquiries that
followed though by June his health was much improved;
and after their reports came out it was too late for anyone to ask him awkward questions. His role receded into

the past. His hair turned white during his illness, but he remained the great shipbuilder. Indeed the business done by his world-beating yards actually boomed, because they reconstructed many ships after the disaster to make them conform to the new rules officially imposed as a result of the defects exposed in their prize product. In World War I, Lord Pirrie was in charge of all British merchant shipbuilding. He was made a baron in 1909 and became a viscount in 1921. He died at sea in 1924 from pneumonia in the Panama Canal, returning with his wife from a voyage on Harland & Wolff business to South America.

To find the source of Pirrie's grand ideas and confidence, we need to look back at the atmosphere of those early years. Belfast had a long shipbuilding tradition, but it was only around the time Pirrie became an apprentice that Harland & Wolff started on its rapid rise to world dominance. The founding father was a restless engineering genius from Yorkshire, Edward Harland, who in 1858 bought a small boatbuilding business on Queen's Island, which is still part of the Harland & Wolff site today. Harland was no traditionalist. His main reforms, according to his successors in Belfast, were two: he replaced wooden upper decks with iron decks, thus in effect turning the hull into a box girder of immensely greater strength; and he changed the shape of the hulls by giving them a flat bottom and square bilges, thus increasing their capacity. He also did away with the relics of sailing-ship days, bowsprits and figureheads, although his steamships were still carrying sails until nearly the end of the century.

The stroke of luck in Harland's career was to catch the eye, early on, of Hamburg Jews. One of them, a financier named Gustavus Schwabe, came to Liverpool and put money into a rising local shipping firm, the Bibby Line, and gave repair and building contracts to Harland.

Schwabe's nephew, an engineer like Harland, became Harland's partner. His name was Gustav Wolff. In Harland & Wolff's present-day order book, which lists in numerical order the 1,700 ships they have built in their hundred-and-fifty-year history, numbers one, two, and three are Bibby Line ships.

Harland and Wolff joined forces just before Pirrie arrived in their yards as an apprentice. With every year that passed, their business expanded. In 1864 the gross tonnage of the ships they built was 30,000 tons. In 1884 the figure was 104,000. Pirrie's career was contemporaneous with the development of steel shipbuilding, and he himself was in the forefront of all the important advances in naval architecture and marine engineering. He took over as chairman when Harland died in 1894; so he was thirty years under Harland, and thirty years on his own as chairman.

He was more than chairman: he was a dictator. Physically, he was small and ferociously energetic. He craved public recognition. He stood out from his rivals because he was not only a master-technocrat but a master-businessman. The members of his board were ciphers. He secured the orders for ships himself, built them to his own designs with little more than a general specification from the clients, and charged them the building costs plus a 4 percent commission for Harland & Wolff—a highly satisfactory way of doing business. (It was when the firm built the *Canberra* for P&O on a fixed-price contract that it lost millions and nearly went broke.) Apart from Pirrie, nobody knew or was even allowed to discuss his firm's finances; one of the ship architects who inadvertently became involved in financial talks with a shipowner "stood down," supposedly due to bad health. When Pirrie was away from Belfast, meetings were chaired by his wife.

Though forgotten now, Pirrie was lauded in his own

day, when engineers were national figures. The celebrated journalist W. T. Stead, who was drowned in the *Titanic,* praised Pirrie's "foresight, optimism, incessant industry and selection of able lieutenants (a sure sign of superior ability)" and proclaimed that he had developed "the greatest business of the kind that has existed in the world since men first began to go down to the seas in ships." The verdict of the *Dictionary of National Biography* is that he was "the creator of the big ship."

How did this happen? The starting point may be said to have been the alliance between Harland & Wolff and White Star.

The important new figure who enters the story here is the formidable T. H. Ismay. His father had been a boatbuilder in a small way in Maryport, Cumberland. In 1869 — not long after Pirrie joined Harland & Wolff—T. H. Ismay bought, with Schwabe's financial backing, the flag of White Star, a company that had made a name on the Australian run, shipping optimistic emigrants to the goldfields.

White Star's history, as it happened, contained an odd prelude to the *Titanic.* In 1863 the company took delivery of a fine ship called the *Royal Standard,* advertised as the latest word in seagoing comfort: "Her saloons are spacious and handsomely furnished, with everything requisite for the voyage, including bedding, linen, piano, library, etc." She was launched in the summer of 1863 and on April 4, 1864, fourteen days out of Melbourne and homeward bound, she struck an iceberg. "Destruction seemed inevitable," said her master. She was making ten knots under sail when she struck; the iceberg towered 600 feet above her, he said. The main and mizzen masts snapped, the starboard lifeboat was smashed, and her starboard quarter was stove in, even though her hull was of iron. For half an hour the ship rubbed along the flank of the iceberg, reckoned by the master to be a quarter of a mile long, before she could break away; thirty-five days later she limped into Rio.

The Australian run was profitable, but it was small beer, as Schwabe and Ismay saw, by comparison with the glittering new opportunities offered by the Atlantic. The whole secret of the growth of the shipping companies and the size of the ships they built is to be found in the extraordinary expansion, unparalleled in history, of the population of the United States. During the half century between 1840, when Samuel Cunard's *Britannia* inaugurated the first transatlantic steamship service, and 1890, trade between the United States and Britain rose sevenfold, in cotton, tobacco, and wheat, with Liverpool as its focus. At the same time, the population of the United States quadrupled. Cunard was not slow to realize that its business could not expand by relying on mail, cargo, and first-class passengers alone; so it also started to carry steerage passengers, cashing in on the flood of immigrants from Britain as well as continental Europe. Bigger ships and longer passenger lists were the keys to profit; but the expanding market also attracted competitors. Ismay's White Star, financed by Schwabe and building all its ships at Harland & Wolff yards, was challenging Cunard on the Atlantic routes by the early 1870s; and by the 1880s the great German shipowners joined the battle as well.

Then came the Americans and J. P. Morgan. The impact of American capital on the shipping business had been long delayed, partly because of the American Civil War, and partly because the new breed of industrialists and financiers had been fully occupied opening up the continent with oil, steel, and railways. But when it came it was devastating. It started when a company that later became part of the Morgan combine acquired Inman Lines of Liverpool, which gave the Americans access to British shipbuilding technology. At White Star, correctly identifying the threat,

T. H. Ismay attempted to assemble a consortium of British shipowners to save the ailing company, but the other shipowners would not listen to him. The issues and arguments were much the same as those of 1986, when the British Cabinet split over whether Westland Helicopters should be sold to the American giant, Sikorsky. Ismay's warnings, like those of the Minister of Defence, Michael Heseltine, went unheeded.

It was one of the few failures of Ismay's career and one that he always regretted. Shortly before he died in 1899, leaving more than a million pounds, an interviewer asked him about his principles of business success. He named two. First, he said, don't be too greedy; always let someone else make a bit. Second, never let a weak man go out of your trade if it means letting a strong one in. He instanced the shipowners' refusal to save Inman. "And now," he said, "we have an American railway company come into the trade, with millions at its back, running under a well-known British flag, and setting us all to work building whether we want it or not."

Morgan's aim was to establish in the Atlantic the same sort of business that he was used to at home: a monopoly. With Pirrie's help, he forced through an amalgamation with the big German lines, North German Lloyd and Hamburg-Amerika. He then launched the most vicious fare war in shipping history, offering third-class transatlantic passages for as little as £2. His principal target was Cunard. Having driven the company into financial trouble by his price cutting, he then tried to buy it and was only repulsed when the British government, alarmed by the idea of a great British asset passing into foreign hands, came to the rescue with substantial and favorable subsidies. The condition of the subsidies was openly nationalistic. "Under no circumstances shall the management of the company be in the hands of, or the shares of the company held by, other than British subjects."

Pirrie had quickly seen the Morgan threat. The source of much of his business, White Star, was as vulnerable as Cunard, with profits reduced by the fare war causing a shortage of capital for new ships. Schwabe had died in 1890, Ismay in 1899. Ismay's son, J. Bruce Ismay, was relatively inexperienced. Pirrie saw that unless drastic action was taken White Star would drop further and further out of the battle and build fewer and fewer ships in Pirrie's shipyards. His solution was unattractive but practical. Instead of opposing Morgan's ambitions, he supported them. Three years after Ismay senior died, Morgan, with Pirrie as an intermediary, swallowed White Star. The head of Cunard, Lord Inverclyde, acquired considerable prestige from the skillful way he exploited Morgan's bid in order to extract favorable loans from the government, while yielding none of his company's independence. But at the very time that Inverclyde was concluding these advantageous arrangements, J. Bruce Ismay was being forced to sell—not least by the pressure of his father's old ally, Pirrie.

The transaction was a financier's cat's cradle. It had been the International Navigation Company of Philadelphia, with the Pennsylvania Railroad Company, that had acquired Inman Lines. In 1902 the International Navigation Company changed its name to the International Mercantile Marine Company. This company, with Pirrie on the British board, acquired practically all the shares in the Oceanic Steam Navigation Company, which had always owned the ships of the White Star Line, of which Ismay, Imrie & Co. were managers. Morgan then registered the Oceanic Company shares in the name of the International Navigation Company of Liverpool, a subsidiary of the International Mercantile Marine Company, which in its turn transferred the shares to two trust companies in the United States as security for certain bonds.

Given the intricate nature of Morgan's combine, it is not surprising that the absoluteness of his control of White Star was not fully appreciated. The *Titanic* was generally regarded as a British ship. Even Lord Mersey, with his Liverpool background, was taken aback in the Board of Trade inquiry into the *Titanic*'s sinking when he learned that the White Star Company's seagoing rules, under which the *Titanic*, like all other White Star vessels, had been operating, had been drawn up in the United States. Morgan had seen how his bid for Cunard had alarmed the British. With White Star, the appearance of control stayed firmly in Britain. All White Star ships were to be officered by British subjects and to fly the British flag. A majority of the directors were to be British. The original Ismay company of Ismay, Imrie & Co. became a shell, but J. Bruce Ismay remained chairman of White Star and was soon persuaded by Morgan to become president of International Mercantile. The appointment looked impressive on paper, but for J. Bruce Ismay it was a humiliation.

These were significant events in the tilting of industrial power away from Britain and toward the United States. One great British company, Cunard, had had to be bailed out by the government—an early example of state intervention. Another equally prominent British company, virtually a national institution, had been taken over. The effect of the White Star deal was to bring together British technology, in the shape of Harland & Wolff, and American capital. This was the conjunction that produced the *Titanic*.

But it was not changes of ownership alone that produced the drive toward bigger and bigger ships. Despite Ismay senior's complaint that it was the American newcomers who kept the British shipowners building whether they liked it or not, it was an economic force much more fundamental than J. P. Morgan's aggression that constantly pushed the owners forward. Once the technology was available, the growth in the size of ships was unstoppable, whether anyone wanted them or not. Taking emigrants to the United States was more profitable than government mail contracts or high-class passenger traffic. Nor was the emigrant traffic all one way. At one stage, 100,000 disappointed or homesick Britons were annually heading home. The snag was that the emigrant market was wholly unpredictable, depending as it it did on famine or repression or fashion. The seesaw demand meant that the owners needed to look sharp to make the most of it; hence the fare wars, and hence the need to attract and carry more and more passengers, to cover rising costs and make a modest return on capital. As the chairman of the White Star line wrote in Lloyd's List in 1924, looking back at "steamships of the monster type" and their history: "This extensive third-class business has been a very potent factor in the development of the fleets of the principal companies, and has culminated in the superliners of today."

Influenced by narrative paintings of the nineteenth century, we are inclined to assume that the desperate emigrants who poured from the slums of Europe into the slums of New York or Chicago took any ship they could find. But the images of women on deck wearing shawls and surrounded by wide-eyed children are misleading. Cunard took most seriously a complaint from one steerage passenger, evidently representative of many, who said that he had been treated as if the company was doing him a personal favor in conveying him across the Atlantic. It was not only first-class passengers who could be attracted by extra space; so could the huddled masses. Every pressure was in the direction of size. Cunard built the *Bothnia* of 4,555 tons in 1874, the *Umbria* of 7,718 tons in 1884, the *Campania* of 12,950 tons in 1893. White Star replied with the *Teutonic* and the *Majestic*. The Germans by the turn of the century had deployed an imperial race of four-funneled monsters with names to match: *Kaiser Wilhelm der Grosse, Kronprinz Wilhelm, Kaiser Wilhelm II, Kronprinzessin Cecile*. In 1899, as Ismay senior was dying, White Star came up with the *Oceanic*, 17,274 tons and 705 feet long, the first ship to be longer than Brunel's white elephant of 1858, the *Great Eastern*, and the largest steamship in the world.

In the archives of Harland & Wolff is a book of photographs of the *Oceanic* presented to Thomas Andrews, Esq., Pirrie's nephew and later one of the designers of the *Titanic*, with the compliments of Ismay, Imrie. The frontispiece is of Thomas H. Ismay, his hair slightly curled and his determined mouth in a faint smile. The internal decor of the ship is that of an Edwardian country house, not surprisingly, as one of the architects was R. Norman Shaw. The principal saloon featured Ionic pillars. In the smokeroom was a representation of a bacchanalian procession inspired by a poem of Dryden. Carved trophies of fruit and flowers in the style of Grinling Gibbons decorated other parts of the first-class accommodation, and so did allegorical female figures of Great Britain, America, Liverpool, and New York, the last holding a rudder and a coil of rope. A Harland & Wolff archivist has tucked into the back of this lavish book an article from a contemporary magazine, which featured a series of statistics and cartoons to dramatize the size of the new ship. A hen would have to lay an egg every day until the middle of 1967 to produce the number of eggs carried on each trip. The volume of "jams, jellies and marmalade" aboard would fill a jar 6 feet high and 14 feet and 1¾ inches in diameter. Alice of *Alice in Wonderland* was shown standing on a ladder gazing in wonder down into the jar.

The century opened with both White Star and Cunard in a position to move their new ships up a few notches in size. Cunard moved first. The government had given them the subsidies partly so that they would build two big ships that could be turned into armed transports in time of war. By 1907 these two were ready for service, the *Lusitania* and the *Mauretania,* both of them not only larger but much faster than anything afloat. The *Mauretania* at once became especially loved and fashionable. Henry James crossed to England on her in 1911 and met Thomas Edison on board; the liner lifted James across the seas "as if I had been carried in a gigantic grandmother's bosom and the gentle giantess had made but one mighty stride of it from land to land." When she was broken up in 1935, President Franklin D. Roosevelt presented a model of her to the Smithsonian Museum in Washington and wrote a sentimental private memorial, calling her an "old dowager" and recalling the hand-carved panels of Latvian oak in her dining room.

This was the daunting new competition that White Star had to beat. They were running a regular express service from Southampton to New York with the *Teutonic,* the *Oceanic,* and the *Adriatic,* but these were no match for the crack Cunarders. How was White Star to reply? It would be hopelessly uneconomical to try to compete with Cunard for speed. More speed would mean less passenger and cargo space. The leapfrog move must be to go for extreme size, and to attract the urgently needed extra passengers by providing special luxury for the rich and more spacious accommodation for the poor.

It would be wrong to give the impression that everyone was enthusiastic about bigger ships. Complaints about size went back a long time. In 1776 William Julius Mickle

published his translation of *The Lusiad,* Camoens's epic
poem about the discovery of India by Vasco da Gama. He
described *The Lusiad* as "the Epic Poem of the Birth of
Commerce." But he added, in one of his voluminous notes
expounding the growth of trade, that "the Portuguese historians ascribe the shipwreck of many Portuguese vessels
on the voyage between Europe and India to the avarice of
their owners, in building them of an enormous bulk, of
400, 500, and 600 tons." Captain Cook's two vessels, he
observed, had been of 462 and 336 tons. In the nineteenth
century, professional misgivings surfaced when a royal
commission was appointed in 1873 to inquire into "unsea-
worthy ships." One of the leading partners in Cunard,
Charles McIver, told the commission about the danger of
building ships that were too long in relation to their width.
Another prominent Liverpool shipowner, Alfred Hold,
agreed. So did McIver's sons, who were also employed
by Cunard. All three McIvers were forced to resign, and
Cunard set out to rebuild its fleet faster, heavier, and longer
than ever.

Twenty years later, the greatest and most prophetic of
American historians, Henry Adams, visited the World's
Columbian Exposition in Chicago, a display of the wonders of the industrial and artistic world. Eight or ten years
of study, as he explained, had led Adams to think that he
might use the thirteenth century as the unit from which he
could measure motion down to his own time. What could
he learn from the Exposition about the course of history,
and the effect on it of the new sciences? He was especially
concerned to try to understand "the law of acceleration,"
the speed of progress. Fifty years earlier, he reflected, science had taken it for granted that the rate of acceleration
could not last: scientists encouraged laymen to think that
force would be limited in supply. It then emerged that

force was inexhaustible . . . Nothing so revolutionary had happened since the year 300. . . . Impossibilities no longer stood in the way. One's life had fattened on impossibilities. Before the boy [he meant himself] was six years old, he had seen four impossibilities made actual—the ocean steamer, the railway, the electric telegraph, and the Daguerreotype; nor could he ever learn which of the four had most hurried the others to come. He had seen the coal-output of the United States grow from nothing to 300 million tons or more.

Adams was born in 1838, the year when crossing the Atlantic by steamship became feasible for the first time. Railroads had begun by then to radiate out from the eastern cities; Samuel B. Morse sent the first electric telegraph message in 1844. Daguerreotype, the first successful photographic process, was invented in France by Louis Daguerre in 1839. Force, or power, ruled the rate of man's progress, and society had by common accord agreed in measuring its progress by coal output, the world's principal source of energy. The coal output of the world, said Adams, had roughly doubled every ten years between 1840 and 1900. This rate of acceleration might seem exaggerated, but it could be tested. "Perhaps the ocean steamer is nearest unity and easiest to measure, for anyone might hire, in 1905, for a small sum of money, the use of 30,000 steam-horse-power to cross the ocean, and by halving this figure for every ten years he got back to 234 horse-power for 1835, which was accuracy enough for his purposes."

In Chicago, Adams studied with special attention the exhibit by Cunard.

Historical exhibits were common, but they never went far enough; none were thoroughly worked out. One of the best was that of Cunard steamers, but still a student hungry for results found himself obliged to waste a pencil and several sheets of paper trying to calculate exactly when, according to the given increase of power, tonnage, and speed, the growth of the ocean steamer would reach its limits. His figures brought him, he thought, to the year 1927; another generation to spare before force, space, and time should meet. The ocean liner ran the surest line of triangulation to the future, because it was the nearest of man's products to a unity.

It was, in short, the best single example of man's multifarious skills.

Henry Adams published *The Education of Henry Adams,* which contained these reflections, in 1906. They were already out of date, for even he had underestimated the "rate of acceleration." He had written about an ocean steamer generating 30,000 horsepower in 1905. But the Cunarder *Lucania* already generated that amount of power in 1893, and the *Lusitania,* launched the year after *The Education* was published, generated 68,000 horsepower. (His prediction about the date of the biggest ocean liner was only a decade too early: Cunard's *Queen Elizabeth,* whose maiden voyage had to be postponed because of World War II, was the biggest genuine liner ever built, at 83,673 gross tons.)

The decision to build White Star's three monsters was taken as the *Mauretania* and the *Lusitania* were coming into service. According to tradition, Pirrie and Bruce Ismay met one evening at Pirrie's London house in Belgravia and sketched out their plans "over coffee and cigars." The *Olympic* and the *Titanic* were to be a hundred feet longer than the Cunarders, only four or five knots slower, and at 46,000 tons no less than 15,000 tons bigger. They were to be built regardless of cost, and regardless of complaints from harbor boards that there was no room for them. New York was especially angry. To make the boards realize they were living in the past, Pirrie replied that it was his ambition to build a liner of a thousand feet long, and he did not rule out the possibility of a ship of 100,000 tons.

He certainly thought on a grand scale. At the time he was drawing up the plans, not only was there no dock big enough on either side of the Atlantic to take the new ships, but no yard big enough to build them either. Harland & Wolff had to construct specially strengthened slips to bear the weight.

They are still there. Not long ago, I went to see them, wondering what traces were left of Lord Pirrie's ambitions. At the Belfast docks, in the main Harland & Wolff offices—red brick and little changed since Pirrie's day—I met my guide, Mr. Tommy McCluskie, who led me a hundred yards out of the back door and stopped. We stood surrounded by a wasteland of cracked and discolored concrete, empty apart from a row of parked company cars and scattered piles of rusty metal. "This is where she was built," he said. Then he added wryly, "The *Titanic* is one of our better known vessels."

Away to our right rose two huge yellow gantries, known as Samson and Goliath. Like enormous goal posts, they straddle a dry dock in which four banana boats for Vestey's were recently built all at the same time, a dock so huge that it could accommodate, if a mad latter-day Pirrie required such a thing, a vessel of a million tons. So no theoretical limit to the size of ships had yet been reached? Mr. McCluskie shrugged. "A million tons is possible," he said, "though improbable."★

★ McCluskie was talking about ships of 1,000,000 tons deadweight, about half the size of the largest oil tankers yet built.

In one of the first books written about the *Titanic* after she went down, the journalist and man of letters Filson Young called her "monstrous," an "evil dream," and "unthinkable." Standing in the concrete wasteland, I remembered his rhetoric about her construction. As his mail steamer from Fleetwood glided through the mud flats, he had heard, he claimed, a noise like bees in a giant hive. This "sonorous murmuring," as he drew closer, turned into "the multitudinous clamour of thousands and thousands of blows of metal on metal coming from a veritable forest of iron, a leafless forest of thousands upon thousands of rusty trunks [carrying] a multitude of pigmy men swarming and toiling amid the skeleton iron structures." It was "in this awful womb," Filson Young goes on, "that the *Titanic* took shape." At the sight of it, men held their breaths:

> It was the shape of a ship, a ship so monstrous and unthinkable that it towered high over the buildings and dwarfed the very mountains beside the water. It seemed like some impious blasphemy that man should fashion this most monstrous and ponderable of all his creations into the likeness of a thing that could float upon the yielding waters. . . . Yet, like an evil dream, as it took the shape of a giant ship, all the properties of a ship began to appear and increase in hideous exaggeration. A rudder as big as a giant elm tree, bosses and bearings of propellers as big as the size of a windmill—everything was on a nightmare scale.

Old photographs pinned up in the company photographer's office show that the gantry dominated the shipyard and the city. These days, the biggest structures in the yard, apart from Samson and Goliath, are grain silos, massive sheds, and a fertilizer factory. But harbors and shipyards change slowly. Ships still use the four-mile Victoria Channel between the flats, as the *Titanic* once did. Cave Hill and Black Mountain are unchanged, except for television masts. The spire of St. Joseph's, the church in Dock Road, is still a landmark. One floating relic of *Titanic* days, moored in Milewater Basin, is an old light cruiser, HMS *Caroline*, built by Harland & Wolff and a survivor of the Battle of Jutland, scrupulously cared for and used now as a training base for the naval reserves, and still with her original funnels, masts, and fighting top.

The row of huts used by the foremen who supervised the *Titanic*'s construction is still standing, though now tumbledown, with broken windows. So is the long concrete ramp some thirty feet across with a slope of four or five degrees on which the *Titanic*'s hull was built. Its purpose, Mr. McCluskie explained, was to tilt the hull so that when launched it would slide easily over the greased keelblocks wedged underneath and into the water. The bow would have projected over the end of the ramp. One could estimate where the pygmies had lifted and riveted the plates of the 300 feet of hull ripped open by the iceberg.

Other relics were embedded in the concrete: narrow rails, like tramlines, for the cranes bringing in the plates; and holes the size of half an orange. Mr. McCluskie gouged the mud out of one of these holes with his toecap and revealed a rusty iron ring that would have held the base of one of the wooden posts supporting the scaffolding's outer skeleton. We walked to the far end of the slipway, where it met the water. In the old days, massive dock gates like a high wooden fence stood here to stop incoming tides from flooding the slipway. Because water inevitably seeped through, a pump was needed to pump out the ditch between gates and slipway. This pumping station, built underground, survives, though flooded; peering down into the brown water, you can see the submerged wheel that controlled one of the valves. Somebody turned this wheel on May 31, 1911, when, shortly after noon, in the presence of J. P. Morgan, the dock gates were withdrawn, the hydraulic rams restraining the *Titanic* on the slipway were released and the ship was launched while (according to Filson Young) the "thousands of pigmy men who had roosted in the bare iron branches, who had raised the hideous clamour amid which the giant was born, greeted their handiwork, dropped their tools, and raised their hoarse voices in a cheer. The miracle had happened."

Big ships are not launched at Harland & Wolff today, since—unlike the shorter *Titanic*—they would bend in the middle as the first half reached the water. They are built in the giant dry dock and then floated out. Nor are they riveted; they are welded by machines controlled by computers. In its heyday, Harland & Wolff employed 40,000 or 50,000 men; now, partly because of new technology and partly because of a slump in shipbuilding, it employs 6,300, which accounts for the deserted nature of much of its 300 acres and for the silence that is the most striking difference between the yards now and the yards in 1911.

The glories as well as the decibels have declined since 1911, but it is still easy to find old men whose self-esteem is grounded on the skill they showed at the shipyards in the days when Harland & Wolff led the world.*

---

* Since this book was first published, Harland and Wolff has undergone many changes. For some years after Davie's visit it continued to build ships, including very large oil tankers and highly specialized vessels for the offshore oil industry. Its finances were always shaky and highly dependent on government handouts. It eventually fell into the hands of Fred. Olsen Energy PLC. Its last ship was *Anvil Point,* hull number 1742, which was delivered to the Ministry of Defence in 2003. In the following years its staff declined to as few as 120 and it eked out an existence as an engineering consultancy.

Today the staff has increased to more than 500 and the company is deeply involved with offshore wind farms and other specialized structures. All kinds of ship repairs and maintenance are carried out, using its building dock, the largest in Western Europe. It has renewed its ties with *Titanic* by winning a contract to refurbish *Nomadic,* the tender

One of them, Mr. Dick Sweeney, keeps a rivet of *Titanic* vintage in his house for old times' sake, a big squat nail three inches long, made of pure iron and as thick as a man's thumb. Three million rivets like this went into the *Titanic;* some of them are visible in the underwater photographs of the wreck taken in the summers of 1985 and 1986. In his trim front room on a hillside overlooking the shipyards, Mr. Sweeney, a wiry man, said he had worked in the yards for most of his life, and his uncle and grandfather had worked on the *Titanic.* Most Belfast people, he said, thought the sinking not so much a night to remember as a night to forget. "They were ashamed it wasn't as unsinkable as they said it was. It wasn't a good achievement, was it, to build the boat and get it sunk? That's the way Belfast people looked at it."

Remembering Joseph Conrad's simile about the *Titanic* being ripped open like a Huntley & Palmer biscuit tin, I asked Mr. Sweeney to tell me exactly how its hull had been put together. The plates of the *Titanic,* he said, were of iron.

They called it steel-plate, but it was not really high-class steel in those days; it was really raw hard iron. Most ships now are made of high-tensile steel, which is much tougher. I was a welder. They built the first oil rig in the world at Harland & Wolff and the caulkers—the men who trim off the steel after it has been automatically welded—couldn't cut that metal; it turned their tools. Of course the whole of the *Titanic* was hand-riveted, a massive job. They started at six in the morning and went on until half past five at night,

built to ferry passengers to the liners at anchor at Cherbourg. The company's future appears bright.

Those interested in the rapidly changing situation in Belfast should consult the Internet. Much is afoot, including a rediscovered pride in *Titanic,* under the motto, "She was all right when she left here!"—DG working in squads of four. First the "heater boys" heated up the rivets. They were called heater boys, but they might be fifty. They had a long pair of tongs and they poked the rivets into a coke brazier for three or four minutes, keeping the brazier hot by working a bellows with their foot. Then they threw the rivet to a "catch boy" and he put the stalk of the rivet into a hole through two overlapping plates. Then a man called the "holder up" put a big heavy hammer under the panhead on the rivet, which was of pure iron, and held on to it while the fourth man beat it and flattened it into the hole. The outside hull, the shell, was worked on by special men called "shell-riveters," and the men who hammered in the rivets were divided into the right-handers and the left-handers, who were known as "cloot-men," cloot meaning left. They used a light sledge hammer weighing about five pounds. You didn't need to be big and tough so much as wiry, with skill in using your muscles. They'd do about 200 rivets a day in the *Titanic* time, provided it didn't rain. If it did, the wet horn would sound and they would all have to go home. For the time they had to be at home they didn't get paid; they were paid from horn to horn by the number of rivets they put in.*

I asked him about the *Titanic*'s double bottom, claimed at the time to be an effective safety feature, although it only came up seven feet above the keel. The outer skin was an inch thick, the idea being that if this skin was pierced the inner hull, although thinner, would keep out the water. An inch thick, I said, did not sound very thick to me. Mr. Sweeney demurred. An inch was very thick; most ships now would have a hull of seven-eighths- or three-quarter-

---

*Davie's informant misled him. Almost all the ship's hull was hydraulically riveted, using steel rivets. Hand riveting, using wrought iron rivets, was confined to curved areas and other parts that could not be reached by the hydraulic machines.

inch plate. The bulkheads of the *Titanic* were half an inch thick—the divisions inside the ship that the boilers were thought to have crashed through when she stood on end before sinking. Mr. Sweeney offered me a cup of tea and shook his head. "They thought it was really unsinkable."

Before I left, Mr. Sweeney hinted at something special about the *Titanic*'s construction, something I found hard to interpret. He recalled that, at the time, Ireland was rent by the Home Rule controversy. The country was divided, he said, so it would be only natural, would it not, if the shipyards were divided also? He implied that he had heard, from his uncle and grandfather, stories of political disaffection among their fellow-workers. Certainly, given that many of the men, if not most, believed that the government at Westminster was planning to betray them, they had no reason to feel pro-English, and it was an English company—or they thought it was an English company—that was building the ship. Pirrie himself cannot have been popular; he was a Home Ruler and on one occasion clashed violently with Orangemen. Was Mr. Sweeney implying that political disaffection had led to sabotage, or at least that the job had not been done as well as it might have been? He retreated from any such allegation; but it hung in the air. I thought of a photograph I had seen earlier in Harland & Wolff's offices. It showed men pouring out of the yards at the end of a day's work, some smoking clay pipes—the picture was pin-sharp—and some wearing peaked caps, led by two small boys with bare feet; in the background rose the scaffolding of the *Titanic* and the *Olympic*. The picture seemed laden with doom. The *Titanic* was doomed, and so were the men. Some of them joined the volunteer force raised by Sir Edward Carson to resist Home Rule, and later the Ulster Division that was cut to ribbons on the Somme. Mr. Sweeney probably had heard tales of work deliberately skimped by these men, but even if the tales were true their secret protests would not have affected the *Titanic*'s fate, although the men could have thought differently, which might account both for Mr. Sweeney's readiness to plant the idea in my mind and for his reluctance to enlarge on it. His hesitant testimony seemed still more interesting in retrospect, after the 1986 Woods Hole expedition reported that the *Titanic* had burst open down a seam of rivets.

He said again before I left, "They really thought it was unsinkable." But did they? I found it hard to believe that anyone, even at the height of Edwardian self-confidence, could ever have believed in the possibility of an "unsinkable" ship, least of all the hard and experienced shipbuilders and shipowners of Belfast and Liverpool.

The answer, as I learned later, is that although the owners and builders were confident that they had done everything possible to make the *Titanic* safe, there is no evidence that they thought or said she was unsinkable—although plenty of other people did. One of the early journalists into the field after the sinking was Sir Philip Gibbs, a prolific popular author. In his pamphlet *The Deathless Story of the Titanic,* a paradoxical title, he quoted what he said was the owner's description of the watertight doors: "Each door is held in the open position by a suitable friction clutch, which can be instantly released by means of a powerful electric magnet controlled by the captain's bridge, so that, in the event of an accident, or at any time when it might be considered advisable, the captain can, by simply moving an electric switch, instantly close the doors throughout—practically making the vessel unsinkable." Gibbs said that the last five words were written in italics. They read now, he said, "with a dreadful irony." A contemporary shipping journal also used the words "practically unsinkable." The idea spread, and the qualifier was lost. Time and again at the official inquiries passengers and crew testified that they had reacted slowly to the collision because they thought the *Titanic* unsinkable. Several people continued to think so even after they were in the lifeboats. The explanation of this extraordinary but widespread delusion—nobody today could think a ship unsinkable—must have had something to do with the spirit of the times, the confidence exuded by believers in progress like Pirrie, and the consequential confidence engendered in others, whether they knew anything about ships or not. That anyone should be drowned in a Harland & Wolff ship was highly improbable. True, one of their ships had been shipwrecked on her maiden voyage, but the captain had been drunk, which was scarcely the fault of the shipbuilders. As for White Star, the managing director Harold Sanderson told the Board of Trade inquiry that the total number of passengers carried in the ten years before the *Titanic*'s voyage had been 2,179,594 and the loss of life three—when the *Republic* collided with the *Florida* in 1902. Besides, the construction of the ship paid special attention to safety. The wireless installation was particularly powerful, with three different sources of supply: one from the ordinary electric-light plant in the engine room, one elsewhere in case the engine room flooded, and a third from storage batteries in the Marconi Room itself. The double bottom was deep enough to allow a man to walk through it upright, and was bigger than usual, being carried above the bilge instead of stopping short under it. The pumping arrangements were exceptional, since every boiler compartment had its own pumping equipment. Finally, the structure featured plating and connections of extra strength, and an unusual number of watertight bulkheads, fifteen in all.

Descriptions of the *Titanic* in the technical journals before she sailed took pride in her sheer size. *Engineering,* a very sober publication, called the *Titanic*'s height "splendid": 104 feet from keel to navigating bridge. It gave the statistics of the biggest ship in the world: length overall of 882 feet 9 inches, extreme breadth of 92 feet, gross tonnage of 46,328 tons— about 1,000 Registered Tons larger than her sister ship the *Olympic*—and an anticipated "continuous sea speed of 21 knots." Twenty-nine boilers, the journal continued, having in all 159 furnaces, were arranged in six separate watertight compartments. She was certified for 905 persons in first class, 564 in second, 1,134 in third, and a crew of 944—a total of 3,547. The machinery was exhaustively described and accompanied by many precise drawings and some photographs, of which the most startling shows a man dwarfed by a receding row of monstrous boilers. Particularly notable from *Engineering*'s point of view, apart from the size, was the combination of quadruple expansion engines operating the two-wing propellers and a low-pressure turbine for the center screw.

Having dealt thoroughly with the boilers, *Engineering* took a tour of the passenger accommodation. It concluded that the *Titanic*'s special attractions lay in the Turkish baths with shampooing rooms, the swimming bath, the gymnasium with gym instructor, and the squash court, which was 30 feet long and 20 feet wide (a little smaller than the modern standard dimensions). *Engineering*'s big ship reporter was plainly not a squash player. He conceded that the court was "an interesting development," but added that "the game is most popular with the Americans." He singled out the swimming bath as the new feature that "should appeal particularly to passengers. It is arranged much on the lines of an ordinary swimming bath on land, and is fitted with dressing boxes and fresh-water sprays." One arrangement he approved of was the fully carpeted first-class restaurant in which (unlike the dining room) you could dine à la carte, an advantage "more consonant with modern ideas as to diet."

After the *Titanic* went down, posthumous descriptions concentrated on her conspicuous display. In beauty and luxury she had no rival, wrote Sir Philip Gibbs.

All that the genius of modern life has invented for comfort and adornment was lavished upon her in a prodigal spirit; all that wealth and art can attain in splendour was given to her decoration. The imagination of old story tellers writing of fabulous ships paled before the actuality of this magnificence. . . . Here any passenger might sit in a tropical verandah restaurant, where vines grew upon the lattice work of windows through which there streamed—artificial light! It was called the Café Parisien, and here at night the band played the gayest tunes of life. . . . The dining rooms, state rooms, and common rooms were furnished in various periods and styles, copied faithfully from old models, so that English gentlemen might sit in rooms panelled and adorned like those of Haddon Hall, and fair women might have their beauty reflected in oval mirrors hanging upon walls like those of Versailles when Marie Antoinette played with her ladies. For the payment of £870 per voyage the richest man on earth would not lack a single comfort that his wealth might buy.

All this was, in a sense, true, and Sir Philip omitted the feature of the *Titanic* that seems most extraordinary today: the Edwardian opulence of the best cabins. Some of them had Adam fireplaces that burned coal in their sitting rooms and, in the bedrooms, full-size double four-poster beds. The two grandest suites, fifty feet long, had private promenade decks. Every style of architecture was represented: Elizabethan, Dutch, Adam, Louis Quatorze, Louis Quinze, Queen Anne. In the reading room there were sash and bow windows. Even the third-class (or steerage) cabins were perfectly adequate for a five-day trip: four bunks to a cabin, with washbasin. From the photographs, it looks as though the standard of comfort in the third-class public rooms was about the same as it is on a present-day cross-Channel ferry. The great difference between the third and first class was that the third class still looked like a ship, with pipes and girders showing, whereas in the first class all the construction was hidden behind paneling or tapestries.

The idea of decorating a ship so that it seemed like a very large house or hotel reached a climax in the *Titanic*. But the idea itself was not new. Beatrice Lillie's famous quip as she stepped aboard the *Queen Mary*—"Say, when does this place get to New York?"—could have been made at the turn of the century. Pirrie visited the best hotels in England, on the Continent, and in the United States to work up the interior designs of Harland & Wolff liners. The Liverpool *Daily Post* had said the *Oceanic* would cross the Atlantic "with the speed and certainty of an express train— the conquest of the mighty force of matter by the mighty force of mind," and then described her as "a triumph of art, as the last thing, so far, in the way of floating hotels . . . now mahogany; now oak; now satinwood." The lavatories were of "costly marble. It is the literal truth to say that the *Oceanic* is the Hotel Cecil afloat."

Boastfulness as well as decor reached a climax with the *Titanic*. No record survives of who thought of the name that has helped to make her famous. In the old days, names had been more modest: *Golden Hind* for Drake, *Endeavour* for Captain Cook. Ismay senior started the custom of giving White Star ships names that ended in "-ic": *Oceanic, Atlantic, Baltic, Republic, Adriatic*. One, a tender, was called *Traffic* and another *Arctic*, until the line thought better of it and renamed her *Baltic*. Running out of seas and oceans, they turned to the gods.

One can see how their minds were working. Advertising, with new mass-circulation newspapers booming on both sides of the Atlantic, was a significant part of salesmanship and was becoming more and more extravagant in its claims. The booklet written by Sir Philip Gibbs gives the flavor.

The title page is faced by an advertisement of a man, looking like Mr. Asquith, who is offering, under the headline
"Discard Your Truss," not merely an alleviant but a certain
cure for rupture. "Words of Wisdom to Wage Earners" rec-
ommends Mother Seigel's Syrup as a herbal remedy that will
"surely and speedily" cure indigestion forever. Bovril claims
that in recent experiments upon human subjects reported to
the Medical Association, Bovril was "proved" to produce
an increase in flesh and muscle, or "body-building power,"
from ten to twenty times the amount taken. The master of
the late barque *Colorado,* shipwrecked on Staten Island off
Cape Horn, states that he and his crew of twenty-five men
were kept alive for six months "on this barren island, in a
region of perpetual ice," entirely by drinking Epps's Cocoa.
Similar extravagances were appearing about ocean liners.
"What more appropriate setting," said an advertisement for
the *Titanic,* "than this dignified Jacobean room, redolent of
the time when the Pilgrim Fathers set forth from Plymouth on their rude bark to brave the perils of the deep!"
Large claims and grandiose words—"conquest," "titanic,"
"unsinkable"—were in the air. Edith Wharton, in her novel
The Custom of the Country, published in 1913, invented a fashionable transatlantic liner ironically named the *Semantic.*

The basic flaw of the *Titanic* was not technical. Her fate
is better explained by the theories of Henry Adams than by
drawings of her watertight compartments. Adams saw the
modern world being propelled at an ever-increasing speed
by the new energies released through scientific discovery,
ruled by men who worshipped the dynamo with blind faith
and lacked all understanding of where they were leading
mankind. Pirrie, Adams's contemporary, is a classic example of a dynamo-worshipper. But he was not alone. Faith in
the dynamo was so pervasive that it infected even an old sea
dog like the *Titanic's* captain, Captain E. J. Smith.

2

"ICEBERG RIGHT AHEAD!"

By the time the *Titanic* sailed from Belfast docks for her trials in Belfast Lough she had been visited and examined by Board of Trade inspectors, according to evidence given at the British inquiry, more than two thousand times. She performed her trials satisfactorily, then sailed for Southampton arriving on April 2. There she filled up with coal. In Southampton, White Star's newest triumph was received with acclamation, and not entirely because of her size. She was a source of jobs. Belfast built her, but it was Southampton that supplied most of her crew, including Captain Smith.

Southampton still regards the *Titanic* as a Southampton ship. The disaster was felt there more than anywhere else. An old copy of the *Southern Daily Echo* contains a group photograph of forty small children, all from the same school, and all deprived of a father or a brother or an uncle by drowning. The inhabitants of one short street near the docks lost thirteen relations among them. The little two-story houses of Milbank Street have been replaced by light industry, but Winn Road, Westwood Park, where Captain Smith used to live, is still leafy and residential and recognizably turn-of-the-century, although many of the substantial old houses have been demolished to make way for flats. *Kelly's Directory* for 1911–12 lists the houses—Ballencrieff, Lyndale, Speranza, Cranbourne, Boldrewood—and the residents, among them Rear-Admiral Charles Winnington-Ingram. Captain Smith is eighth on the list, at Woodhead. His house has gone, but the social status of the road is unchanged, with blocks of flats called Brookvale Court, Pinehurst, and Sandringham Court. Captain Smith had seen service as a commander in the Royal Naval Reserve, and Winn Road still houses an R.N.R. officer, also on the south side.

Elsewhere in Southampton are no fewer than seven memorials to the men who died in the sinking, one of them prominent in East Park, with bas-reliefs commemorating the engineers, a neat flower bed at the foot, and floodlit at night. Until recently, an anonymous woman used to leave a wreath beside the flower bed every year on the anniversary of the disaster. The other *Titanic* memorials are a drinking fountain, a bronze tablet in the post office, a memorial in the seamen's chapel of St. Mary's Church, two in Millbrook Church, and another in St. Augustine's, Northam, which contains a reference that sounds sardonic now regarding "her presumed indestructibility." Captain Smith was probably one of those who so presumed.

Ships' captains came up the hard way in those days. Smith started his apprenticeship at the age of sixteen in sailing ships. He served in the Boer War as a commander with the Royal Naval Reserve. He was sixty-two by the time he took over the *Titanic* and had been with White Star for thirty years, a captain for twenty-five. Someone calculated that by the time of the *Titanic*'s maiden voyage he had sailed two million miles for White Star. The company had complete confidence in him; they invariably gave him their best and newest liners. Before the *Titanic,* he had captained the *Olympic.* His salary was the highest of any man afloat—£1,250 a year—while the captain of the *Californian,* the ship that failed to come to the *Titanic*'s rescue, was earning £240 a year. Newsreel film of Captain Smith survives; in his uniform frock-coat, four rings on each sleeve, and stiff collar, and with his fluffy beard, he looks upright, dignified, and above all reassuring. It was as advantageous then for a ship's captain to look the part as it is for an airline pilot now.

His standing in society at large, not merely in the maritime community, is shown by what happened after he went down with his ship. Two years later, in 1914, the mayor of Lichfield decided that it would be appropriate if the town erected a memorial to him. Smith was a Staffordshire man, and Lichfield was halfway between Liverpool and London. It was pointed out, in support of Lichfield's claim, that Anna Seward, praised by Dr. Johnson as the "Swan of Lichfield," had written movingly of icebergs around the North Pole in her ode on the death of Captain Cook. A subscription list was opened, and the widow of another national hero who had lost his life among ice, Captain Scott, was commissioned to produce a slightly larger than life-size statue. The subscribers, and those who attended the unveiling, represented the higher reaches of British society. Waldorf Astor, M.P., elder son of the first viscount and first cousin once removed of the colonel J. J. Astor who had gone down in the *Titanic,* was on the list. So was the Duke of Sutherland. So was the Dowager Countess of Arran. Among those who wrote tributes to Captain Smith were the Marquess of Salisbury, who was a former president of the Board of Trade, and the publisher J. G. Hodder Williams of Hodder & Stoughton. Lady Diana Manners (later Lady Diana Cooper), the most brilliant social figure of the day, attended the unveiling ceremony, together with her sister the Marchioness of Anglesey. Addresses were given by Lord Charles Beresford and the Duchess of Sutherland.

The navy was represented by Captain Smith's old South-ampton neighbor, Rear-Admiral Winnington-Ingram.

The captain had met most of these prominent people, and had come to know them, because they had sailed in a ship under his command. Then, as now, it was an important part of a liner captain's job, if the weather allowed, to cultivate the grander passengers; for their part, a certain cachet attached to knowing the captain. On the night the *Titanic* sank, Captain Smith had been entertained at dinner by Mr. and Mrs. George D. Widener, with Mr. and Mrs. John B. Thayer among the other guests—the cream of Philadelphia society. Later, a woman survivor wrote to the United States senators inquiring into the disaster to tell them that Captain Smith had been drinking at the dinner; but she had not been at the table, and two women who had, Mrs. Widener and Mrs. Thayer, both signed written depositions saying that the captain had not drunk alcohol at all. Apart from this solitary wild traducer, not one survivor, whether passenger or crew, had anything but good to say of Captain Smith. Five conflicting accounts of the manner of his death were given; the most dramatic was that he drowned while swimming toward a lifeboat with a baby in his arms. All the accounts are creditable to Smith. The senior surviving member of the crew, Second Officer C. H. Lightoller, remembered Smith all his life—and he did not die until 1952—as the best captain he had known.

Somewhere, though, there was a flaw. Smith said some strange things. In 1907, arriving in New York as captain of a new White Star liner on her maiden voyage, he told *The New York Times* that he had never been in trouble at sea in all his long career, although of course he had seen storms and fog; nor did he expect to be in the future. "Modern shipbuilding," he was reported as saying, "has gone beyond that." Beyond what? the reporter should have asked. Five years later, the impression that Captain Smith gave both passengers and crew was of total confidence in his new ship. His crew certainly had confidence in him. His three senior officers had all served with him before. Captain Smith had brought over his chief officer from the *Olympic*, Henry Wilde, to be chief officer of the *Titanic*—thinking his experience of the sister ship would be valuable on the maiden voyage—which meant that two *Titanic* officers had to move down a rung, W. M. Murdoch to first officer and Charles Herbert Lightoller to second.

Aboard the *Titanic* for her first Atlantic crossing, the crew numbered 891. Some 340 of these worked belowdecks in the engine department: engineers, trimmers, electricians, boilermakers, greasers, firemen. There were some 290 stewards and stewardesses. There was a window cleaner, a linen keeper, a stenographer, a fish cook, an assistant soup cook, a masseuse, an iceman, plate washers, a roast cook, several bakers, a night watchman, an assistant vegetable cook, nine "Boots," and Italian and French waiters in the à la carte restaurant. The number of all-around seamen on board was much less than the number of crew looking after the passengers.

Of those passengers, there were 324 in first class, 284 in second class, and 709 in third class. The British well-to-do were not tempted by a maiden voyage, preferring the Cunarders, so the first class was dominated by Americans. The second class was mainly Anglo-Saxon. The third class, largely immigrants, included Armenians, Italians, Syrians, Chinese, Russians, Scandinavians, Dutch, and Irish.

The *Titanic* sailed from Southampton on April 10 shortly after noon, bound for Cherbourg to pick up more passengers. Captain Smith must have known that the latest leviathans required careful handling. Six months earlier, when he was taking the *Olympic* out of Southampton on her sixth Atlantic crossing, she had collided with a cruiser, HMS *Hawke,* whose bow had torn a jagged and ugly gash ten feet deep in the *Olympic*'s starboard quarter. An Admiralty Court held that the *Olympic* had gone too close to the cruiser and that White Star, and hence Captain Smith, were to blame for the collision. Smith had not been pleased; he wrote to a friend to say that "we are not taking it lying down." He meant that White Star would appeal, which it did; but the verdict was upheld. It was thought at the time that the huge bulk of the *Olympic* might have drawn the cruiser toward her. Two of Smith's officers on the *Titanic,* Lightoller and William Murdoch, who was on watch when the *Titanic* hit the iceberg, were also aboard the *Olympic* when she hit the *Hawke.*

Smith must have been reminded of the *Hawke* when he stood on the bridge of his latest command as she in her turn left Southampton. A local paper described what happened. "The departure of the *Titanic* on her maiden voyage on Wednesday was marred by an untoward incident, which caused considerable consternation among the hundreds of people who had gathered at the quayside to witness the sailing of the largest vessel afloat," said the *Southampton Times & Hampshire Express.* The wash of the *Titanic* caused all six ropes holding the liner *New York* alongside the jetty to part. The greatest consternation was among the sightseers who had trespassed onto the *New York* to get a better view, for they thought a collision "inevitable." A touch ahead on the port engine by Captain Smith and the rapid intervention of two tugs saved the day. But it had been very close. The *Southampton Times* interviewed Captain C. Gale of the tug *Vulcan.* "We got hold of the *New York* when she was within four feet of the *Titanic,*" he said. The paper ended its report by remarking that the trespassers aboard the *New York* "will doubtless retain for years vivid recollections of the first sailing of the *Titanic* from Southampton docks." The episode showed, for the second time, that lessons still had to be learned about the giant ships' maneuverability.

Was Captain Smith, behind the obscuring beard, a risk taker? Of all the characters in the *Titanic* drama, he seems now particularly hard to understand. Here was a ship's captain of vast experience, universally regarded as a highly responsible man, who behaved at times in a manner that appears, in retrospect, positively reckless. In his reminiscences, Lightoller recalls with approval the dash with which Smith used to take his ships into New York— "at full speed," says Lightoller, although the word "full" must be an exaggeration. "One particularly bad corner, known as the South-West Spit, used to make us fairly flush with pride as he swung her round, judging the distances to a nicety; she heeling over to the helm with only a few feet to spare between each end of the ship and the banks." According to Lightoller, Smith as a mailboat captain was relentless in the way he pressed on despite heavy seas and fog to get the mail through on time; this was one of the reasons why Lightoller admired and respected him. Robust captaincy was a function of intense competition between rival companies. But Cunard historians maintain that the White Star Line, which Cunard eventually took over, followed a particularly bold policy.

Did Captain Smith choose a daring route across the Atlantic for the *Titanic*? Well-connected elderly Englishmen recall well-connected friends saying years ago that the secret of the *Titanic* disaster was that she was taking a shortened route, too far north, because she was lacking coal as a result of the great 1912 coal strike. True, the strike gravely embarrassed the transatlantic-liner business. The *Olympic,* in New York on one crossing, crammed every available part of the ship with coal in order to boost White Star's reserves. The *Titanic* had to get coal in Southampton from other ships, which were consequently delayed. But the route she followed was normal. There were, and indeed still are, two recommended transatlantic tracks, the northern and the southern, which are alternated according to the time of year. *Titanic* was on the southern, not the northern, route. Immediately after the disaster, the recommended southern route was moved further south, and then further south again, to avoid any risk of a second collision. But though the *Titanic*'s route turned out to be fatal, there was nothing unusual about it.

Trying to understand Captain Smith's state of mind before the disaster, one is tempted to take his own word for it, as expressed to *The New York Times,* and conclude that his errors stemmed from a belief that the dangers of the Atlantic had been neutralized by technology—that modern transatlantic travel had become safe and predictable. But there was too much daily evidence to the contrary for Captain Smith to have really believed anything of the sort. Newspapers reported shipping accidents then as faithfully as they report airline accidents or alarms today. The files of *The New York Times* in the months before the sinking are full of such reports. On the first day of the new year the White Star liner *Arabic* arrived in New York a day late because of a gale. During the next few weeks, three crewmen of an American ship were swept overboard during a storm off Key West, Florida; the U.S. Atlantic Fleet lost two seamen when all of its ships were struck, and some of them badly damaged, by an Atlantic gale; a British battleship at Portsmouth broke its moorings in a storm and crashed into a dreadnought; fifty-three out of a crew of fifty-seven were drowned when a British steamer sank off Aberdeenshire during a gale; the White Star liner *Adriatic* arrived in New York thirty hours late because of high seas; the British steamer *Birchfield* arrived in New York having had a seven-day fire in its coal bunkers; the *Lusitania* was a day late because of bad weather and ice.

No doubt Captain Smith, after a lifetime at sea, regarded these incidents as regular, familiar hazards of seagoing. Can he have thought the same about icebergs and failed to take them seriously? If not, why on the fourth day of the maiden voyage did he take his ship at high speed into a region he knew to contain icebergs?

There does seem to have been general underestimation of the fact, fully accepted now, that icebergs are the most dangerous hazard of all, more dangerous than storms, collisions, or fog. It is a pity that a small book published in 1898 was not more widely read. It was written by the American Morgan Robertson, who held a first mate's certificate and had eight years' experience at sea. It told how a huge ocean liner called the *Titan* collided with a North Atlantic iceberg, with the loss of almost all her company. Its title was *Futility*. In 1912 *Futility* was hastily republished as *The Wreck of the Titan*. The displacement and power of the *Titan* were increased, making her larger and faster than the *Titanic*.

	Titan 1898	*Titanic* 1912	*Titan* 1912
Overall length	800'	882'9"	800'
Displacement	45,000 tons	52,310 tons	70,000 tons
Service speed	25 knots	21 knots	25 knots
Horsepower	40,000	51,000	75,000
Watertight compartments	19	16	19
Propellers	3	3	3
Capacity	About 3,000	3,547	About 3,000
Flag	British	British	British
Time of voyage	April	April	April
Number on board	Almost 3,000	2,208	Almost 3,000
Lifeboats	24	20	24
Lifeboat capacity	500	1,178	500
Deaths	About 3,000	1,496	About 3,000

Robertson's story is much loved in some quarters as a supposed foretelling of the *Titanic* disaster. However, even after the 1912 changes, there are many differences between fiction and fact. The *Titan* was on her sixth Atlantic crossing and was sailing from America to Britain. She had many features the *Titanic* lacked, such as a theatrical company and two brass bands. She carried no cargo. The book remains an interesting curiosity but if we demand accuracy from our prophets, it fails the test.

Only after the *Titanic* went down was the story noticed and alleged to have a special significance as an example of second sight.

Also unlike the *Titan,* the *Titanic,* before she hit the iceberg, had received by wireless telegraph no fewer than six ice warnings. Decades later, a member of the Titanic Historical Society read a newspaper item that led to a visit to the small German industrial town of Leisnig in Saxony, where an old gentleman suddenly fumbled in his desk, produced a crumpled scrap of paper, and exclaimed, "If only they had heeded my warning!" The man's name was Otto Reuter; in April 1912 he had been first wireless officer aboard the German liner *Amerika;* and a scrawl on the piece of paper was the text of the radio telegram he sent via the Cape Race station to the U.S. Hydrographic Office in Washington at 11:20 a.m. on Sunday, April 14, the day the *Titanic* hit the iceberg. It read: "*Amerika* passed two large icebergs in 41 degrees 27 minutes N. 50 degrees 8 minutes W. on the 14th April Knuth." Knuth was the captain. The message was intercepted by the *Titanic* and passed on to Washington.

But Herr Reuter was only one of the message senders. On Friday the 12th the French liner *Touraine* told the *Titanic* she had crossed a "thick ice field." Besides the *Amerika,* on the fatal Sunday, the *Caronia* sent a message reporting "bergs, growlers and field ice"; the *Noordam,* after congratulating Smith on his new command, reported "much ice"; and the *Baltic* soon after midday passed on a report from a Greek steamer which said she had passed "icebergs and large quantities of field ice." How many of these wireless messages did Captain Smith see? One point to remember about wireless telegraphy in 1912 is that although not brand new, it was relatively new and not properly organized to meet a ship's needs. Wireless operators aboard the liners were employed not by the shipping company but, if they used the Marconi system, by the Marconi Company. No iron routine had yet been drilled into the operators about the treatment of wireless messages, although they were under instructions to give priority to any messages about navigation; still more inefficient, Marconi operators thought of themselves in competition with other wireless companies and often either declined to accept signals or treated them in a cavalier fashion. Smith certainly saw four messages. It came out in the inquiries that around lunchtime on Sunday the 14th he handed the *Baltic's* message to Bruce Ismay, the White Star chairman traveling on the ship's maiden voyage, who put it in his pocket. The last warning to come in, two hours before the collision, was from the *Mesaba,* reporting "much heavy pack ice and a great number large icebergs"; but nobody saw it because the *Titanic* operator put it under a paperweight and forgot it.* Even without this ominous final message, nobody could deny—though some tried to—that the *Titanic* had been warned. Captain Smith and his officers knew they were heading into ice.

These days, the people in the world who know most

---

*The paperweight story is from Charles Lightoller, writing in 1935, and its accuracy is dubious.

about icebergs are the members of the International Ice
Patrol. This indispensable organization was set up as a
direct result of the *Titanic* disaster. The IIP's headquarters are at New London, Connecticut. Its lone Hercules
C-130 operates out of St. John's, Newfoundland. Though
responsible to the United States Coast Guard, it broad-
casts regularly to all Atlantic shipping and is financed by
the nations that make most use of the North Atlantic
lanes, including Britain, France, Belgium, Canada, Den-
mark, Germany, Greece, Israel, Italy, Japan, Liberia, the
Netherlands, Panama, Poland, the United States, and
Sweden.

The Ice Patrol officers, who fly Hercules C-130 aircraft
with side-looking airborne radar to monitor iceberg movements, take a keen interest in the *Titanic,* partly because
she brought them into existence, and partly because the
memory of the disaster keeps them on their toes. There
have been one or two serious collisions since 1912—the
most serious being in 1959, when the *Hans Hedtoft,* on
her maiden voyage, equipped with all the latest electronic
equipment, struck an iceberg off Cape Farewell, Greenland, and sank without a trace, taking with her ninety-five
passengers and crew. But within the area monitored by the
Ice Patrol, which encompasses only those regions of the
North Atlantic through which the main transatlantic shipping tracks pass, not a single life has been lost because of
icebergs since 1912, although a Canadian bulker smashed
her bows to pieces on one not long ago. Nevertheless, even
with all the advances in radar and satellite navigation and
the Ice Patrol's computerized predictions about icebergs'
whereabouts, there is still no reason why a ship today could
not suffer exactly the same fate as the *Titanic.* The iceberg
"menace," says an official Ice Patrol publication, is a "natural hazard which man, in all his ingenuity and resource-

fulness, has not been able to control, regulate, or entirely avoid."

With seventy years' study and records behind them, the Ice Patrol is familiar with the state of iceberg knowledge in 1912. Captain Smith, they say, would have known perfectly well that April is one of the worst months, because it is then that the rising spring temperatures melt the sea ice that has imprisoned the bergs, letting them float free. Icebergs start as the seaward tips of glaciers. Of the 10,000 to 15,000 icebergs that break off every year, some 85 percent come from the west coast of Greenland, the largest island in the world, where the ice cap is nearly two miles thick. They are "calved" by the hundred or so glaciers there (each glacier has a name, mainly Danish but sometimes Eskimo), head north along the Greenland coast, around the western side of Baffin Bay, and then drift south past Labrador and Newfoundland toward the Grand Banks. Most of them disintegrate, but on average about a thousand a year survive to reach the Grand Banks and the shipping lanes—the record is 2,202 (the Ice Patrol counts every iceberg) in 1984. The survivors by that time will have traveled some 1,800 miles and taken anything from eleven months to three years for the journey, depending on whether or not they grounded for a time on some Arctic island or were sidetracked into a Labrador cove.

Icebergs come in all shapes and sizes, though not in all colors—which was a crucial point at issue in the *Titanic* inquiries. In an attempt to explain why the fatal iceberg had not been spotted earlier, it was said that it must have been black; but the Ice Patrol is skeptical, saying it has never seen a black iceberg.

One fact about icebergs that Captain Smith would not have known is that they are virtually indestructible. The U.S. Navy has conducted numerous experiments in the past twenty years to find a technique of breaking them up and rendering them harmless. Nothing has worked. Demolition of an average-size iceberg, the Ice Patrol concludes, would take 1,900 tons of TNT. To melt an average-size iceberg would take the heat of combustion generated by 2.4 million tons of gasoline.

The Ice Patrol classifies icebergs as small, medium, large, and very large. The small ones go up to fifty feet above water, the medium-size ones to a hundred feet, the large ones to two hundred feet, and the very large ones to anything over that. The Patrol's commanding officer told me that the biggest authenticated iceberg he had ever heard of would have weighed six million tons. If the iceberg that hit the *Titanic* was fifty feet high, which is perhaps the likeliest of many guesses, then—given that seven-eighths of any iceberg lies below water—its weight would have been something like 100,000 tons.

On the fatal night, the *Titanic* was steaming at 21 or 22 knots. However, she was not trying to break the transatlantic speed record. In the archives of the public library of Southampton is a letter written in the 1960s by an old surviving crew member in which he says categorically that Captain Smith, urged on by the owner, J. Bruce Ismay, was trying on White Star's behalf to capture from Cunard the Blue Riband, the record for the fastest transatlantic passage by a passenger liner. This notion is and always has been absurd. No ship can go faster than another ship that is lighter and has more power, which was the relation between the *Titanic* and the crack Cunarders. At both inquiries, Ismay was closely questioned about trying to break the record and he categorically and repeatedly denied it. His indignant testimony was wholly plausible. It was simply not possible for the *Titanic* at full speed to go faster than the lighter and more powerful Cunard liners at full speed. Nor was it

ever intended, either by the owners or by the builders, that
the *Titanic* should be able to match them.

Many questions were asked at the inquiries about
whether the *Titanic* was going flat out, or only nearly flat
out, at the moment of impact. Ismay said she was not; a
stoker discovered by Senator Smith, the chairman of the
American inquiry, gave evidence to suggest that she was.
The difference is unimportant. The point is that the ship
was going very fast. Still more significant, both Smith and
Ismay had it in mind that the ship would be tried at full
speed the following day. The idea of slowing down was
evidently far from their thoughts.

Experts were produced by counsel for White Star at the
British inquiry who said there was nothing untoward about
the *Titanic*'s speed. Other ships' captains said that Captain
Smith was merely following the practice, established many
years past, of maintaining course and speed in regions of
ice provided that the weather was clear. But even if that
was the practice, was it a safe practice? One man with
experience of navigating among ice thought it dangerous
and told the inquiry as much; this was Ernest Shackleton,
recently returned from his first expedition to the Antarctic.
He said his own custom in the vicinity of ice was to slow
down to 3 or 4 knots. The lawyers defending White Star
remarked that that might be so, but his own ship was very
small, was it not? Naturally, Shackleton had to concede
that by comparison with the *Titanic* his ship was indeed
very small. But the difference in size was scarcely pertinent. The *Titanic* also was very small by comparison with
the icebergs she was liable to meet and indeed did meet:
50,000 tons compared with 100,000 tons.

The Ice Patrol says that hitting such a massive though
largely hidden object would have been like hitting a small
island, icebergs being not only virtually indestructible but

unyielding. One member of the patrol who spent three years in a U.S. Coast Guard ship in northern waters says it was their custom, when ice was in the vicinity, to proceed at no more than 3 or 4 knots. The captain of a U.S. oceanographic vessel says the same: 4 knots is fast enough. Even a "growler," the smallest sort of iceberg—defined by the Ice Patrol as being fifteen feet high or less, and fifty feet long or less—should be, he says, treated with extreme care.

At the American inquiry, great hilarity was caused when Senator Smith asked Fifth Officer Harold Lowe of the *Titanic* what an iceberg was made of, and Lowe replied, "Ice." But the question was not quite so foolish, nor the answer quite so witty, as might at first appear. When more snow falls on a glacier, the pressure forces air out from between the snow particles and presses in ice instead. This process produces a very tight, very dense crystalline structure. The commander of the Ice Patrol said he had heard glacial ice described as "metamorphic rock," and he thought the description apt: "You could call it a mineral." With time, it gets harder. The bottom layer of the older glaciers has been estimated by carbon-dating to be some 100,000 years old; the average age of icebergs is some 3,000 years old.

Asked why, in their opinion, Captain Smith was traveling at nearly full speed when he knew he was in an ice region, the Ice Patrol says that in those days captains seem to have thought of ice and icebergs simply as one more natural hazard, like rough seas or fog. They did not instinctively regard icebergs, as any ship's captain would today, as uniquely menacing. This seems to approach the heart of the mystery. The Ice Patrol is also inclined to think that the flaw in Captain Smith's judgment was compounded by arrogance. He must have believed that the combination of his vast experience and the new technology of his ship would surmount any conceivable emergency. What he was doing on April 14, in effect, was to take his ship, at night, at speed, toward a slow-moving archipelago of rock-hard islands without even the benefit of a chart showing their approximate whereabouts.

From Southampton, the *Titanic* had called at Cherbourg and Queenstown, taking on mail and more passengers—more than a hundred Irish immigrants joined in Queenstown. Over the years, every *Titanic* relic has been carefully preserved, and a few postcards and letters posted in France or Ireland have survived. They are all humdrum, though in retrospect poignant. Mrs. Straus, wife of one of the owners of Macy's in New York, wrote to the owner of Harrods in London to thank him for sending flowers to the ship. Mrs. Thayer of Philadelphia wrote to a friend to say that her husband, John, had taken five photographs of the near miss at Southampton (they were lost with her husband, alas). Sotheby's, the auctioneers, exhibited in January 1986 a letter on *Titanic* writing paper, posted in Queenstown four days before the sinking, from J. H. Loring giving instructions about the installation of a new horn on his Daimler. "This is a huge ship," he added, "and I think will be most comfortable."

A high proportion of the survivors have been exhaustively interviewed over the years, some of them many times. Every story of what happened after the collision is interesting; every account of life aboard the *Titanic* before the collision is unexceptional: the weather was fine and shipboard life at its most predictable. This couple met that couple; deck quoits were played; the ship's daily run guessed; the gymnasium, the swimming pool, and the squash court tried out and admired. Mr. W. T. Stead, on his way to a peace rally in New York, talked politics. Mr. Lawrence Beesley, a schoolmaster from Dulwich making his first trip outside England, discussed in the second class the comparative virtues of Oxford and Cambridge as character-forming institutions with a Church of England clergyman, and observed that the ship's elevators, operated by a smiling young man, were invaluable in helping the old ladies to get about. One or two trivial events were later magnified into omens: in Queenstown, for a joke, a stoker climbed up inside one of the enormous funnels, a dummy for ventilation, and stuck his head out of the top; for some reason his blackened face was subsequently seized on as a portent. Two nervous elderly ladies expected disaster; one of them refused to undress at night because she wanted to be ready for the crack of doom.

Four days out of Southampton, Sunday was properly observed. Smith presided over a service in first class at which two American ladies, Martha Stevenson and Elizabeth Eustis, were surprised that they did not sing the hymn "For Those in Peril on the Sea." In second class, the purser held a service. It was after the services, going on deck before lunch, that some passengers noticed that the weather had turned very cold. A second-class lunch menu survives: "Consommé Fermier, Cockie Leekie; Fillets of Brill; Egg à l'Argenteuil; Chicken à la Maryland; Corned Beef; Vegetable Dumplings. From the grill: Grilled Mutton Chops; and mashed, fried, and baked jacket potatoes." For pudding, a choice was offered between custard pudding, apple meringue, and pastry. Across the bottom of the menu was printed, "Iced draught Munich Lager Beer 3d and 6d a Tankard."

One routine that should have been followed before lunch was a boat drill, with all hands, passengers, and crew assembling in lifejackets at their boat stations. In White Star ships, Sunday morning was always supposed to include a boat drill. Why on this occasion did Captain Smith skip it? There are two possible reasons: one is that he thought the chance of anyone having to take to the boats so remote that a boat drill would be a waste of time; the other is that, well aware of the gap between the capacity of the boats and the numbers on board, he considered that a boat drill would make the discrepancy too obvious and perhaps disturb some of the passengers.

That Sunday evening, after dinner with his Philadelphia hosts, Captain Smith went up to the bridge shortly before 9:00 p.m. It was a clear, starry night and the sea was flat calm.

The officer on watch when the captain arrived, Charles Lightoller, had already had an adventurous life. His family had originally been well-to-do, in Lancashire cotton, but their prosperity had suffered from the American Civil War, and the young Lightoller, to his own delight, had gone to sea at the age of thirteen. Since then he had been wrecked four times, survived a fire at sea, and prospected for gold in the Yukon. He had also become a Christian Scientist. Besides possessing great physical courage and being a first-rate seaman, Lightoller was ambitious; he had been with White Star twelve years when he joined the *Titanic* at the age of thirty-eight, and he was very put out when he was required to move down from first to second officer as a result of the captain's last-minute reshuffle in Southampton. The *Titanic* disaster determined the course of Lightoller's future, as of many others; he performed magnificently in the crisis, but during the subsequent inquiries found himself in the delicate position, as the senior surviving officer, of having to answer all the most awkward questions and to try to protect the reputations both of his employers and of Captain Smith. He got little thanks for his pains; White Star had no wish to remind potential customers about the *Titanic,* and Lightoller was never accorded the distinction he sought and deserved: a ship of his own. But he com-manded a destroyer as a Royal Naval Reserve officer in World War I and rammed and sank a U-boat; and in World War II he was one of the boldest of the old-timers—he was by then sixty-seven—who took a private boat to join the makeshift armada of small ships that evacuated the British Expeditionary Force from Dunkirk.

The conversation on the bridge between Lightoller and Captain Smith at 9:00 p.m., two hours and forty min-utes before the *Titanic* hit the iceberg, was subsequently described in detail by Lightoller. He remarked on the cold and the calm. Both men were aware that ice was probably in the vicinity, although neither had seen the latest warn-ing, which would have told them that icebergs had been sighted no more than forty miles ahead. Captain Smith observed that it was an exceptionally clear night and added that if it came over at all hazy they might have to slow down. Then he left the bridge, with the usual captain's reminder that he should be called if the weather changed.

At 10:00 p.m. Lightoller was relieved on the bridge by First Officer Murdoch, an experienced Scotsman. Ligh-toller told him, "We might be up around the ice any time now." They discussed the weather and agreed that "we seemed to be able to see a long distance." Lightoller told Murdoch he had given the lookouts instructions to keep a sharp watch for ice, including growlers. Then Lightoller left the bridge to carry out his nightly rounds. Murdoch seems to have been the only officer who took any special action before the collision. At about a quarter past seven that evening, a forty-three-year-old lamp trimmer from Southampton, Samuel Hemming, whose job was to mix paint and trim lamps, had reported to Murdoch that all was in order with the lamps, and Murdoch said, according to Hemming's later testimony, "Hemming, when you go forward see the fore scuttle is closed as we are in the vicinity of ice, and there is a glow coming from that, and I want everything dark before the bridge." Hemming had closed the scuttle.

Lightoller finished his rounds and turned in; so did most of the passengers. There was no dancing aboard White Star ships on Sundays, and the bars shut at half past eleven. During the evening Lawrence Beesley's new friend, Mr. Carter the clergyman, had organized, by permission of the purser, Sunday-night hymn singing attended by a hundred people; Beesley had thereafter visited the library with its open fire before going to his cabin. Colonel Gracie, an American, had spent an energetic morning on the squash court with the resident professional and taken a swim. A few men were playing cards. Outside, it was freezing. Below, the men working in the engine department sweated in a temperature of about 100 degrees.

As the officers of the watch changed, so did the lookouts; and here we come to one of the cruxes of the *Titanic* story. Given that Captain Smith and Lightoller agreed that visibility was particularly good, even though there was no moon, and that they could even see the stars "heading down toward the horizon"—proof that there was no haze—how was it that in these conditions nobody saw a fair-sized iceberg until it was too late to get out of the way?

The *Titanic* carried six specialist lookouts, more than any other ship afloat. They worked in pairs, two hours on and four hours off, and their place of work was the crow's nest, reached by a ladder inside the forward mast. Hogg and Evans had been on watch from six to eight; Symons and Jewell from eight to ten; Fleet and Lee had come on at ten. At the inquiries, Lightoller was asked whether, since ice was a possibility, extra lookouts had been posted. "No, sir," he said. It is hard to understand why not. One Ice

Patrol officer told me that when ice is about at night (the Ice Patrol operates ships as well as aircraft), it was standard practice to post as many lookouts as possible, especially in the bows. Even today, with radar, the only reliable way to detect icebergs, the Ice Patrol says officially, is with the human eye. Still more cavalier, the *Titanic* lookouts were not supplied with binoculars.

This was one of the awkward facts that Lightoller had to explain and try to defend later on. "We never had night glasses," Hogg testified. "Just the naked eye. I have always had night glasses in the White Star boats. I asked for the glasses and I did not see why I should not have them. I had them from Belfast to Southampton, but from Southampton to where the accident occurred we never had them. . . . I asked for the glasses several times." Symons said, "It is always customary to have glasses in the crow's nest. . . . I served three years and five months on the *Oceanic,* and they had glasses all the time. . . . They have glasses in all the other ships."

The tangled story of the binoculars is found in snippets of evidence from several witnesses. During *Titanic's* passage from Belfast to Southampton, the then second officer, David Blair, had seen fit to lend the lookouts a pair of zoom binoculars originally intended for his own use and marked accordingly. He may have done this because of the amount of traffic to be expected in the Irish Sea and the need to sight navigational marks. When Blair left the ship, the new second officer, Charles Lightoller, took charge of them. No binoculars were ever specifically allotted to the lookouts. The lookouts were resentful, judging by their replies at the inquiries. They had been deprived of the tool of their trade; and they maintained that if they had had binoculars they might well have seen the iceberg earlier and the ship could have been saved. Fred Fleet, described by one of the lawyers at the British inquiry as the man who "discovered the iceberg," was insistent on the point and remained so for the rest of his life. The insistence might have been a form of self-protection; he might secretly have felt guilty that he had not seen the iceberg earlier. Lightoller on the other hand maintained that binoculars, though a useful aid, were not an essential piece of equipment. He himself relied first and foremost on the naked eye, using binoculars to survey what he had already seen. A captain from another ship supported him; he never supplied his lookouts with binoculars.

Still, whether the lack of binoculars was or was not decisive, the fact is that they were regarded as standard in White Star ships at the time and have been so regarded by the merchant navy and the world's fighting navies ever since. In the British Navy, lookouts are taught to sweep the horizon—each lookout having a defined sector of sea and horizon—first with the naked eye, then with binoculars, and so on. The Ice Patrol trains its lookouts to scan with the naked eye, to cover the field, and to use binoculars for identification. "You can get captivated by binoculars," they say. To see things at night you must first concentrate on surveying a large visual field, and then you will be able to pick out any anomaly; when you do, you use the binoculars to narrow the field, enlarge the anomaly, and examine it. Exactly the same principle applies, they say, to side-looking airborne radar: big sweeps first with a wide field, searching for anomalies, then close-ups.

All this is pertinent to what happened in the *Titanic*'s crow's nest in the moments before impact. The crow's nest accommodated two lookouts standing up; there was a locker for binoculars, which was empty; a telephone to the bridge; and a bell with a clapper, rung by hand. It was very cold, very calm, and the stars—as everyone noticed—were very bright.

Now Fred Fleet was perhaps the most important man in the entire drama: the man who sighted the iceberg, the man who always insisted that if he had had binoculars he might have seen it earlier. If he had seen it even a few seconds earlier, the action taken by Murdoch on the bridge might have been effective and the iceberg might have slid harmlessly by. In that case, probably nobody would ever have heard about it. Fleet and Lee would not have wanted it known that they as lookouts on a clear night had failed to see an iceberg until the ship nearly hit it; and Murdoch would not have wanted to be marked down in the White Star head office as the officer who nearly rammed an iceberg with their newest and largest liner. Not all near misses by aircraft are reported now; and the Ice Patrol wonders how many near collisions by ships were reported then.

But although Fleet was the key figure aboard the *Titanic* at 11:40 p.m. that Sunday night, he was scarcely cast for the role. The Philadelphia Maritime Museum possesses letters he wrote in 1964 and 1965 to Mr. Edward Kamuda of the Titanic Historical Society in the United States, who had written to ask about his career. Fleet wrote back from Southampton, mentioning that he kept two framed photographs of survivors in his bedroom. A month later he wrote again, a sad letter:

> I don't know who my parents where [*sic*], I have been an orphan all my life my Mother left when I was a baby she went to a place called Springfield Mass [oddly enough, Mr. Kamuda's hometown] I have been brought up in one of those homes Dr. Barnadoes till I was twelve and then

went to a training ship till I was sixteen then pushed out to look after myself. I started out as a deck boy worked up till I was an Able seaman, been all kinds of company's ships, finished up with the sea in 1936 the *Olympic* was my last ship, from the time I started deep sea, 1903 I was no better off, pay in those days was very poor, I was always without money always in debt.

On January 8, 1965, he wrote to Mr. Kamuda again: "My dear Friend, Just a few lines to let you know I am in deep trouble I have just lost my wife, also I am leaving my house the place where I have been living their [*sic*] is only my brother-in-law and myself we cannot agree. From yours sincerely, Fred Fleet."

The letter was posted in Southampton at 1:30 p.m. on January 9. It may well have been the last letter that Fleet wrote. On January 11 the *Southern Evening Echo* (having changed its name from the *Southern Daily Echo* in the interim) reported that Mr Fleet the day before had been found hanged from a clothes post in the garden of his brother-in-law's house in Norman Road, Fremantle, a suburb of Southampton.

The paper recalled that in later life Fleet had worked as an occasional newspaper seller for the *Echo*. Every now and again, the paper had carried stories of the "little do the people who buy papers from the seller at the corner of Market Street realize" variety. Interviewed for these stories, Fleet would always repeat that if he had had binoculars the *Titanic* might have been saved.

He was even more definite at the inquiries. Mr. Scanlan, the lawyer representing the National Sailors' and Firemen's Union in London, asked him if with glasses he would have seen the iceberg sooner. "Certainly," he replied.

Q: How much sooner do you think you would have seen it?

A: In time for the ship to get out of the way.

Q: So that it is your view that if you had had glasses it would have made all the difference between safety and disaster?

A: Yes.

Q: After all, you are the man who discovered the iceberg?

A: Yes.

Q: Would you have used them constantly?

A: Yes.

Fleet, however, may have been a difficult character. After his death, his brother-in-law wrote to Mr. Kamuda to say that he did not "hold any pleasant memories of Mr. Fleet." He mentioned domestic differences to which, perhaps, little significance should be attached. But at the inquiries Fleet came out as truculent, even paranoid.

The Court was trying to establish whether or not there had been any haze. Lightoller said there was none; if there had been, either he or Murdoch should have told the captain. But Lee had testified that the haze was serious: "We had all our work cut out to pierce through it just after we started"—that is, after he and Fleet went on watch. He said Fleet had remarked to him, "Well, if we can see through that we will be lucky." Fleet himself said there was a "slight haze," but it was "not difficult at all" to see. A lawyer asked him to account for the conflict between his "slight haze" and his remark as reported by Lee. "Well, I never said that," he replied.

Conducting the inquiry, Lord Mersey at that point dismissed Lee's testimony altogether, saying it was inconsistent with everything else the Court had heard. "This man was trying to make excuses for not seeing the iceberg," he said, which was surely true.

But then Fleet was asked about Lightoller's testimony. Lightoller had talked to Fleet after they were rescued, and Fleet had not said anything about haze.

SIR ROBERT FINLAY, K. C.: Is that right?
A: Well, I'm not going to tell him my business. It is my place in court to say that, not to him.
LORD MERSEY: You really do not understand. This gentleman is not trying to get round you at all.
A: But some of them are, though.
MERSEY: They are not. I can see you think most of us are, but we are not.

When another lawyer asked Fleet, not for the first time, about the presence of women on the boat deck after the collision, he declined to give any answer at all. The verbatim transcript records "No answer." Fleet then said, "Is there any more likes to have a go at me?"

A peculiarity of Fleet's emerged at the American Senate inquiry. He could not judge distances. He refused to give any estimate of how far away the iceberg had been when he saw it, despite sympathetic questioning designed to help him. As Senator Smith remarked, an admitted inability to judge distances was a strange defect for a professional ship's lookout. Fleet drew a picture to show how the iceberg looked when he sighted it: the iceberg is on the horizon, which cannot have been accurate. Lookouts' eyesight was supposed to be regularly tested, and Fleet's had been tested five years earlier. In England, Board of Trade officials thought the Court should order a newer and more thorough test for all the *Titanic*'s lookouts, but their advice for some reason was not followed.

Fleet saw the iceberg, rang the bell three times, reached across Lee to the telephone, and called, "Iceberg right ahead!" On the bridge, the sixth officer said, "Thank you" and repeated the warning to Murdoch, who at once ordered, "Hard-a-starboard!"—which meant, under the system of helm orders then in force, that the ship's head would go to port. Then Murdoch ordered, "Stop. Full speed astern." He pulled the switch that closed the watertight doors in the boiler and engine rooms. The ship's head swung slowly to port. In the crow's nest, Fleet thought they had missed the iceberg altogether; on the bridge they felt the impact.

Captain Smith came rushing out of his room.

"Mr. Murdoch, what was that?"

"An iceberg, sir."

The British inquiry concluded that the iceberg had torn a three-hundred-foot gash in the hull on the starboard side, above the double bottom. The Woods Hole underwater inspections have thrown doubt on this conclusion. At all events, within minutes the water had reached fourteen feet above the keel. Six watertight compartments were breached. The transverse bulkheads, or upright partitions, had not been built all the way up to the deck-heads; so that as the ship's bow went down, adjoining compartments filled up too, like—as someone said later—the sections of an ice-cube tray. If only three of the *Titanic*'s compartments had been flooded, the ship could have stayed afloat, but with six gone she was doomed.

3

SURVIVAL OF THE RICHEST?

In all disasters, it is the fate of the rich and famous that attracts the most fascinated attention; and of this squalid but universal truth the *Titanic* is a glaring example. Like the poor on land, drowned steerage passengers have no history. Common humanity has little interest in knowing what happened to other common people like themselves; shocked by the sudden intervention of chance and chaos in human affairs, they draw reassurance from the knowledge that even the privileged can come to an untimely end.

Privilege has rarely, in modern times, been more blatantly on display than it was aboard the *Titanic*. Soon after the news of the disaster came through, newspapers and magazines such as the *Illustrated London News* published sectional drawings of the ship. Nothing could have exposed more starkly the social structure of the civilized western world. There on the top decks in the lavishly furnished and spacious cabins were the rich, "the great merchants, the princes of trade, the controllers of the world's markets," as Sir Philip Gibbs called them in his pamphlet; next down were the second class, in more modest conditions; and there toward the bottom of the ship were the lower classes, four to a cabin. Finally, down below the water-line were the laboring class, in heat and noise and steam, shifting coal by shovel and barrow, stoking the fires in the boilers, tending the pumps, the electricity generators, the dynamos, and the engines. The illustrations showed social inequality at its most extreme and at its most vertical, with the classes ranged one above the other, the richest visibly on top and the poorest visibly at the bottom. The drawings were almost caricatures of social stratification.

It was the rich who attracted most attention from the beginning. Sir Philip Gibbs went so far as to draw up a list of millionaires—"men known to have represented a total capital of at least £120 million"—with the richest at its head. His list began:

Colonel J. J. Astor	£30 million
Mr. B. Guggenheim	£20 million
Mr. I. Straus	£10 million
Mr. G. Widener	£10 million

He then listed those thought to be worth between five million and a million.

But there was another circumstance that caught the public's attention besides the extreme wealth of some of the passengers. Soon after the disaster, the Board of Trade published tabulated statistics that showed the number of passengers, male and female, in each class. The same tables showed what proportion of passengers and crew had been saved. The figures were startling, and their implications inescapable. A far higher proportion of first-class passengers had survived than of any other class. Thirty-four percent of male first-class passengers had been saved, by compari-son with 8 percent of second-class males and 12 percent in third class. There could be no arguing with these figures: the rich, defined as anyone in first class, must have had privileged treatment. Suddenly it looked as if death and disaster were not such great levelers after all.

It may have been for this reason that Colonel Astor's name became so closely identified with the name of the *Titanic*. Professor P. N. Furbank has shown with a wealth of scholarship that in Britain the idea of class and classes emerged during the first half of the nineteenth century. He has demonstrated the artificiality of the concept, and its subjectivity. But the class system aboard the *Titanic* was real, and seems particularly bleak and crude because it was based entirely on money. In the enclosed and temporary society of the great transatlantic liners it was logical that Colonel Astor, being the richest man on board, should be treated by everyone, not simply by the White Star Line servants but by other passengers, by newspapers, and by newspaper readers, as the most significant and important. But there was more to it than that. He was not only the richest, but he had been drowned. Looking back through the files, it is clear that "Astor" was the evocative name that every newspaper wanted in its *Titanic* headlines.

The colonel, as it happens, was an interesting man. Photographs of Astor from around this time reveal a conventional figure with a trim, military moustache, an upright bearing, and a confident gaze. There is nothing American-looking about him. He could be one of a thousand similarly dressed Englishmen on his way to the City of London.

Behind the orthodox exterior, however, Colonel Astor, besides being fabulously wealthy, was enterprising and mildly eccentric. The Astors had (and still have) a confusing though understandable habit of naming sons after the founding father, John Jacob Astor, who emigrated to the United States from Waldorf in Germany in 1783 and made a fortune from the fur trade and subverting the Indians. The

colonel, his great-grandson, was the fourth descendant to
be named after him. He went to Harvard and developed a
keen interest in mechanical engineering that came out in a
passion for motorcars (he was once fined by a British court
for exceeding the speed limit in Croydon). He invented a
brake for bicycles, which was successfully marketed, and
a pneumatic device for flattening road surfaces that won a
prize. He experimented with a new sort of ship's turbine
and waived the rights to its patent. He wrote a novel which
has been classified as an early example of science fiction,
in which Colonel Bearwarden, president of the Terrestrial
Axis Straightening Company, pumps out the Arctic to put
the globe on an even keel.

He was also, in a mild way, a man of action. In the
Spanish–American war, he raised and financed his own
unit, named after himself, and in Cuba attended one of
the principal battles; hence the rank of colonel. He was
an intrepid yachtsman and once disappeared for sixteen
days aboard his private yacht *Nourmahal* in the Carib-
bean, affecting real-estate markets in New York, causing
a United States revenue cutter to be sent to search for
him, and provoking, after he appeared safe in San Juan,
an irritated leading article in *The New York Times* which
said crossly that national concern for the colonel's safety
had been unduly exaggerated. (The paper changed its tune
when he disappeared on the *Titanic*.)

In business, he maintained and extended the family's
vast real-estate holdings in New York, showing a special
fascination with hotels. At the time of his death he owned
more hotels and skyscrapers in Manhattan than anyone had
ever owned; he had built the Knickerbocker and the St.
Regis. The old Astor family town house had been at the
corner of Fifth Avenue and Thirty-fourth Street; after the
property was divided between J. J. Astor and his cousin,

the cousin put up a hotel and called it the Waldorf, and J. J. Astor put up an adjoining hotel and called it the Astoria; hence the Waldorf-Astoria, which at once became, as it has remained, the best-known hotel name in the city. (The Waldorf was given as a present to one of the English Astors, William Waldorf Astor, the M.P. and husband of Nancy Astor; he sold it to the du Ponts in 1916.) Not long before Colonel Astor was drowned, he was assessed for tax on his Manhattan holdings; they were revealed to be an astounding accumulation of no fewer than 700 different lots.

The public was even more interested in his matrimonial affairs. In 1909, to the particular amazement of the residents of Dutchess County, where the colonel had an estate, it was abruptly announced that his wife was suing him for divorce. A month later, all legal proceedings having been kept secret—to the indignation of the New York press—and the papers in the case sealed, Mrs. Astor was granted a divorce. She was discovered living under an assumed name in French Lick Springs, Indiana. Two years afterward, the colonel allowed it to be known that he proposed to marry an eighteen-year-old New York girl named Madeleine Force. The announcement set off an uproar among the churches. The judge who granted the divorce said that Astor could not remarry in New York State; but the Episcopalian bishops said he should not be remarried at all, and they were supported by the president of the Federation of New York Churches. Astor thereupon offered a Baptist pastor a thousand-dollar fee to perform the ceremony. He refused. Astor repeated the offer to a Methodist, who also declined. Two volunteers came forward: a clergyman in Norwalk and another in Providence, Rhode Island. Finally, the couple were married on September 9, 1911, by the Reverend J. Lambert of the Elmwood Temple in Newport. The Berkshire, Massachusetts, Ministers Club instantly condemned Lambert, as did the Chicago Congregational Ministers Union; and the Rhode Island Congregational Ministers Association passed a resolution deploring the marriage. Two months after he had performed the ceremony Lambert resigned—bowing, he said, to the criticism of his fellow clergymen. It was in the wake of these disputes that Colonel Astor, having spent most of the autumn of 1911 cruising up and down the east coast of the United States in his yacht, being assailed by newspaper reporters every time he put into harbor, decided to escape both the winter and the controversy by taking his young wife abroad on a trip to Egypt, followed by a few days in Paris before catching the *Titanic* back to the United States. By this time his wife was pregnant.

The second name on Sir Philip's list, Benjamin Guggenheim, was scarcely less interesting than Colonel Astor, though the £20 million attached to his name turned out to be an exaggeration. He was born in 1865, the fifth of seven sons of Meyer Guggenheim, a Swiss emigrant. The family had made their vast fortune principally in smelting, in Leadville, Colorado. Benjamin had moved from mining into mining machinery; he owned a plant in the United Kingdom. Then he went into the manufacture of pumps, some of them big enough to feed a city's main water supply with twenty million gallons a day. The story of how he met his death is well attested. When he heard the ship was doomed he went below and reappeared in full evening dress, saying that if he was going to die he wanted to die like a gentleman. Then he told a steward to tell his wife, if he was lost and the steward saved, that Ben Guggenheim had done his duty, a message the steward was able to deliver. The family went to the quayside to meet the *Carpathia* when the ship arrived in New York with the survivors, but down the gangplank came not Ben Guggenheim but the blonde singer reputed to be his mistress. His daughter Peggy Guggenheim, who became a celebrated collector of modern art and patron of artists, always believed that the woman was paid by the family to return at once to Europe to avoid scandal. A further blow was in store for the young Peggy when her father's will was proved. He had left one-third of his money to his wife and two-thirds to his daughters; but the fortune had dwindled away and Peggy inherited only $450,000, which was much less than she had been brought up to expect.

The third name on Sir Philip's list became, with his wife, one of the *Titanic*'s principal heroes. Isidor Straus arrived in the United States shortly before the American Civil War. Settled in Georgia, he and his family found themselves in what one descendant calls "the world of *Gone with the Wind*" and became salesmen for Confederate bonds; Isidor traveled to Liverpool to sell them. After the war, when many Southerners defaulted, Straus senior did not; having thus acquired a reputation for exceptional probity, he was able to raise credit in the North, and the family went into the glass and china business. In New York, the big new store of R. H. Macy was flourishing; Isidor and his brother asked if they could have a corner of the store to sell glass and chinaware; in return, they would give the store 10 percent of the takings. In ten years they owned the store. Today, there are more than eight hundred branches nationwide.

Several eyewitnesses told substantially the same story about the Strauses' behavior while the *Titanic* was sinking. Colonel Gracie described how Mrs. Straus declined a seat in one of the lifeboats in order not to be separated from her husband, to whom she had been married for forty years; how he, Colonel Gracie, suggested that Mr. Straus should be allowed to be an exception to the rule of women and children first, since he was old and infirm and would have little hope of surviving by his own efforts; how Mr. Straus scotched the idea, refusing to accept special treatment; and how the colonel last saw the couple taking their seats in steamer chairs on the boat deck to await their end.

Seventy-three years later a footnote was added to the story. Iphigene Ochs Sulzberger, an elderly daughter of Adolph Ochs, the founder of *The New York Times,* wrote a brief article in the paper saying that the discovery of the wreck was perhaps the time to make generally known what she had known since 1912, when she was a student at Barnard. Mrs. Straus's maid survived. On the ship, before the maid got into a lifeboat, Mrs. Straus had taken off her fur coat and said, "Wear this, it will be cold in the lifeboat, and I do not need it any more." When the maid arrived back in New York, she took the coat to Mrs. Straus's daughter, who told the maid to keep it, as it was her mother's gift to her. Isidor Straus, a man of modest tastes, had been a considerable philanthropist. A memorial service for him and his wife was attended by no fewer than forty thousand New Yorkers, some of them from the tenements of the Lower East Side. At Broadway and 107th Street a small park was dedicated to their memory and presented to the city by the family; it was land that had once formed part of Isidor Straus's dairy farm. Macy's employees collected money for a plaque to be placed over the 135 West Thirty-fourth Street entrance, still known as the Memorial Entrance.

As for the fourth name on the list, the sinking of the *Titanic* resulted in Harvard University acquiring a substantial library. The Wideners had made their money as tramway kings; Harry Widener, aged twenty-seven and a Harvard graduate, was less interested in transport than in books and was already respected on both sides of the Atlantic as a bibliophile, a friend and customer of the two leading antiquarian booksellers of the day, Bernard Quaritch in London and A. S. Rosenbach in Philadelphia. It was for Harry Widener that Rosenbach had recently bid a record £18,000 for a first folio Shakespeare. Before going to Europe with his mother and father, Harry Widener had attended in New York the first part of the Robert Hoe library sale and had been the underbidder, at $49,000, for a Gutenberg Bible; Henry Huntington had bid a thousand more. Widener had also looked over the books due to form the next part of the sale and had shown interest in one particular rarity, the Caxton edition of John Gower's *Confessio Amantis.* Both he and his father were drowned; and in Harry's memory his mother—the hostess at the last dinner party aboard the *Titanic*—gave Harvard the great library that bears his name. It is one of three American cultural institutions with a *Titanic* connection; the other two are the Guggenheim Museum in New York and the New York Public Library, which inherited Colonel Astor's collection of rare books.

There were other well-off people aboard: a Washington banker, a telephone company widow, a yachtsman from Marblehead, Massachusetts, a cotton manufacturer, a Guernsey businessman going to Toledo to visit relatives, and a fifteen-year-old heiress from St. Louis with an allowance of $7,500 a year for her education and clothes. Mr. Clarence Moore was in first class; he was the Master of the Chevy Chase hunt, who had bought "25 brace of hounds," said the papers, in England. So was Charles M. Hays, the Canadian president of Grand Trunk Pacific Railroad Companies, who had built a new bridge over the Niagara

River at Niagara Falls and was ranked second in North America as a railwayman to the late Edward H. Harriman. There may well have been some professional gamblers on the ship, too; and there was certainly a well-known man-about-town, Clinch Smith, who had been present in 1906 when the adulterous architect Stanford White was shot dead by a jealous husband in New York City. One person who had planned but failed to take the trip was the ultimate owner of the *Titanic,* J. P. Morgan himself; it had been said that he was in poor health, but a reporter found him, just after the ship went down, "in excellent health" at the Grand Hotel, Aix, where he was undertaking the cure. The reporter was writing a seventy-fifth-birthday piece, but no one would think Mr. Morgan seventy-five, he said; he was hale, with "the bright critical eyes of the connoisseur." He took no exercise, and at Aix was concentrating on sulfur baths and massage, with "occasional Naunheim treatment." Apparently as an afterthought the reporter asked him about the *Titanic,* whereupon, toward the end of the article as published, J. P. Morgan indicated extreme distress.

It was to try to get a better understanding of this aspect of the disaster—to see what lay behind the statistics showing that the rich came off best, which might well be thought the most scandalous part of the whole story—that I went to Philadelphia to visit John Thayer, whose grandfather, vice president of the Pennsylvania Railroad, perished in the sinking, but whose grandmother and father survived. Mr. Thayer—the fifth John Borland Thayer—is in his sixties, trim and alert. He has retired from farming and lives with his wife in a comfortable house well outside the city. On the telephone Mr. Thayer had said he had "nothing much" to show me, and so I was taken aback when he ushered me into his study, which is a maritime museum. Paintings and photographs of ships covered the walls; a glass case displayed ship models, some of them made by Mr. Thayer himself; here were books about ships and relics of ships, and most of the collection had to do with the transatlantic liners of the past century. His lifelong absorption with his hobby started at school, when he used to write to the captains of the big liners asking for their autographs, and he has never stopped since, buying in London as well as in the United States.

After he had shown me some of his prize items, including a group of framed representations of ships assembled by montage, partly using silk and velvet, to give a three-dimensional effect, he went to a corner and pulled open the drawer of a filing cabinet. Everything in the study is ship shape, and the drawer contained neat folders from which Mr. Thayer carefully drew out an original first-class *Titanic* passenger list which he said his grandmother had happened to bring away from the ship in the pocket of her coat. Next he pulled out and handed to me a carbon copy of a typed document on good onionskin paper turned slightly yellow with age, four pages fastened by a rusty pin. The document was headed "In the matter of an inquiry into the loss of the *Titanic*" and began as follows:

I, Marian Longstreth Morris Thayer, widow of John B. Thayer, of Haverford, Montgomery County, in the State of Pennsylvania, United States of America, hereby make oath and say:

I was a first-class passenger on the *Titanic*. My husband and I were guests at a dinner in the restaurant on Sunday evening, the 14th of April, given by Mr. and Mrs. Widener. Captain Smith was there, also Major Butt [President

Taft's favorite aide] and others. We entered the restaurant at 7:35 p.m. I am sure that our party, including Captain Smith, left the restaurant, to have coffee, before 8:30 p.m., as the dinner was served very quickly. We went out into the hall by the companionway for that purpose. Captain Smith had left our party and gone towards his own quarters by a quarter of nine o'clock, at the latest.

My husband, my son, and I were the only persons at the Captain's table in the Saloon. The Captain usually took his meals in the Saloon, but did not do so for about the first day and a half after sailing. I noticed that the Captain never took any alcoholic liquor of any kind at any meal.

I do not remember hearing, during the dinner on Sunday night, any mention made by any person of ice being in the neighborhood, or that we might expect to see ice, as Mr. Widener, Major Butt, and I were deeply engrossed in conversation on other subjects during the entire time of the dinner.

The collision occurred at fourteen minutes before twelve o'clock, and at that time I was in my stateroom, No. 68, on the port side of C Deck, awake. I had just rung for the steward to open the porthole. He was in the middle of the room. The jar of the impact was slight, but prolonged. We threw on overcoats and went up to A Deck, on the starboard side. Upon looking over the side of the vessel I saw what looked like a number of long, black ribs, apparently floating nearly level with the surface of the water, parallel with each other but separated from each other by a few feet (two or three feet) of water. These long black objects were parallel with the side of the ship—the nearest one being probably twenty feet from the ship, and they extended from near the bow to about amidship. I saw no high iceberg at that time. We walked around to the port side of the deck. I then remarked to my husband and son that the ship was listing towards the starboard and bow.

I then went down to my cabin to dress. My son and husband told me the accident was serious and that we should put on life belts immediately. Our steward brought life belts to us and helped us to put them on. I saw other stewards helping passengers to put on the life belts. All the stewards were, I think, remarkably good, and quite self-possessed. There was no panic.

It was about five minutes past twelve when I left my cabin. I went up on A Deck with my husband and stayed probably for ten or fifteen minutes in the companionway. Then the women were ordered to go up to the boat deck. Mr Dodd, the Chief Dining Saloon Steward, told us to go there. I saw Captain Smith giving orders on the port side of the bridge, near where we were standing on the boat deck. I also saw Mr. Wild [*sic*] and other officers. There seemed to be very few seamen about. A group of men—some of them with blackened faces, whom I supposed were stokers—came up on deck from below. At this time rockets were going up beside us, and the Morse signal light was begun. All the officers seemed to be very busy, and working hard. I saw only one man (who looked like a foreigner, and was evidently a steerage passenger) who had "lost his head," and he was struggling and fighting, deliriously, near us. I think the steerage passengers had as good a chance as any of the rest of us to be saved. I saw many of them on the deck near us.

While still on the boat deck I saw, on the port side, what appeared to be the hull of a ship, headed in the opposite direction from our ship, and quite near us (perhaps a mile away), from which rockets were being sent up. I am certain of this, for later, on reaching the water, I was disappointed to find she had disappeared. The impression I had received was that the vessel was less than half the size of the *Cedric,* and higher out of the water at her bow than the *Carpathia.*

The order was now given, "All women to the boats," but it was found too difficult to get the women into the boats from the boat deck, as the boats swung too far out from the deck. We were then ordered to go to A Deck. Mr. Wild [*sic*] took us there, and the boat was lowered there. Here again delay occurred on account of there being no means of getting from the ship into the boat—the boat being too far away from the ship. Ladders were called for, but there being none it was necessary to lash two steamer chairs together to serve as a sort of gang plank to enable the women to get into the boat.

The lifeboat that I was in was No. 4. As the boat was being lowered, and when it was still about twelve feet above the water, we heard the order given above to "Let her go," and only our shouts and protestations to those above prevented the letting go of the tackles while we were yet that distance above the water. As evidence of the danger we were in from this error, we passed an overturned boat shortly after reaching the water. There were two seamen at the oars of our boat, and one steering. There was also a man in the bow of the boat who said he was a Quartermaster. He was absolutely inefficient, and could give us no direction or aid whatever, and besides this was most disagreeable. I do not think he was a Quartermaster. There was no light in the boat—a search was made but nothing found but a bailer. There were forty-five women and some children in the boat when it was lowered, besides the seamen. Just as we reached the water and were about to cast off the boat at least two men from steerage slid down the davit ropes into the boat.

I think it was about 1:40 a.m. when our boat reached the water. . . .

Here was one survivor, at least, who was saying—whatever the efficiency or lack of it with which the evacuation was handled—that first-class passengers were not given special treatment: that steerage passengers had as good a chance of escaping as anyone else.

Mr. Thayer handed me another document, this time the copy of a letter that his father, then seventeen years old, wrote from Haverford to Judge Charles L. Long of Springfield, Massachusetts, on April 23, 1912—eight days after the disaster.

My dear Sir:

I received your letter this morning. Mother and I were very touched by it. Words cannot express how much we sympathize with you and Mrs. Long.

The newspaper clipping is accurate as far as it goes, but it does not give any of the details relating to my short friendship with your son. These I will try to tell you now, giving our own words as I can recall them.

I was sitting in the room outside the main dining saloon, waiting for the music to begin. I had dined alone and was sitting alone, my father and mother having been invited out to dine in the restaurant. There was a box of matches on the small table at which I was sitting. Your son was sitting in front and to one side of us, with his back toward me. He took out a cigarette and, having no matches, came up to my table and asked if he might take a match. I said "Yes." In a few minutes he came back for another one. I told him he might take them back to his table if he wanted, as I didn't smoke. He looked lonely, sitting all alone, and

I was lonely, so I pulled my chair up to his table and asked if I might join him. He smiled and said "Yes, certainly." I started the conversation by telling him that I had just been in Switzerland, Holland, Germany, Austria, and England. He said he had just been in St. Moritz, and he told me all about the winter sports. He said that he had been skiing mostly, and that he did not go on the "Cresta" because he was your only son and you did not want him to run into any danger for nothing. He said that he expected to go back to England in a few months, to spend the summer and go to several house parties. We talked about cricket and baseball. He told me of his trip around the world and of getting shipwrecked near Alaska. He said he only got his feet wet, as he jumped from the boat to the shore. I asked him if he ever collected stamps, with his wonderful advantages for it while traveling. He said he did, but had lost interest in it. I told him it was my hobby. We talked about stamps for a while. Then we talked over different things we had seen, and he connected with some dates. I expressed some surprise, thinking he was about twenty-one or twenty-two. He laughed and asked me to guess his age. So as not to be too far out either way I guessed twenty-six. Then he told me he was thirty, but had been masquerading in Switzerland as twenty-two. We kept on talking about different things, which I do not remember. We talked for about two hours and a half together. Then I saw mother and father come downstairs, so I said good-night to your son. He asked me to come and sit with him or walk with him on deck the next morning. He then went to walk on deck before going to bed. I went to bed with mother and father.

The *Titanic* struck the ice at fourteen minutes to twelve. There was only a slight shock and bumping—then all was still. It was about five minutes after twelve when I again saw your son. Father and mother and I were just going up the stairs, having dressed completely and tied on life preservers under our overcoats, when we met your son on A Deck. He had on an overcoat over his dress suit, and a life preserver on under his overcoat. I think he had just been sitting in the smoking room or had come in from his walk on deck. He came up to me and said "Do you mind if I stick with you?" I replied "No; come ahead; keep with us." We all went up and walked around the boat deck for a while. Father and I said goodbye to mother at the top of the stairs on the boat deck, when they called all the women to the port side. Then your son and myself and father walked around to different boats, only to be directed to others. We then went to the port side. We met Dodd, the dining saloon steward. He took us to mother, as she had not yet gotten into a boat. We stayed with her for a few minutes when Mr. Wild [*sic*], the Chief Officer, told us to go down onto A Deck and get into a boat that they were loading from there. Father and mother went ahead—your son and I followed. A crowd pushed ahead of us and we could not find my mother or father when we were able to pass on, so thinking they had managed to get off in a boat we went to the starboard side of the boat deck. There was an awful crowd around the last boat on the forward part of the starboard side, pushing and shoving wildly. We thought it best not to try to get in it, as we thought it would never reach the water right side up, but it did. We went and stood by the davits of a boat which had left. There was such a big list to port that it seemed as if she would turn over on her side as she sank. In such a case we would not have had the slightest chance, so I told him I was going to jump out and slide down the davit ropes into the water and try to swim to the boats in the distance. I started to do this three times, and each time he caught hold of me and asked me to wait awhile. In a few minutes she straightened up on an even keel. We hurried back and stood by the rail about even with the second funnel. She started to shoot down fast at an angle of about thirty degrees. We shook hands, said goodbye and wished each other luck. We did not give each other any messages for home, because neither of us thought we would ever get back. Then we jumped upon the rail. Your son put his legs over the rail, while I straddled it. Hanging over the side, holding onto the rail with his hands, he looked up at me and said, "You're coming, boy, aren't you?" I replied, "Go ahead, I'll be with you in a minute." He let go and slid down the side and I never saw him again. Almost immediately after he jumped I jumped. All this last part took a very short time, and when we jumped we were about ten yards above the water.

Your son was perfectly calm all the time and kept his nerve, even to the very end. I wish I had more to tell you, but I hope this will be of some comfort to you.

I am sending you my picture, thinking you might like to see who was with him at the end. I would treasure it very much if you could spare me one of his.

Mother and I hope that if you and Mrs. Long feel able to you will come and see us, and let us do what we can for you.

With our heartfelt sympathy, believe me,

Sincerely yours, John B. Thayer, Jr.

Next, Mr. Thayer showed me a statement made by his father as soon as he got back to Philadelphia on April 20; it was typed on foolscap headed "The Pennsylvania Railroad" and went over some of the same ground as the letter to Judge Long, except that he explained in more detail how he tried and failed, because of the crowd, to find

Left: The Harland & Wolff yard in Belfast. The gantry used for the construction of the *Titanic* is in the background.

Below: A White Star Line advertisement for "Triple Screw RMS *Olympic* and *Titanic*, 45,000 tons each. The Largest Steamers in the World."

The *Titanic* leaving Belfast. *Left inset:* Lord Pirrie and J. Bruce Ismay inspecting the *Titanic* before her launching on May 31, 1911. *Right inset:* The boat deck of the *Titanic*.

Opposite: The *Titanic*'s reading and writing room.

Left: A corner of the *Titanic*'s gymnasium.

Below left: Captain E. J. Smith.

Below right: Second Officer Charles Herbert Lightoller.

A section through the *Titanic* from the *Illustrated London News,* April 1912.

Inset: The sinking: a contemporary artist's impression from the *Sphere,* April 27, 1912.

The *Titanic*'s last message: CQD and SOS were distress calls; MGY was the *Titanic*'s call sign.

Colonel and Mrs. J. J. Astor.

Below: Survivors from the *Titanic* approaching the *Carpathia*.

his parents: "That was the last time I saw my father." He also said, which shows the persistence of the idea that the *Titanic* was unsinkable, that even after he had made his three starts toward the davit ropes and had been held back by Long, "we thought she might possibly stay afloat."

I asked Mr. Thayer whether his father used to talk about the *Titanic* and he said he did not; nor did his grandmother. In 1940, however, his father suddenly wrote an extended, reflective account of his experiences and published it in a limited edition of 500 copies. Mr. Thayer said that unfortunately the family had failed to copyright the little book, and it had since been published commercially "at four dollars." The preface strongly suggests that it was World War II that stirred Thayer to think about the *Titanic*'s significance. Evidently his long reticence had not been due to any attempt to suppress the memory. "The whole event passes before me now in nineteen hundred and forty, as vividly and with the same clarity, as twenty-eight years ago in nineteen hundred and twelve." The same seems to have been true of all survivors able to talk about their experiences (some were not): they remembered every detail as long as they lived. Thayer in his preface went on to contrast the uncertainties of 1940 with the certainties of his youth, saying that the world had been moving at "a rapidly accelerating pace ever since, with less and less peace, satisfaction, and happiness." The *Titanic* disaster was to him the event that left the old certainties in ruins.

He adds more details to his 1912 accounts. "I have spent much time on the ocean, yet I have never seen the sea smoother than it was that night." Blackish smoke poured out of the three forward funnels (the fourth was the ventilation dummy). After the impact—"if I had had a brimful glass of water in my hand not a drop would have been spilled"—he told his parents that "I was going up on deck

to see the fun." He and his father learned of the seriousness of the collision from Thomas Andrews of Harland
& Wolff, who told them "he did not give the ship much
over an hour to live." The band was playing "lively tunes"
without being much attended to. Twenty-eight years
later, Thayer was sharply critical of the organization: "It
seemed we were always waiting for orders and no orders
ever came." In the early stages the crowd, which included
second- and steerage-class passengers as well as first, was
"fairly orderly," but he remembered one example of disor-
derly behavior. He saw "one man come through the door
out onto the deck with a full bottle of Gordon Gin. He
put it to his mouth and practically drained it. If I ever get
out of this alive, I thought, there is one man I will never
see again. He apparently fought his way into one of the
two last boats, for he was one of the first men I recognized
upon reaching the deck of the SS *Carpathia*. Someone told
me afterwards that he was a State Senator or Congressman
from Virginia or West Virginia."

Thayer was one of the last to leave the ship voluntarily.
He describes how, at around 2:15 a.m., as the ship went
down by the head and water crept up the deck and right
up to the bridge, the crowd gradually moved back toward
the stern, keeping away from the rails—"a mass of hopeless, dazed humanity." He and Long kept near the rail,
thinking their best chance was to stay clear of the crowd.
The collision had been followed by the deafening hiss of
steam escaping from the boilers, but now the noise had
stopped, "making a great quietness" occasionally interrupted by a thud or muffled explosion. Then, as without
warning the ship seemed to start forward, moving into the
water at an angle, the water no longer creeping but rushing toward the stern, a new clamor began: "a rumbling roar
mixed with more muffled explosions; it was like standing

under a steel railway bridge while an express train passes overhead, mingled with the noise of a press steel factory and wholesale breakage of china." Then he jumped.

His son next handed me another private document which, he said, like his grandmother's affidavit and his father's letter, had never been made public. From one point of view it was the most interesting of all, in its artless candor and detail, and it "pretty well confirmed," as Mr. Thayer remarked, his grandmother's account. It was headed "The *Titanic*—Our Story" and was "by M.E.S. and E.M.E.," two sisters, Martha Eustis Stevenson and Elizabeth Eustis, who were neighbors of the Thayers in Haverford.

The story, written by Martha, begins with the sisters, thoroughly appreciating every moment of their trip. On that Sunday they had written letters before morning service, spent the afternoon reading, taken tea on deck, walked on the boat deck, and enjoyed "a delicious dinner with souvenir menus." After dinner they listened to "a fine musical program in the reception room" and at about 9:30 went up to the lounge, "a most beautiful room with an open fire." Because she had finished all her own books, Martha borrowed Shackleton's book about the South Pole from the library steward and spent half an hour looking at pictures of icebergs and ice fields. Before turning in, she remarked to Elizabeth that they only had two more nights to go and "neither of us had had one bit of discomfort from seasickness." Their friend John Thayer, I thought, would have considered their orderly day an excellent example of how life was lived by persons of his circle in the pre-*Titanic* era, when "the world had an even tenor to its ways." "It seems to me," Thayer wrote, "that the disaster about to occur was the event which not only made the world rub its eyes and awake, but woke it with a start."

Martha's account of this seminal event is as follows:

I was sound asleep when at a quarter before twelve I was awakened by a terrible jar with ripping and cutting noises which lasted a few moments. [The sisters were among the very few who were alarmed by the impact.] We were both much frightened, sitting up in bed and turning on the electricity. Our door was on the hook and we soon heard voices in the hall so that Elizabeth put on her wrapper, slippers, and cap and ran out. I was bitterly cold, and, shivering from fright and cold, sat undecided as to what to do. Our steward came down to close the port and I asked him if the order had been given to close all the ports, but he said "No, it's only cold, go to bed; it's nothing at all." Before Elizabeth returned I decided to get dressed as I had seen a gentleman in one of the rooms opposite pull his shoes in from the passageway. When she came in she told of many people outside half-dressed, one woman having a thin white pigtail down her back and a feather hat; also that some man was fastened in his inside room unable to open his door. He was much worried, calling for help, and young Williams [a well-known amateur tennis-player and a friend of young Thayer's] put his shoulder to the panels and broke it in. The steward was most indignant and threatened to have him arrested for defacing the beautiful ship.

I had my shoes nearly buttoned, and she said, "Why, Martha, are you dressing?" and I said I should feel much safer with my clothes on and could go to bed later if it all was right. She then decided to dress also. We did not hurry, and dressed fully as if for breakfast, putting on our burglar pockets containing our letters of credit and money. I determined also to do my hair and put on a lined waist and old winter suit as it was so cold. While Elizabeth was doing her hair the ship suddenly settled, frightening me very much, and I urged her not to take pains but to hurry.

Just as I was wholly dressed and she was hooking her waist Mr. Thayer [Mr. Thayer senior] appeared at the door, which we had opened, and said he was very glad that we had dressed. He thought there was no danger, but we had struck ice and there was much on deck and he urged us to come up and see it, saying we would find him and Mrs. Thayer on the deck. I put on my fur coat over everything and Elizabeth said she thought she would wear her watch, which reminded me that mine was hanging by the bureau and I quickly put it on. I took my glasses and small change purse, also a clean handkerchief. We then left our room, leaving the electric lights on, also the electric heater so it would be warm on our return. We closed the door and started down the long passageway and up the stairs.

On the next deck we met the Thayer family, who seemed to be waiting for us, and started up to go on the deck when a steward called "All back to staterooms for life preservers." We turned around and I cannot remember that we ran but we walked quickly to our rooms and Elizabeth climbed up, pulling down two life preservers from off the top of her closet. We said then we felt it must be serious if they had ordered the life belts, and we were much frightened though very quiet. We again went up the stairs, with our life preservers in our hands and once more joined the Thayer family. We quietly read the notices of "inside front" and "inside back" and put them on over our heads, Elizabeth tying mine and I tying hers. We put ours on over our heavy coats. After our life preservers were on, Mrs. Thayer suggested getting Jack's coat, and Elizabeth and I followed to the steward's room, and when Mrs. Thayer took the coat we each took our steamer rugs, not knowing why, but simply that we were there.

My mind is a blank as to the trip we took to the boat deck, when I distinctly remember being beside the gymnasium on the starboard side and seeing Mr. Ismay come out, noting the fact that he had dressed hurriedly, as his pyjamas were below his trousers. After getting our rugs we were in the companionway of A Deck when orders came for women and children to boat deck and men to starboard side. Elizabeth and I took each other's hands, not to be separated in the crowd, and all went on deck, we following close to Mrs. Thayer and her maid and going up narrow iron stairs to the forward boat deck which, on the *Titanic,* was the captain's bridge.

At the top of the stairs we found Captain Smith looking much worried, and anxiously waiting to get down after we got up. The ship listed heavily to port just then. As we leaned against the walls of the officers' quarters, rockets were being fired over our heads, which was most alarming, as we fully realized if the *Titanic* had used her wireless to ill effect and was sending rockets it must be serious. Shortly after that the order came from the head dining saloon steward to go down to the A Deck, when Mrs. Thayer remarked, "Tell us where to go and we will follow. You ordered us up here and now you are taking us back," and he said "Follow me."

On reaching the A Deck we could see, for the decks were lighted by electricity, that a boat was lowered parallel to the windows; these were opened, and a steamer chair put under the rail for us to step on. The ship had listed badly by that time and the boat hung far out from the side so that some of the men said, "No woman could step across that space." A call was made for a ladder on one of the lower decks, but before it ever got there we were all in the boat. Whether they had drawn the boat over with boathooks nearer the side I do not know, but the space

was easily jumped with the help of two men in the boat.
The only gentleman I remember seeing at all was Colonel
Astor, who was stepping through the window just in front
of me when the crew said, "Step back, sir; no men in this
boat." He remarked that he wanted to take care of his wife
[who was pregnant], but on being told again that no men
could go, he called "Goodbye" and said he would follow
in another boat, asking the number of our boat, which
they said was "No. 4." In going through the window I was
obliged to throw back the steamer rug, for, with my fur
coat and huge cork life preserver, I was very clumsy. Later
we found the stewards or crew had thrown the steamer
rugs into the boat, and they did good service, Elizabeth's
round a baby thinly clad, and mine for a poor member of
the crew pulled in from the sea.

Our boat I think took off every woman on the deck at
that time, and was the last on the port side to be lowered.
Only one man went down with us; the boat was lowered
slowly, first at the bow, then at the stern, and very carefully. When near the water the man gave the order to "Let
her go," but we all called, "Not yet, it's a long way to the
water." On reaching the water they called from the deck
to know who was in command and a man answered, "The
quartermaster." They then said, "Who else?" and he said,
"I am alone." Then they said "We will send you two more
men," and shortly a boatswain and common sailor came
down over the davit ropes and into the boat. . . .

Of the scores of survivors who told their stories at the
time or left private accounts for posterity, John Thayer, his
mother, and the two sisters are among the most persuasive. They had no axe to grind; they knew one another;
they produced the accounts themselves, at home. They had
nothing to hide. None of them had cause to feel guilty

about surviving: the head of the Thayer family had been lost; the women had done as they were told; and John Thayer, Jr., had survived by luck. Martha Stevenson's story about Colonel Astor must be true. Mrs. Astor went to stay with the Thayers in Haverford when they all returned to the United States, and if Martha's memory had been at fault, or if she had confused Astor with another passenger, the Thayers would have known it. Besides, her account is confirmed by Lightoller, who said he was the officer who prevented Astor from leaving.

Colonel Gracie, an amateur military historian, wrote the longest and best-researched account by any first-class passenger. During the crisis he was indispensable, rounding up, with his friend Clinch Smith, women and children for the boats. (Smith, after the collision, picked up a flat piece of ice and told Gracie he could take it home as a souvenir.) One of the surprises in Gracie's book, which he put together with Lightoller's help, was his eyewitness evidence about the number of women among the dazed crowd huddled on the *Titanic*'s stern when she went down. Gracie was washed overboard at the last moment; he saw the women, to his astonishment, in the final minutes. He had thought all women had been rescued.

Gracie made the point that because of the size of the *Titanic* no one could know what was happening except in his or her immediate vicinity, any more than someone standing on a street corner can know what is happening a block away. Nevertheless, from the Thayers, Gracie, and others a reasonably clear picture does emerge of what happened in first class.

The best witness from second class is the young schoolmaster Lawrence Beesley, although his general comments on the cause of the disaster and his recommendations about

the steps that ought to be taken for the prevention of similar disasters are overconfident for someone whose entire
sea-time consisted of four days aboard the *Titanic*. But his
account of his own experiences is level-headed and especially illuminating about the time it took for passengers to
realize that something was seriously wrong. He himself left
his cabin and went on deck not because he was startled by
the collision—he felt "nothing more than an extra heave
of the engines and a more than usually obvious dancing
motion of the mattress"—but because he was curious to
find out why the ship had stopped; he guessed she had
dropped a propeller blade. He went up on deck, which was
deserted, and then into the smoking room, where a game
of cards was in progress, with several onlookers. One man
had seen an iceberg go by, "towering above the decks,"
and had told the others. "They all watched it disappear
but then at once resumed their game." None of them—
incredibly—had been surprised or interested enough to
go out on deck and take a closer look. Their estimates
of its height varied from sixty to a hundred feet. "One of
the players, pointing to his glass of whisky standing at his
elbow, and turning to an onlooker, said, 'Just run along
the deck and see if any ice has come aboard: I would like
some for this.' " The roar and hiss of the steam escaping
from the boilers surprised nobody in the smoking room;
a steam train blew off steam when it stopped, so why not
an ocean liner? It was only when the rockets started going
up that people realized that matters were serious; but even
then they scarcely understood that the ship was sinking.
They felt a "wonderful sense" of security, Beesley said, as
if standing on "a large rock." On the boat deck, about an
hour after the collision, he saw one of the bandsmen running down the starboard side, "his cello trailing behind

him, the spike dragging along the floor." It was soon afterward that the band started playing on the promenade deck and went on playing until the ship went down.

Beesley remembered one incident that helps to explain the statistics. He was on the boat deck when two women walked toward the rail separating the second-class from the first-class part of the deck. They asked an officer, who stood barring the way, if they could pass through to the boats. No, the officer politely told them, their boats were down on their own deck. Beesley concludes: "If the second-class ladies were not expected to enter a boat from the first-class deck, while steerage passengers were allowed access to the second-class deck, it would seem to press rather hardly on the second-class men, and this is rather supported by the low percentage saved." Beesley himself got away because, when he was looking down from the top deck at a boat swinging level with B Deck, a member of the crew told him he had better jump, which he did, having first thrown in his dressing gown.

Beesley jumped some two hours after the *Titanic* was struck. The starboard side of the boat deck was then deserted; and Beesley was advised to take his chance only after the crew on B Deck had searched for and failed to find any more women. Yet more than a hundred women died. Where had they been? And where—at the time that Beesley jumped from a deserted boat deck—was the rest of the "mass of humanity" that Colonel Gracie, half an hour later, suddenly saw flooding up from below just before the ship foundered?

The British inquiry was not interested in these questions; Lord Mersey did not call a single steerage passenger. But they worried the politician from Michigan in charge of the American investigation, William Alden Smith. After the Senate inquiry officially closed in Washington, Senator Smith went to New York to pursue some independent research. He told a reporter he was deeply troubled by the thought of what had happened to the third-class passengers and wanted to find out whether they had been under any restraint. Evidently, he had reservations about the evidence of the *Titanic* officers, since both Lightoller and Lowe had told him categorically that there had been no restraint and that all classes had been given equal treatment. However, it turned out that Lightoller and Lowe had not been precisely accurate. In New York, Smith found a migrant who had seen a member of the crew locking a gate between steerage and the upper decks. But the incident seemed to be isolated and inconclusive, since the migrant went on to say that the passengers had broken the gate down and were thereafter treated the same as other passengers. Elsewhere in the records are reports by third-class survivors about being herded behind ropes by crew members. How many were thus restrained, or for how long, or why, is obscure. There is no evidence that it was general ship's policy to keep the steerage passengers back while the rest escaped.

One enterprising third-class passenger told an innocent tale of how he had found his way onto the boat deck and quietly stepped aboard a lifeboat, evidently entirely unaware, even at the time he was making his statement, that he had done anything in the least deplorable.

Clearly, there was much more confusion and even more bewilderment in steerage than in other classes. By 1912, the balance of migrants heading for the United States had shifted away from northern Europe toward southern Europe, Russia, and the Middle East. There were Syrians and Armenians aboard the *Titanic* and many of the migrants spoke no English. Unlike the first- and second-class passengers, whose immediate instinct was to put on warm clothes, the migrants' instinct was to try to save their belongings, appearing in the passageways laden with parcels and suitcases, or carrying bundles on their backs. Fewer crew members were on hand to tell them what to do. Those who were ignorant of their true plight thought they would be safer on board than in a lifeboat; others were so alarmed that they despaired too early. The American psychologist Wyn C. Wade not long ago was allowed to publish the recollections of a Swedish survivor, the late August E. Wennerström. The Protestant Swede had been irritated by the pious and supine Catholicism shown by fellow passengers: "Hundreds were in a circle with a preacher in the middle, praying, crying, asking God and Mary to help them. They lay there still crying till the water was over their heads. They just prayed and yelled, never lifting a hand to help themselves. They had lost their own will power and expected God to do all the work for them." Besides, the geography of the ship was against them. The route from steerage to the upper decks was long and complicated; the *Titanic*'s designers had not envisaged circumstances in which easy access would be crucial.

Senator Smith told a crowded Senate of his conclusions about the steerage passengers in a speech on May 28:

> The occupants of the forward steerage were the first of the passengers to realize the danger—one or two witnesses said they stepped out of their berths into water probably an inch or two inches deep. Those in the forward steerage knew directly of the impact and of the presence of water which came up from the lower part of the ship into the mail room and the forward steerage. Those steerage passengers went on deck, and as fast as they were able took places in the lifeboats. While the after steerage, more than an eighth of a mile away, was by the operation of the added weight raised out of the water . . . so that these steerage

passengers got their first warning of real danger as the angle of the deck became very great. I feel that the small number of steerage survivors was thus due to the fact that they got no definite warning before the ship was really doomed—when most of the lifeboats had departed.

This analysis begged the question of why "no definite warning" reached them. Captain Smith's policy can only be guessed at. Glimpses of him after the collision have come down to us: exclaiming "My God!" when he saw the degrees of list registered on the inclinometer on the bridge; giving Lightoller permission to take the covers off the lifeboats; telling the wireless operators to call for help; being handed a gun by the first officer; shouting through a megaphone. At the end, he told the wireless operators that they had done their duty and should now look out for themselves; the evidence that he was seen on deck calling, "Every man for himself" is strong; that he urged others to "Be British" is less strong. Why did he not issue a general alarm as soon as he himself knew the seriousness of what had occurred, which was within a very short time of the collision? He had then ordered the carpenter to sound the ship; he had toured her himself with Thomas Andrews, the head of the Harland & Wolff team (none of whom survived); and he conveyed a sense of urgency to those passengers he happened to encounter. He talked to Chief Engineer Bell, who would have agreed that he and his men would do all they could to keep the pumps and power supply working for as long as possible. But neither Lightoller nor Lowe nor Boxhall of the surviving officers seems to have been given any general orders by the captain. When Lightoller was asked whether he was obeying his captain's orders in sending away women and children first, he said he was obeying "the rule of human nature." The presumption must be that Smith thought a general alarm would cause panic belowdecks and chaos above.

At all events, no general strategy was applied to the emergency. This was true even of the lifeboats, where a definite plan was vital—given the lifeboat shortage—if as many lives as possible were to be saved. The government department responsible for lifeboat requirements was the Board of Trade. Its regulations called for ships of 10,000 tons and over to carry a minimum of sixteen boats, with a total minimum capacity of 5,500 feet. It further laid down that "if the boats placed under the davits do not furnish sufficient accommodation for all persons on board, then additional wood, metal, collapsible, or other boats of approved design (whether placed on davits or otherwise), or approved liferafts shall be carried." The additional boats and/or rafts were required to have a capacity equal to 75 percent of the volume of the boats under davits. The *Titanic*'s boat capacity was therefore required to total 9,625 cubic feet. This requirement was exceeded by the *Titanic*'s wooden boats alone. Her collapsible boats brought her total boat volume to 11,325 cubic feet. The Board of Trade allowed 10 cubic feet per person for the *Titanic*'s large lifeboats and 8 cubic feet for the two emergency boats and the collapsibles. The total capacity was calculated to be 1,178 persons.

Under a regulation known as Rule 12, the boat capacity could be reduced if the ship could be shown to have exceptionally good subdivision. In practice, this rule was seldom applied and no application for its use was made.

American regulations were much stricter. They would have required the *Titanic* to provide enough lifeboat space for 2,142 people—still not enough places for a full complement.

The builders and owners of the *Titanic* changed their minds about the lifeboats late in the day. An article in *Engi-*

neering, published while the ship was being built, described a new and improved device for lowering boats on board ship, the quadrant davit for double-banked boats. The article explained the success of the standard Welin quadrant davit, of which 3,000 had recently come into use. Its popularity was due not merely to its mechanical superiority but to the fact that it took up less deck space.

To all familiar with the conditions of modern ocean travel [said the journal] it will be patent what this really means. Nowadays the success of a line of passenger-carrying steamers depends (at least on certain routes) largely upon its popularity among the travelling public. Competition has in many instances afforded a wide choice of routes, and passenger lines must provide, at the present day, vessels not only as safe and well found as possible in all respects, but also boats which are attractive and offer special facilities for the pleasurable occupation of the long hours of enforced leisure. For these and other reasons, saving in deck space is a distinct advantage, and it may be taken that any gear which renders this possible has much to recommend it.

The new and improved davits made it possible to double-bank boats in a way that satisfied Board of Trade regulations. Hitherto, the Board of Trade had said that all boats must be "under davits," which meant that inboard boats did not count. So lifeboats had to be in a long straight line, which took up space and spoiled the view. Now ships could have twice as many boats in much less than twice the space, because one pair of davits could be swung through an arc wide enough to raise and lower two or even, if required, three boats.

This was the system originally planned for the *Titanic. Engineering* published a drawing showing how double-banked boats would provide lifesaving space for 1,700. Triple-banking would have provided space for 2,500. But the plans were revised. Owners and builders decided that, to give the *Titanic* a competitive advantage, more deck space was more desirable than more boats. So the *Titanic* was equipped with sixteen lifeboats and four emergency rafts, enough for some 1,178 people. It should have been possible to get away all these boats fully laden during the two hours or more before the ship sank; the ship took on an increasingly awkward list, but the sea was calm.

Eighteen boats were successfully lowered. Two collapsible boats were washed overboard during the sinking and one of them capsized. About 665 people were loaded and about 50 later managed to scramble on board from the sea. Of the survivors, a sizeable number were crew, not passengers. The operation got off to a slow start. The collision was immediately followed by the order "All hands on deck." At that point Lightoller, according to his own account, used his initiative to tell the bosun's mate of his watch to strip the covers off the boats and clear them away. Then he asked Chief Officer Wilde if he should swing the boats out, but Wilde told him to wait. Next, Lightoller saw Captain Smith leaving the wireless room, "his face stern but haggard." In one Lightoller version he cupped his hand to the captain's ear (because of the noise of escaping steam) and asked if he should swing the boats out; in the other, if he should get the women and children away. Captain Smith in both versions agreed. But Smith did not tell Lightoller that he had just ordered the wireless operators to send out the international distress call. Thus Lightoller did not know the damage was serious until the first few boats had been loaded and lowered the 75 feet from davit to sea level, and even then did not believe the ship would sink. He only came to realize she was doomed after making a series of brief visits to the head of a long narrow stairway, constructed for the use of the crew, that led down from the boat deck to some four decks below; it was the sight of the water creeping further and further up the stairway that gave him a sense of urgency. The form it took was to make him sharply conscious of the "unutterable disgrace of going down with boats still hanging on the davits." He was frustrated and briefly delayed in his work by the refusal of some people, including Mr. and Mrs. Straus, to get into the boats, and he ran out of experienced help, since few of the crew were all-around seamen and those who were competent were needed to accompany the women and children in the boats. Instead of organizing and supervising the efforts of others, he himself had to throw off his overcoat and set to work—lifting women, who stood in a row with their arms held out, bodily across the gap between the boats' gunwales and the ship's deck.

Very soon after the disaster there was a public outcry, especially in the United States, from newspapers and others wanting to know why the *Titanic* had carried so few lifeboats, and why they had not all been filled. The first question was soon answered: the *Titanic* had adhered to British regulations, which were disgracefully out of date. The second question was less rapidly answered, but it eventually emerged at the American inquiry that both Lightoller and Lowe, on the port and starboard sides respectively, assumed it would be hazardous to fill up the boats when still suspended from the davits; either the boats might "buckle up," as Lowe put it, or the davits might give way. They did not know that Harland & Wolff had tested the davits and established that they would carry the weight of lifeboats filled to capacity.

Lightoller's idea was to get the boats into the water safely, though only partly full, and then send them to an open hatch at the bottom of a gangway to fill up with more passengers. But the bosun's mate and team he sent below for this purpose were never seen again. One mystery remains, however. Even if Lightoller and Lowe did not know about the strength of the davits, what about Captain Smith? Supposing that Smith did not know either, what about all the Harland & Wolff representatives on board? They included Thomas Andrews, the Harland & Wolff director, Lord Pirrie's nephew, who had been trained by the firm and had taken a deep interest in all practical details of the ship's design from the initial stages. They also included the chief shipyard draftsman, Mr. R. Chisholm, than whom, said *Engineering,* "no one was more conversant with modern practice in the building of large merchant ships." The other members of the staff were almost equally knowledgeable. They must have seen what was happening. Yet it was only the last boats, after pushing and shoving, that were filled up.

One gets the impression from Lightoller and Lowe that they were fearful of being rushed by panic-stricken passengers. As soon as he heard that the ship had struck, Lowe equipped himself with his own Browning automatic. When about half the boats on the port side had been got away, Chief Officer Wilde came over to Lightoller from the starboard side and asked him where the small arms were. It had been one of Lightoller's jobs in Belfast to receive and take charge of revolvers and ammunition, but when demoted to second officer he had left the weapons in his former cabin, later occupied by William Murdoch. He led Wilde, Murdoch, and the captain to Murdoch's cabin, gave them a revolver each and took one himself. Lightoller deduced that "there had been some trouble" with the starboard-side boats. Lowe told the Senate inquiry he had fired to deter "a lot of Italians" who were "glaring more or less like wild beasts ready to spring" into a boat. Later he issued a statement saying he had not meant that the "wild beasts" were Italian; he meant only that they were "of the types of the Latin races." Lightoller also found his revolver useful. After getting the last lifeboat away he went forward to fill and lower the much smaller No. 2 emergency boat. "I climbed aboard to find three or four men hidden under the thwarts." Nearly a quarter of a century later, Lightoller wrote of this incident: "Let me say at once they were neither British nor American; in fact, never in my life have I been so unspeakably proud of the English-speaking race as I was during that night. The cool, calm unselfish courage exemplified throughout has never been excelled." The "would be stowaways," he continued, were rapidly dealt with. "A few threats, accompanied by the flourish of an empty revolver, soon cleared the boat which was quickly filled and in the water."

The *Titanic's* officers knew from the beginning that there were not enough boats to accommodate all those on board; they soon realized that there was also a shortage of trained crew. It is hard to resist the conclusion that, consciously or unconsciously, their aim in these desperate circumstances was to get away as many first- and second-class passengers as possible—who were in any case the nearest to the boats—before the whole operation was swamped by uncontrollable hordes from steerage.

To that extent, it is fair to say the rich were favored over the poor. But one should remember that of the men in first class only 58 out of 173 were saved: 34 percent is not a high percentage, even though it is strikingly higher than that in the other classes. Money was not enough; many of the richest and best known drowned. Wilfred Scawen Blunt, the writer and adventurer, wrote in his diary that if anyone had to drown, it was best that it should be the Anglo-American millionaires. It was a foolish sentiment, and no doubt widely shared. But it was, and is, incompatible with the notion that all the rich received favored treatment.

4

IN THE LIFEBOATS

Leaving the ship was a fearful experience even for those who found a place in the boats. It was unimaginably terrifying for those who jumped or were swept overboard. For most survivors, though, the hours still ahead were to bring the most horrific moments of all. During that time, some of them faced character tests they failed to pass.

Few of the lifeboats got away smoothly. Falls jammed; the lights required by Board of Trade regulations in all boats were found in some cases to be missing; so were plugs. As Lowe blithely explained to the American inquiry, not every seaman member of a liner's crew was competent to handle a 30-foot lifeboat, or had even set foot in one. True all-around seamen were rare aboard the *Titanic*. "Many of the sailors could not row," said Lowe. Mrs. Thayer concluded that the man in charge of her lifeboat could not be a quartermaster, as he claimed, because he was so "absolutely inefficient." She was mistaken, however; he was Quartermaster Perkis.

Besides Mrs. Thayer and the quartermaster, No. 4 lifeboat contained Martha Stevenson and her sister; Mrs. Astor and her trained nurse and maid; Mrs. Thayer's maid; Mrs.

Widener and her maid; Mrs. Carter, her two children, and
her maid; Mrs. Arthur Ryerson, her boy, two daughters,
governess, and maid; and many women and children from
second and third class—some forty-five in all.

Martha Stevenson described what happened after the
boat was in the water:

> When we reached the sea we found the ship badly listed,
> her nose well in so that there was water to the D Deck,
> which we could plainly see as the ship was lighted and the
> ports on D Deck were square instead of round. No lights
> could be found in our boat and the men had great dif-
> ficulty in casting off the blocks as they did not know how
> they worked. My fear here was great, as she [the *Titanic*]
> seemed to be going faster and faster and I dreaded lest we
> be drawn in before we could cast off.
>
> When we were finally ready to move on, the order was
> called from the deck to go to the stern hatch and take off
> some men [this was the Lightoller plan that failed because
> the bosun's mate and the party sent to execute it disap-
> peared]. There was no hatch open and we could see no
> men, but our crew obeyed orders, much to our alarm, for
> they were throwing wreckage over and we could hear a
> noise resembling china breaking, which we learned later
> was the cracking of the boiler plates. We implored the men
> to pull away from the ship but they refused, and we pulled
> three men into the boat who had dropped off the ship and
> were swimming toward us. One man was drunk and had
> a bottle of brandy in his pocket which the quartermaster
> promptly threw overboard and the drunk was thrown into
> the bottom of the boat and a blanket thrown over him.
> After getting in these three men they told how fast she was
> going and we all implored them to pull for our lives to get
> out from the suction when she should go down.

One of the luckiest men that night was Belfast fireman Thomas (Paddy) Dillon. He went down with the ship, but managed to reach the surface. Taken into lifeboat 4, he collapsed, but recovered to find two dead shipmates sprawled on top of him. Beesley was also lucky. He was young and wide-eyed enough to experience the lowering of himself and sixty others down the liner's black hull as "a great adventure." If anyone wanted to know what the sensation was like, he recommended them to measure seventy-five feet from a tall house or block of flats, look down on the ground, and then imagine themselves being crammed into a boat and descending in a continuous series of jerks. When his boat was in the water no one knew how to release the falls. It was carried parallel to the ship until it was directly underneath another boat being lowered. The crew on the boat deck could not hear the shouts from the Beesley boat, nor the subsequent shouts from the boat being lowered, and Beesley and his sixty companions were about to be crushed when at the last moment a sailor found a knife and cut the falls. The crew members in Beesley's boat were useless:

> I do not think they can have had any practice in rowing, for all night long their oars crossed and clashed; if our safety had depended on speed or accuracy in keeping time it would have gone hard with us. Shouting began from one end of the boat to the other as to what we should do, where we should go, and no one seemed to have any knowledge how to act. At last we asked, "Who is in charge of this boat?" but there was no reply.

Beesley could not be sure exactly who was in his boat, because in the darkness he could see only a few feet, but he thought the list was as follows: no first class; three women, one baby, and two men from second class; and the other passengers steerage—mostly women; a total of about thirty-five passengers. The rest, about twenty-five or possibly more, were crew, including stokers. A stoker, by common consent, was appointed captain. How such a comparatively large number of crew got away is obscure. Of the 891 crew on board nearly a quarter were saved, in comparison with the 16 percent saved of male passengers.

Beesley's boat was launched, he reckoned, about an hour and a half before the *Titanic* sank; yet it contained almost as many crew as passengers. One stoker told him he had been at work in the stokehole when the collision occurred. The whole side of a compartment had caved in and the inrushing sea had thrown him off his feet. He went on deck, but was ordered down again with others to draw the fires from under the boilers; that done, they were allowed back on deck. He must thus have been one of the first to know the extent of the damage, and one of the first to get away; perhaps the facts were linked. The stoker got away because he knew early on that the ship was doomed; many steerage passengers died because they did not know until too late.

The stoker had been safely in his lifeboat for at least an hour, possibly much longer, when John Thayer jumped. Thayer thought later that pure chance, a matter of five seconds, saved him from the same fate as Long, his new friend. Long did not jump but let go of the rail and slid down the side of the ship. Thayer jumped outward, feet first. "I am afraid that the few seconds elapsing between our going, meant the difference between being sucked into the deck below, as I believe he was, or pushed out by the backwash. I was pushed out and then sucked down."

The shock of the cold water, he said, took the breath out of his lungs. Down and down he went, spinning. Fortunately he was a good swimmer. Under water, he swam as hard as he could in the direction he thought to be away

from the ship, and finally came up with his lungs bursting, but without having swallowed any water. Facing him,
about forty yards distant, was the *Titanic*. "I don't know
why I didn't keep swimming away. Fascinated, I seemed
tied to the spot." The ship appeared to be surrounded by
a glare, the water was over the base of the first funnel, and
the people massed on the stern were still edging backward.
As the ship rumbled and roared, a funnel lifted off among
a cloud of sparks and fell, missing Thayer by thirty or forty
feet. Again he was sucked down, struggling and trying to
swim, but "spent." As he came up for the second time he
felt some obstruction near his head and, putting up his
hand to push it away, found it to be the cork fender of a
collapsible lifeboat, floating beside him bottom up. Four
or five men pulled him aboard. Although it seemed like
hours, he had probably been in the water for no more than
four minutes, if that. His watch had stopped at 2:22 a.m.

Lightoller spent his last moments on board freeing this
same collapsible, borrowing Colonel Gracie's pocket knife
to cut the lashings. That was the last boat on the port side.
Lightoller then made sure that all boats on the starboard
side had also been got away and, with nothing further to
be done that could be of the slightest help to those remaining, took a header into the sea from the top of the wheelhouse. First he was sucked up against the wire grating over
the immense airshaft at the base of the forward funnel and
was glued there by the force of water rushing down to the
decks below. He began to sink with the ship. Blown away
from what he thought was certain death by a sudden blast
of hot air at his back, he surfaced briefly among floating
bodies before he was again dragged down by water pouring into a second grating. He could not remember afterward how he escaped from there. When he recovered his
wits, he realized he was alongside the collapsible he had

just freed. He was clinging to a length of rope attached to it when the *Titanic*'s forward funnel went. As it crashed into the sea nearby, the "terrific wash" picked up both the boat and Lightoller and flung them clear.

Gracie's experience was comparable. By the time his useful pocket knife had done its work, Gracie was trapped between the massed crowds astern and the advancing water forward. He tried to climb onto the roof of the officers' quarters, but as he did so the ship took the sudden dive that everyone noticed and a wall of water came at him. He had been hanging onto a rail, but soon let go. He found himself in a whirlpool, under water, terrified that he might be boiled in the hot water coming up from the boilers. However, swimming with what seemed to him to be "unusual strength," he surfaced, got clear, and clambered onto the same upturned boat as the stalwart officer whose conduct in the crisis he had much admired, Lightoller.

The time now, two hours and forty minutes after the iceberg had struck, was about twenty past two in the morning. In the immediate vicinity of the *Titanic,* this was the situation: The ship herself was rapidly foundering. Nobody except the most ignorant or the most credulous can have believed at this stage in the possibility of her survival as a floating hulk and haven. It is probable that the engineers were dead. Almost fifteen hundred people, mainly men but some women, crowded the stern. Many wore lifejackets. An English priest, Father Byles, moved among them, hearing confessions. The last well-attested glimpses of Captain Smith describe him using his megaphone to hurry people into the last boats, telling the crew in the final minutes that it was every man for himself, and then finally taking up a stand on the bridge to await the end.

Near the ship, the sea was strewn with steamer chairs and other wooden debris, thrown down in the desperate hope that it might give someone something to cling to. Further off floated sixteen lifeboats, some full, some half empty. A few of the boats had pulled away from the *Titanic* under the impression, given them by Captain Smith himself, that they would be transferred immediately to another ship that had been seen—many thought—no more than a few miles away. That expectation had proved false. None of the boats, even those under competent leadership, had a clear idea of what should be done next. There seemed no reason to try to head in any particular direction. In many of the boats, the oars were manned not by crew but by women. The night continued to be spectacular; stars of a brilliance that nobody had seen before, the visibility so clear that when a star sank below the horizon, the horizon bisected the star, with half of it shining above and half of it below the water. The sea was still as calm as a backwater of the Thames, but it was bitterly cold, with the temperature of the water 4 degrees below freezing.

"It Was Sad When the Great Ship Went Down" is the first line of a ballad still sung at American summer camps. The line scarcely does the moment justice.

Lightoller was standing on the upturned collapsible:

> I could now see the massive outline of the *Titanic* silhouetted against the starlit sky, her blackness emphasized by row upon row of lights still burning. But only for a matter of minutes. With her attaining an angle of about 60 degrees all the lights suddenly went out, and, with a roar, every one of the gigantic boilers left their beds and went crashing down through bulkheads and everything that stood in their way.
>
> Crowds of people were still on the after deck and at the stern, but the end was near. Slowly and almost majestically, the immense stern reared itself up, with propellers

and rudder clear of the water, till at last she assumed the exact perpendicular. Then with an ever-quickening glide, she slid beneath the water of the cold Atlantic.

Despite our own danger, every one of us had been held spellbound by the sight, and like a prayer as she disappeared, the words were breathed, "She's gone."

John Thayer wrote:

Her deck was turned slightly towards us. We could see groups of the almost fifteen hundred people still aboard, clinging in clusters or bunches, like swarming bees; only to fall in masses, pairs or singly, as the great after part of the ship, two hundred and fifty feet of it, rose into the sky, till it reached a sixty-five or seventy-degree angle. Here it seemed to pause, and just hung, for what felt like minutes. Gradually she turned her deck away from us, as though to hide from our sight the awful spectacle.

We had an oar on our upturned boat. In spite of several men working on it, amid our cries and prayers, we were being gradually sucked in towards the great pivoting mass. I looked upwards—we were right underneath the three enormous propellers. For an instant, I thought they were sure to come right down on top of us. Then, with the deadening noise of the bursting of her last few gallant bulkheads, she slid quietly away from us into the sea.

There was no final apparent suction, and practically no wreckage that we could see.

I don't remember all the wild talk and calls that were going on in our boat, but there was one concerted sigh or sob as she went from view.

The description by John Thayer's mother was a formal statement, made under oath:

All the lights were burning up to the very time the ship sank, as I saw tier upon tier of lights disappear beneath the water as the forward part of the ship slid down as though being launched—at the same time there was a sound as of drawing a boat over a pebbly beach. Then there was a rumbling noise, and a red glare of cinders in the air, and the forward part of the ship sank out of view. The after part of the ship then reared in the air, with the stern upwards, until it assumed an almost vertical position. It seemed to remain stationary in this position for many seconds (perhaps twenty), then suddenly dove straight down out of sight.

The time was 2:20 a.m., according to a wrist watch worn by one of the passengers in Mrs. Thayer's boat.

Martha Stevenson tried not to look. "When the call came that she was going I covered my face and then heard someone call, 'She's broken.' After what seemed a long time I turned my head only to see the stern almost perpendicular in the air so that the full outline of the blades of the propeller showed above the water. She then gave her final plunge."

As the ship went down, Mr. August Wennerström, in collapsible A with George Rheims, Richard Williams, and Rhoda Abbott, saw a man lowering himself down the logline beside the enormous rudder.

"At the last," said one onlooker, "the end of the world. A smooth, slow chute." "She tilted slowly up, revolving apparently about a centre of gravity just astern of midship," Beesley wrote, "until she attained a vertically upright position; and there she remained—motionless! As she swung up, her lights, which had shone without a flicker all night, went out suddenly, came on again for a single flash, then went out altogether."

Then came the noise, described as partly a groan, and partly a smash, that some thought was an explosion, and some, including Lightoller and Beesley, the sound of engines and machinery and boilers coming adrift and crashing their way through the bulkheads. No one, said Beesley, had ever heard anything like it before, and no one wanted to hear anything like it again. "When the noise was over the *Titanic* was still upright like a column: we could see her only as the stern and some 150 feet of her stood outlined against the star-specked sky, looming black in the darkness, and in this position she continued for some minutes—I think as much as five minutes, but it may have been less. Then, first sinking back a little at the stern, I thought, she slid slowly forwards through the water and dived slantingly down; the sea closed over her. . . ."

Many survivors long remembered the sequence of sounds that night: the "tearing calico" when the iceberg struck; the hiss of the boilers that made speech impossible when they were shut down by the engineers; the detonation of the rockets; the stupendous noise from inside the ship as she tipped on end. The silences were remembered, too: the silence after the hiss of the boilers ceased; the silence as the survivors climbed aboard the *Carpathia*. Nobody forgot the most terrible sound of all, the cries of hundreds that came from the *Titanic* after she sank; nor did anyone forget the unearthly silence that eventually followed. Beesley, for one, was taken unawares. He did not know how many boats the *Titanic* carried, nor how many people were still on board. He would not have been surprised to learn that everyone was safe. "Unprepared as we were for such a thing, the cries of the drowning floating across the quiet sea filled us with stupefaction." John Thayer remembered "one continuous wailing chant . . . It sounded like locusts on a midsummer night, in the woods of Pennsylvania. This terrible continuing cry lasted for twenty or thirty minutes, gradually dying away, as one after another could no longer withstand the cold and exposure. Practically no one was drowned, as no water was found in the lungs of those later recovered. Everyone had on a life preserver."

Then Thayer posed the question that had troubled him for twenty-eight years:

> The partially filled lifeboats standing by, only a few hundred yards away, never came back. Why on earth they did not come back is a mystery. How could any human being fail to heed those cries?
>
> The most heart-rending part of the whole tragedy was the failure, right after the *Titanic* sank, of those boats which were only partially loaded, to pick up the poor souls in the water. There they were, only four or five hundred yards away, listening to the cries, and still they did not come back. If they had turned back, several more hundred would have been saved. No one can explain it. It was not satisfactorily explained in any investigation.

Some boats did their best. On Thayer's overturned boat, people were helped aboard "until we were packed like sardines. Then out of self-preservation we had to turn some away." No. 4 boat went back. "We rowed back and pulled in five more men from the sea," wrote Martha Stevenson. "Their suffering from the icy water was intense and two men who had been pulled into the stern afterwards died, but we kept their bodies with us." Mrs. Thayer, despite her disapproval of the "disagreeable" and allegedly incompetent Quartermaster Perkis, helped to row No. 4; and it was Perkis who decided to go back. They rescued another four or five who were standing up on a capsized collapsible boat, until they were so full that there was nowhere to sit except on the gunwales and they were taking in water.

Fifth Officer Lowe made a valiant attempt to organize a rescue in a seamanlike manner. His lifeboat, No. 14, was virtually full. Assembling four emptier boats, he redistributed the passengers among them, picked a crew of seamen to join him in No. 14, and took it back among the wreckage, turning over bodies for signs of life. Many were dead, apparently frozen rather than drowned. Lowe and his men rescued four people alive, including one "Japanese or Chinese young fellow." Passenger William Hoyt died in the boat shortly after being picked up.

One officer who did not go back was the third officer, Herbert John Pitman. He was thirty-four, from Castle Cary in Somerset, and appears in contemporary photographs wearing a walrus moustache. He had served a four-year apprenticeship, then spent three years with James Nourse Ltd., a year with Blue Anchor running to Australia, six months running to Japan, and five years with White Star.

After the collision, he had worked on the starboard side under First Officer Murdoch, uncovering and swinging out No. 5 lifeboat and helping women climb aboard. He had been impressed by the modern davits, a great improvement on the old-fashioned kind. "I thought what a jolly fine idea they were, because with the old-fashioned davits it would require about a dozen men to lift her, a dozen men at each end." With five or six men, he swung out No. 5 in two or three minutes. When there were "no more ladies," he allowed a few male passengers aboard, and then five male crew. (On the port side, Lightoller was adopting a more rigorous policy; no male passengers, and only two crew to each boat.) When the boat was, as he thought, reasonably full, with forty-five people aboard, Pitman jumped back on deck, whereupon Murdoch told him, "You go in charge." He obeyed with some reluctance, thinking he would be better off on the ship. Once in the water, he told the crew to row to the north and then to lie on their oars, "awaiting further developments." An hour and a half later the *Titanic* went down.

Nine days later he was in Washington before the Senate committee of inquiry, where Senator Smith, like John Thayer twenty-eight years later, was wondering why some lifeboats, though not full, had failed to go to the help of the drowning. There followed this verbatim exchange between Smith and Pitman, as set down in the official Senate record.

SENATOR SMITH: Did you hear any cries of distress?
A: Oh, yes.
Q: What were they, cries for help?
A: Crying, shouting, moaning.
Q: From the ship, or from the water?
A: From the water, after the ship disappeared; no noises before.
Q: There were no noises from the ship's crew, or officers, or passengers, just preceding the sinking?
A: None.
Q: Immediately following the sinking of the ship you heard these cries of distress?
A: Yes.
Q: But, as I understand you, you were not in close proximity to those uttering the cries?
A: I may have been three or four hundred yards away; four or five hundred yards away.
Q: Did you attempt to get near them?
A: As soon as she disappeared I said, "Now, men, we will pull towards the wreck." Everyone in my boat said it was a mad idea, because we had far better save what

few we had in my boat than go back to the scene of the wreck and be swamped by the crowds that were there.

Q: As a matter of fact, do you now know your boat would have accommodated twenty or twenty-five more people?

A: My boat would have accommodated a few more, yes; certainly.

Q: According to the testimony of your fellow officers—

A: My boat would have held more.

Q: Your boat would have held about sixty or sixty-five people.

A: About sixty.

Q: Tell us about your fellow passengers on that lifeboat. You say they discouraged you from returning or going in the direction of these cries?

A: They did. I told my men to get their oars out, and pull toward the wreck—the scene of the wreck.

Q: Yes.

A: I said, "We may be able to pick up a few more."

Q: Who demurred to that?

A: The whole crowd in my boat. A great number of them did.

Q: Women?

A: I could not discriminate whether women or men. They said it was rather a mad idea.

Q: I ask you if any woman in your boat appealed to you to return to the direction from which the cries came?

A: No one.

Q: You say that no woman passenger in your boat urged you to return?

A: None.

MR. BURLINGHAM (APPEARING FOR WHITE STAR): It would have capsized the boat, Senator.

SENATOR SMITH: Pardon me, I am not drawing any

unfair conclusion from this. One of the officers told us that a woman in his boat urged him to return to the site of the ship. I want to be very sure that this officer heard no woman asking the same thing. (*To the witness*) Who demurred, now, that you can specifically recall?

A: I could not name any one in particular.

Q: The men with the oars?

A: No. They did not; no. They started to obey my orders.

Q: You were in command. They ought to have obeyed your orders?

A: So they did.

Q: They did not, if you told them to pull toward the ship.

A: They commenced pulling toward the ship, and the passengers in my boat said it was a mad idea on my part to pull back to the ship, because if I did, we should be swamped with the crowd that was in the water, and it would add another forty to the list of drowned, and I decided I would not pull back.

Q: Officer, you really turned this No. 5 boat around to go in the direction from which these cries came?

A: I did.

Q: And were dissuaded from your purpose by your crew—

A: No, not crew; passengers.

Q: One moment; by your crew and by the passengers in your boat?

A: Certainly.

Q: Then did you turn the boat toward the sea again?

A: No; just simply took our oars in and lay quiet.

Q: You mean you drifted?

A: We may have gone a little bit.

Q: Drifted on your oars?

A: We may have drifted along. We just simply lay there doing nothing.

Q: How many of these cries were there? Was it a chorus, or was it—

A: I would rather you did not speak about that.

Q: I would like to know how you were impressed by it.

A: Well, I can not very well describe it. I would rather you would not speak of it.

Q: I realize that it is not a pleasant theme, and yet I would like to know whether these cries were general and in chorus, or desultory and occasional?

A: There was a continual moan for about an hour.

Q: And you lay in the vicinity of that scene for about an hour?

A: Oh, yes; we were in the vicinity of the wreck the whole time.

Q: And drifted or lay on your oars during that time?

A: We drifted toward daylight, as a little breeze sprang up.

Q: Did this anguish or these cries of distress die away?

A: Yes; they died away gradually.

Q: Did they continue during most of the hour?

A: Oh, yes; I think so. It may have been a shorter time. Of course I did not watch every five minutes—

Q: I understand that and I am not trying to ask about a question of five minutes. Is that all you care to say?

A: I would rather that you would have left that out altogether.

Q: I know you would; but I must know what efforts you made to save the lives of passengers and crew under your charge. If that is all the effort you made, say so—

A: That is all, sir.

Q: And I will stop that branch of my questioning.

A: That is all, sir; that is all the effort I made.

Pitman's conduct did not concern the British inquiry. On the whole, Lord Mersey and his commissioners avoided matters of individual behavior except when they bore on the reasons for the wreck. Rather against the will of Lord Mersey, however, the British court was inadvertently driven to look into the actions of one first-class passenger and his wife after they had been described in an unfavorable light by a member of the crew.

Sir Cosmo Duff Gordon, Bart., was of Scottish descent. One of his ancestors, James Duff, was British consul in Cadiz during the Peninsular War and kept Wellington's armies so efficiently supplied that at the end of the campaign he was given a baronetcy. As consul, he had a finger in every pie; he went into the sherry business, which remained in the family for much of the nineteenth century. He never married, however; and at his death the title passed to his nephew William Gordon, a grandson of an earl of Aberdeen (and a cousin of Lord Aberdeen the prime minister of the 1850s), who added "Duff" by special license to his surname of Gordon. Sir Cosmo, the fifth baronet, was a tall, fine-looking man remembered in the family circle as someone who could be difficult. He was a good bridge player and had fenced for England in the now unofficial 1906 Olympics.

His wife, Lucy, was better known than he was: a sister of Elinor Glyn, the novelist and mistress of Lord Curzon. Lady Duff Gordon was a brilliant and sought-after dress designer with a very successful salon, Madame Lucile, in Hanover Square, where she was the first dress designer to require her models to move about. She taught Molyneux. She owned other establishments in Paris and New York, and the purpose of the trip to the United States was for Lady Duff Gordon, traveling with her secretary, Miss Laura Mabel Francatelli, to conduct business in Chicago. Sir Cosmo was her second husband.

The Duff Gordons' names came up in the British inquiry as a result of a decision to question one person from each lifeboat. For No. 1 emergency boat the choice fell on a leading fireman, Charles Hendrickson of Southampton.

Hendrickson's story was that after finishing his duties below he had gone on deck and, without particularly being ordered to do so, had started to help clear away and lower lifeboats on the starboard side.

He had spent an hour or an hour and a half at this work when he was told to get into No. 1 emergency boat. Two emergency boats were kept swung out and ready to be lowered at all times; they were smaller than the other lifeboats, with a capacity of forty as against sixty-five. The No. 1 boat went away, however, with one of the lookout men, Symons, in charge as coxswain, and only eleven others: six crew (five firemen and trimmers, and one seaman) and five passengers, of whom only two were women. The women were Lady Duff Gordon and her secretary; one of the three male passengers was Sir Cosmo.

The arresting point about Hendrickson's story was that "there was plenty of room for another dozen in the boat," despite the space taken up by four oars and a mast, yet no one except himself had proposed going back after the *Titanic* sank to pick up other people. Once in the water, with members of the crew at the oars, the boat had pulled away about two hundred yards from the ship and had been at that distance when she went down. When they heard the cries, Hendrickson had made a general appeal, he said, not addressed to anyone in particular, that they should look for survivors. "I proposed in the boat that we should go back, and they would not listen to me," he said. He never heard anyone else propose going back. But who was it, he was asked, who objected? "Well, the passengers," he said. "I think it was the women objected." There were only two women in the boat: Lady Duff Gordon and her secretary.

The force of Hendrickson's allegations came out most sharply when he was questioned by Harbinson, the counsel representing the third-class passengers. Hendrickson had said that the coxswain had not paid any attention to his proposal to go back.

> Q: You say that that attitude of his [the coxswain's] was due to the protests of the Duff Gordons?
> A: Yes.
> Q: You say you heard cries?
> A: Yes.
> Q: Agonizing cries?
> A: Yes, terrible cries.
> Q: At what distance?
> A: About two hundred yards.

And later:

> Q: They said it would be too dangerous to go back, we might get swamped. Who said that?
> A: Sir Duff Gordon.

The original objection to going back had been made by Lady Duff Gordon, Hendrickson said, and her husband had backed her up. Hendrickson had been sitting close to them. "Duff Gordon asked me if I wanted a smoke, and he gave me a cigar."

That was not the only thing Duff Gordon had given him. "In the early hours of the morning before we were picked up he said he would do something for us"—"us" being the members of the crew. After they had been picked up by the *Carpathia,* Duff Gordon gave them all "an order for £5." (Lady Duff Gordon had asked them to sign their names on her life-preserver.) Here was a sensational piece of news. Had Duff Gordon bribed the crew not to go back?

Hendrickson did not shift his position under cross-examination, although he was caught out on one minor point. He said there had been no sea anchor in the boat but admitted under questioning that he had never looked for one, nor had anyone else.

The burden of his story, however, was supported by another member of the crew, Taylor, also a fireman, who said he had been sitting on a thwart next to a man he later found out to be Sir Cosmo. He had heard Hendrickson's proposal about going back; he had also heard a woman whom he later found out to be Lady Duff Gordon say that the boat would be swamped if it did.

The coxswain, Symons, denied hearing any proposal or any protests. Symons in the witness box sounded extremely self-important, constantly using two phrases about being "master of the situation" and "using my discretion." He was not in a very easy position himself. For one thing he had told the U.S. inquiry that there had been between fourteen and twenty people in the boat, whereas in London he was forced to admit that there had been only twelve. Why had he given a wrong figure to the Senate, the attorney general asked him. "I think myself, sir, that the mistake I made then was through the way they muddle you about there."

Symons claimed that the boat was much farther than 200 yards away from the *Titanic* when she went down, and that he had in fact started to head in the direction of the cries; but they had stopped and so had he.

From the Duff Gordons' standpoint, Symons's most damaging assertion concerned the way they had gotten into the boat in the first place. According to him, the two women had come running down the deck and jumped in, rapidly followed by Duff Gordon and two Americans.

A further allegation damaging to Sir Cosmo came from one of these Americans, a Mr. C. E. H. Stengel. He had been asked at the American inquiry whether he knew who was giving directions in the boat. "I think between Sir Duff Gordon and myself we decided which way to go." ("Duff" was widely supposed to be Sir Cosmo's first name, not part of his surname.)

There was one more awkwardness. Lady Duff Gordon, as part of her professional life, had written articles for a Hearst newspaper, the *Sunday American*. The morning after the *Carpathia* arrived in New York, the paper's stable mate, the New York *American*, had printed an article about the disaster signed by her. Immediately syndicated to England, as elsewhere, it said, among other things: "We watched her—we were 200 yards away—go down slowly, almost peacefully." It also said: "Women and men were clinging to bits of wreckage in the icy water. . . . And it was at least an hour before the awful chorus of shrieks ceased, gradually dying in a moan of despair."

Thus the behavior of the Duff Gordons—together with the conduct of J. Bruce Ismay, which we shall come to later—became the focus of rumor and scandal, all the more so since it appeared to contrast shamefully with the courage and self-sacrifice displayed by others: the musicians, playing on as the ship went down; the engineers, who had given their lives to keep the ship afloat and the lights burning as long as possible; Captain Smith, who had gone down with his ship; the Strauses, who had refused special treatment; the bravery of the Marconi operator Phillips; the stoicism and sang-froid of the American millionaires. The list of heroes was long. Had a British baronet let down the side?

On May 20 the Duff Gordons appeared before the British inquiry at their own request. Fashionable London turned out for the occasion. Sir Cosmo, represented by Henry Duke, K.C., M.P., faced three troublesome questions. How had he, as a man of honor, found a place in a lifeboat when women were still on board? Why had the lifeboat he was in not gone back to rescue others? What inspired him, alone of all the passenger survivors, to hand out money to the crew?

Sir Cosmo was first examined by the attorney general, Sir Rufus Isaacs. Sir Cosmo explained that his wife had awakened him just after the impact with the iceberg; he had not at first gotten up, but when he did so he went to the top deck, where the noise was "perfectly indescribable," and spoke to Colonel Astor. "Who went down with the vessel?" "Yes." The attorney general had made a point.

Sir Cosmo next described how he had watched men stripping down a lifeboat, had gone below again to fetch his wife and her secretary, and how they had all watched three further lifeboats being filled, almost entirely with women, and lowered. His wife and Miss Francatelli had been asked two or three times to go but had refused. Once, "some men got hold of her [Lady Duff Gordon] and tried to pull her away," but she still would not go. Then, after the three lifeboats they had all been watching had left, when the deck seemed deserted, and the rockets started going up, his wife said to him, "Ought not we to do something?" and he replied, "No, we have to wait for orders." Then an officer had told a group of crew to "man the emergency boat," at which Sir Cosmo had asked him, "May we get into the boat?" "and he said, 'Yes, I wish you would' or 'Very glad if you would' or some expression like that." The officer put the ladies in and helped Sir Cosmo aboard as well. There were no other passengers at all near, said

Sir Cosmo. Finally two Americans came running up, and the officer allowed them in, told two or three firemen that they might as well go too, and put a seaman—Symons—in charge.

The attorney general soon persuaded Sir Cosmo to concede that "of course there was room for more people." In that case, the attorney general asked, exaggerating slightly, how did he explain the contrast with the other lifeboats, which had been filled with as many as they could possibly carry? No one else was visible, said Sir Cosmo; no one else on that side of the deck. He knew there were people still aboard, but he "certainly thought all the women had got off."

And where had the lifeboat been when the *Titanic* went down? Sir Cosmo's impression was that Symons had been ordered by the officer to row as fast as he could for the first two hundred yards; they had then proceeded by fits and starts, rowing and resting, until by the time the ship went down he thought they were about a thousand yards away. He had only one eye and was "presumed not to be a judge of distance"; however, he felt confident that the figure was about a thousand yards.

Had he heard the cries? "Yes, I heard the explosion first, and I heard, I will not say the cries, but a wail—one confused sound."

SIR RUFUS ISAACS: We do not want unnecessarily to prolong the discussion of it, but they were cries of people who were drowning?

A: Yes.

Q: There is no doubt about that?

A: Yes, I think so without a doubt.

Q: Did it occur to you that with the room in your boat, if you could get to these people you could save some?

A: It is difficult to say what occurred to me. Again, I was minding my wife, and we were rather in an abnormal condition, you know. There were many things to think about, but of course it quite well occurred to one that people in the water could be saved by a boat, yes.

Q: And that there was room in your boat; that they could have got into your boat and been saved?

A: Yes, it is possible.

Sir Cosmo had heard no suggestion that the boat should go back to the place the cries were coming from. The men had begun to row again immediately after the cries. "In my opinion it was to stop the sound." He was asked once more if at the time he had thought about whether or not his boat would have been able to save any of the people in the water. "I do not know; it might have been possible; but it would have been very difficult to get back, the distance we were, and in the darkness, to find anything." He was not thinking about it; he was attending to his wife; "we had had rather a serious evening, you know." He had said nothing about the danger of being swamped. No notice was taken in the boat of the cries from the drowning people, and there had been no conversation on the subject.

The attorney general kept probing the failure of the boat to go back.

Q: I understand from what you said, and correct it if it is wrong, that no thought entered into your mind that you ought to go back and try to save some of these people?

A: No, I suppose not.

LORD MERSEY: The last witness [Hendrickson] told us that in his opinion it would have been quite safe to have gone back. What do you say to that?

A: I do not know, my lord, whether it would have been

safe. I do not know. I think it would have been hardly possible.

ATTORNEY GENERAL: Why not possible?

A: I do not know which way we should have gone.

LORD MERSEY: When I say "gone back" I mean towards where the cries came from.

A: I do not know about that. I could not speculate.

It was put to Sir Cosmo that two witnesses had said that a suggestion was made that the boat should go back. Sir Cosmo replied that he could only say that he himself had not heard any such suggestion.

The attorney general asked his final questions on this theme.

Q: You know now, do you not, that you might have saved a good many if you had gone back?

A: I do not know that.

Q: You know that your boat would have carried a good many more?

A: Yes, I know that is so, but it is not a lifeboat, you must remember; there are no air-tanks.

Later, Sir Cosmo was asked about Symons's evidence. Symons had said they did not go back when they heard the cries but did go back later; however, he had strained his ears and heard nothing. Had Sir Cosmo heard Symons give that order to the men rowing in the boat? No, he had not.

Next came the money.

There was a man sitting next to me [Sir Cosmo said] and of course in the dark I could see nothing of him. I never did see him, and I do not know who he is. I suppose it would be some time when they rested on their oars, 20 minutes or half an hour after the *Titanic* had sunk, a man said to me, "I suppose you have lost everything," and I said, "Of course." He said, "But you can get some more," and I said "Yes." "Well," he said, "we have lost all our kit and the company won't give us any more, and what is more our pay stops from tonight. All they will do is to send us back to London." So I said to them, "You fellows need not worry about that; I will give you a fiver each to start a new kit." That is the whole of that £5-note story.

Aboard the *Carpathia,* he asked Hendrickson to give him a list of the men's names, which he did. It was Sir Cosmo's usual practice to draw checks on his bankers, Coutts, on notepaper, and he told Miss Francatelli to make out checks in this way to all the men. He saw Hendrickson, asked him to assemble the men, "and just gave them each their cheque, asking each fellow what his name was. . . . I said, 'I am sorry I cannot give you money; but if you had it you would probably spend it all in New York, so it is just as well it should be in a cheque which will enable you to start your kit again.' "

Lady Duff Gordon followed her husband to the witness box, after her counsel had told the Court that she insisted on doing so. She took the Court from the moment of impact and into the boats in a single answer.

I had quite made up my mind that I was going to be drowned, and then suddenly we saw this little boat in front of us—this little thing (*pointing to a model*)—and we saw some sailors and an officer apparently giving them orders and I said to my husband, "Ought we not to be doing something?" and he said, "Oh, we must wait for orders," and we stood there for quite some time while these men were fixing up things and then my husband went forward and said, "Might we get into this boat?" and the officer said in a very polite way indeed, "Oh certainly; do; I will be very pleased." . . . They hitched us up in *this* sort of way into the boat and after we had been in a little while the boat was started to be lowered and one American gentleman got pitched in and one American gentleman was pitched in while the boat was being lowered down.

She was "awfully sick" and very hazy about what happened thereafter, but she saw the *Titanic* sink. She heard "terrible cries" before the ship sank, and afterward her impression was that there had been "absolute silence." She certainly had never said it would be dangerous to go back.

As for the article in the New York *American,* what happened was that the night they reached New York and the Ritz-Carlton Hotel she and Sir Cosmo had had dinner with six ladies and a "great friend of ours," Mr. Merrett, the editor of the *Sunday American.* "After he had left us about half an hour he telephoned to me and he said, 'Mr. Hearst has just rung me up, and must have your story of the *Titanic* wreck for tomorrow's newspaper.' He said, 'May I tell your story as I have heard it?' . . . I said 'Yes,' and he tells me afterwards he telephoned to their head office all he knew about it, and then a clever reporter put all that into words and it appeared next morning in the New York *American.*" It had been, she said, "rather inventive," and much of it "quite untrue," including the statements about being only 200 yards away when the ship went down and the shrieks lasting an hour.

Mr. Harbinson had no questions for her.

What is one to make of the Duff Gordon episode? The lawyer Harbinson asked Sir Cosmo whether he would be stating the position accurately if he summed it up by saying that "You considered when you were safe yourselves that all the others might perish." Harbinson did his best to make it sound as if Sir Cosmo had promised the crew five-pound notes in order to induce them to row away from the drowning people. A whiff of class antagonism was in the air; Lord Mersey thought so, at any rate. He told Harbinson it was his duty to assist him, Lord Mersey, in arriving at the truth, "not to try to make out a case for this class or that class or another class," or to make out a case against one person or another. Harbinson, before this intervention, had been suggesting to Sir Cosmo that his promises of financial help to the crew had coincided with the audible "harrowing cries" of the drowning.

One interesting point about Lady Duff Gordon's testimony is that she denied telling the New York *American* that the lifeboat had been only 200 yards away when the *Titanic* sank—a figure that would have been in sharp contrast to her husband's, and Symons's, estimate of 1,000 yards. But whatever else the "clever reporter" invented, would he have invented 200 yards? It was at the least a strange coincidence that his invention agreed with Hendrickson's estimate.

Seventy-two years later, I learned from Sotheby's, the auctioneers, of a remarkable and apparently unrecorded letter that came up for sale. It was written in pencil by Miss Francatelli on Ritz-Carlton Hotel writing paper and dated April 28, 1912, thirteen days after the sinking. Miss Francatelli was writing to a Miss Marion Taylor in London, and the salient points, interspersed in the original with emotional comments on her ordeal, are as follows:

> I was just getting into bed. Madame, & Sir Cosmo . . . were up on A deck the top, and I on E, the bottom deck for saloon Passengers. . . . two Gentlemen came up . . . and told me . . . we had run into an iceberg, but we were quite

safe. . . . I still stood there quite 20 minutes . . . the water
was on my deck, coming along the corridor. . . . I found
all the people, running up, & down the stairs . . . Oh Marion that was a sickening moment, I felt myself go like Marble. . . . Sir Cosmo then took us up on top deck. Crowds
were up there . . . several lifeboats had been lowered, they
were preparing the last two, on that side of the ship, the
Starboard side, they cried out, Any more women, saw us,
& came to try & drag Madame & I away from Sir Cosmo,
but Madame clung to Sir Cosmo . . . after all the lifeboats
had gone, everybody seemed to rush to the other side of
the boat, & leave ours vacant, but we still stood there, as Sir
Cosmo said, we must wait for orders, presently. An officer
started to swing off a little boat called the "Emergency"
boat . . . he saw us, & ordered us in, they were then firing
the last rockets beside us . . . two other American gentlemen jumped in, & seven stokers . . . The dear officer gave
orders to row away from the sinking boat at least two hundred yards. . . . We saw the whole thing, and watched that
tremendous thing quickly sink, there was then terrible, *terrible,* explosions, and all *darkness,* then followed the Awful
cries & screams of the 1,600 dear souls, fighting for their
lives in the water. *Oh never shall I forget* that awful night. . . .

The letter in general bears out the Duff Gordons' statements that they got into the boat under an officer's auspices and did not come running down the deck as alleged
by Symons. But it tends to weaken the assertions that the
boat was a thousand yards away from the sinking *Titanic;*
it sounds as if Miss Francatelli was nearer than that to the
explosions and the cries.

Lord Mersey in his report found any suggestion of brib-
ery by Sir Cosmo "unfounded." But he added: "I think,
that if he had encouraged the men to return to the position

where the *Titanic* had foundered they would probably have made an effort to do so and could have saved some lives."

The verdict sounds just. Other boats went back and did their best.

Sir Cosmo died in 1931. He was deeply distressed by the aftermath of the sinking and spent much of his time abroad, some of it in Cairo. Otherwise, he stayed in Scotland.

The present, eighth baronet, Sir Andrew Cosmo Lewis Duff Gordon, said not long ago in defense of his great-uncle that any man who survived that nightmare ordeal by getting away in a lifeboat, when so many others perished, was likely to be regarded with suspicion. The slur on the fifth baronet's name notwithstanding, the ninth baronet will be another Sir Cosmo Duff Gordon.

5

THE CONUNDRUM OF CAPTAIN LORD

The *Titanic* disaster had many subplots, but the most dramatic and mysterious concerns the stony-faced Captain Lord of the *Californian*. Were it not for Captain Lord, there would have been no disaster, because nobody aboard the *Titanic* would have been drowned.

At least, that is the official view. The American inquiry pronounced an unqualified and damning verdict. "There is a very strong possibility that every human life that was sacrificed through this disaster could have been saved," Senator Smith told the Senate. The senator did not spare the captain. His failure on the night the *Titanic* sank, said Smith, "places a tremendous responsibility upon this officer from which it will be very difficult for him to escape." The senator was right. The British inquiry condemned him also. "She [the *Californian*] might have saved many if not all of the lives that were lost," the inquiry concluded. Since then, the Board of Trade and its successors have resisted repeated attempts to get the case of Captain Lord reopened, so that the verdict of 1912 may still be said to stand.

In Britain, the fight to clear Captain Lord's name has

been led by the Mercantile Marine Service Association, supported by Captain Lord's son. After I read the evidence given both in the United States and in London, I agreed with the official view. It appeared incontrovertible. On a subsequent visit to the United States, however, I met two people, Mr. Kamuda of the Titanic Historical Society in Springfield, Massachusetts, and Mr. Russ Lownds, late of the Maritime Museum in Halifax, Nova Scotia, who both called themselves "Lordites," as supporters of Captain Lord have come to be known in *Titanic* circles. Both men are convinced that the official inquiries, partly because they were looking for a scapegoat, arrived at too hasty and definite a conclusion about Captain Lord, and compelled me to wonder whether I had not done the same.

As in an old-fashioned detective story, I shall first set out the complicated circumstances of the mystery. Then I shall summarize the case against the captain and the case for him.

Stanley Lord (no relation of Walter Lord, the author of *A Night to Remember*) was born in Bolton in 1877. He went to sea in 1891, serving first in sailing ships. When he was twenty-three, he obtained an extra master's certificate, which is the highest voluntary qualification open to an officer in the British Mercantile Marine. At the early age of twenty-nine he was appointed by the Leyland Line, which he had joined nine years before, to captain their passenger cargo liners.

On April 14, 1912, the 6,223-ton *Californian*—which had a passenger certificate but was not carrying passengers at the time—was bound from London to Boston under Captain Lord's command when she ran into field ice. Prudently, Lord stopped, telling the wireless operator to send out a general ice report. That was shortly after 10:21 p.m.

At 5:15 a.m. the *Californian*'s engines were briefly turned over and at 6:00 a.m. he got underway, steering for the *Titanic*'s distress position. While the *Californian* was hove to, some 1,496 people from the *Titanic* died.

The *Titanic* hit the iceberg at 11:40 p.m., and some time after that Fourth Officer Boxhall, as he was helping to lower lifeboats, heard that someone had reported a light ahead. He went to the bridge to see what it was. Through glasses, he saw the two masthead lights of a steamer.

Meanwhile he had sent for some distress rockets.* He told Captain Smith he had seen the light and asked permission to send off the rockets. Captain Smith told him to carry on. As he sent off the rockets—"between half a dozen and a dozen"—he was "watching the steamer approach." The rockets—larger than ordinary firework rockets—were a distress signal, with a luminous tail behind them; they exploded loudly in the air and burst into white stars. They were sent off at intervals of "probably five minutes." At one stage, "the vessel got close enough, as I thought, to read our electric Morse signal, and I signalled to her. I told her to 'Come at once, we are sinking.' The captain was standing . . . with me most of the time when we were signalling." The captain also saw the vessel. There was no answer to the Morse signal.

After Boxhall left the *Titanic* in No. 2 lifeboat—perhaps at about 1:45 a.m.—he continued to see the vessel "for a little while, but then lost it." He judged that she had headed away in a westerly direction; her distance from the *Titanic* had been about five miles.

---

*Though often referred to as "rockets," *Titanic*'s distress signals were what were called socket signals. They were packages of pyrotechnics fired from a small mortar, much as is done for entertainment today. They produced two explosions: one on firing and another on bursting into stars at a height of 600–800 feet.

Second Officer Lightoller had also seen the lights of a ship five or six miles away.

So much for what was seen and done on the *Titanic*. A ship was sighted by the *Titanic*'s officers; she was judged to be five or six miles away; she was signaled by lamp, and failed to respond; rockets were fired—these facts are not and never have been in dispute.

But was the ship the *Californian*?

At 11:00 p.m. on the stationary *Californian* the officer of the watch, Third Officer Groves, saw a steamer's lights approaching from the east. Captain Lord told him to call her with the Morse lamp. No answer. Lord then went into the wireless cabin and asked the inexperienced young operator, Evans, whether he had been in communication with any ships. Evans said he had had the *Titanic* and judging by the strength of her signals she was about a hundred miles away. Lord told Evans to call up the *Titanic* and let her know that the *Californian* was surrounded by ice and stopped. Evans started to send a cheery informal message beginning, "Say old man we are surrounded by ice and stopped," but was told by the *Titanic*'s chief operator, Phillips, to shut up as he was busy talking to the wireless relay station on Cape Race.

11:30 p.m. Evans heard the *Titanic* sending passengers' telegrams.

11:35 p.m. Evans turned in.

11:40 p.m. Groves, the officer of the watch, observed that the unknown vessel had stopped and thought he saw the steamer's lights go out. Captain Lord said he didn't believe she was a passenger steamer. Groves said she was.

Just before midnight, on his way to the bridge to relieve Groves, Second Officer Herbert Stone met Captain Lord at the door of the wheelhouse. Lord pointed to the steamer and said she was stopped. Lord told Stone to let him know if the ship came any nearer, and added that he was going to lie down on the chart-room settee. On the bridge, Stone observed that the other steamer was showing one masthead light, her red side light, and one or two small indistinct lights around the deck that looked like portholes or open doors. Stone judged her to be a tramp steamer, about five miles distant.

Stone tried and failed to raise the steamer by Morse lamp.

12:15 a.m. approximately. The apprentice on watch with Stone, James Gibson, came up to the bridge with coffee. He too tried the "tapper" and got no answer. Gibson left the bridge to attend to the log line. While he was away, the captain called up Stone and asked if the steamer had moved. Stone said no.

12:45 a.m. approximately. Stone saw a flash of light in the sky just above the steamer which he thought was a shooting star. Soon afterward he saw what this time he identified as a white rocket. In the next half-hour or so he saw three more rockets, all of them white. He saw no flash on the steamer's deck or any indication that the rockets were coming from her, and had the impression that they came from a good way beyond her.

In 1912, each company had its own private recognition signals, which were sometimes shown when passing other ships at night. They might be Roman candles, flares, or rockets of different colors. Each signal was displayed for a few minutes at the most. The use of white rockets in company signals was practically unknown and rockets of any color were normally only used inshore, when signaling to lighthouses or ports. Distress signals could be of any color, but were usually white. When in the form of socket signals, they made a considerable noise, being propelled by a gunpowder charge equal to that used in a twelve-pounder gun.

1:15 a.m. approximately. Stone whistled down the speaking-tube to Captain Lord, who went from the chart room into his own room to answer. Stone told Lord about the rockets. Lord told Stone to call the steamer on the Morse lamp and try to get some information from her. Lord also asked if the rockets were "private signals," to which Stone replied that he didn't know, but they were all white. Lord then said, "When you get an answer let me know by Gibson."

Gibson and Stone next observed three more rockets going off at intervals. They also noted that the ship, which had not replied to their continual signaling, was apparently steaming away to the southwest.

2:00 a.m. Stone observed that the ship was steaming away fast, by now showing only her stern light and a glow at the masthead. Gibson went down to wake the captain. He told the captain that, in all, he and Stone had sighted eight rockets, and that the steamer was moving out of sight. The captain said (according to Gibson), "All right. Are you sure there were no colors in them?" Gibson replied, "No, they were all white."

2:45 a.m. Stone again whistled down and told the captain that they had seen no more lights and that the ship was out of sight.

4:00 a.m. Chief Officer Stewart came onto the bridge to relieve Stone. Stone told him of the events of the past four hours. Stewart woke up first Captain Lord and then Evans the wireless operator and told him to find out what was going on and what was wrong. Evans picked up a message from the Canadian Pacific liner *Mount Temple;* the message said the *Titanic* had struck an iceberg and was sinking.

Meanwhile, the *Carpathia,* a Cunarder commanded by Captain Arthur Rostron, sailing from New York to Gibraltar, had picked up the *Titanic's* distress calls. At once, she went at full speed, past scores of icebergs, to the rescue. As dawn broke she began to pick up survivors.

5:15 a.m. approximately. The *Californian* got under way and made for the last radioed position of the *Titanic.*

Soon after 8:00 a.m., the *Californian* was within semaphore distance of the *Carpathia* and learned that the *Titanic* had gone down. Captain Rostron signaled Captain Lord to tell him that he had taken aboard all lifeboat survivors and was setting course for New York. He asked Lord to stay in the area and pick up bodies.

Between 9:00 a.m. and 10:00 a.m. the *Californian,* having failed to sight any bodies, resumed its voyage to Boston.

By this time the horrified attention of much of the world was focused on the *Titanic* disaster, though not at this stage on the *Californian.* Brief reports on the day after the sinking noted that the ship was on the scene picking up bodies, but when she found none she was forgotten. On Thursday, April 18, the *Carpathia* and the survivors arrived in New York among mourning and chaotic crowds. That night the *Californian* docked at a freight pier in east Boston, met only by a pilot boat. On disembarking, Captain Lord was met by reporters from the Boston press. He began a campaign of deception, refusing to give his position during the night of April 14 and claiming to have been thirty miles from the scene of the sinking when he first heard of it. His story appeared the next day in several papers. As late as April 24 he was telling the Boston *Post* that the *Californian* "had sighted no rockets or other signals of distress."

The ship and her captain remained in obscurity over the weekend while newspapers and public concentrated on the Senate hearings already starting in the Waldorf-Astoria hotel. During the hearings, however, it was mentioned that, after the iceberg was struck, a ship had been sighted five miles from the *Titanic* and had not answered signals. Someone on *The New York Times* remembered the *Californian*. A reporter went to interview Captain Lord.

On Tuesday morning *The New York Times* carried the interview on the front page, datelined Boston. It was not much of a story, but the reporter gave it the strongest lead he could. "The Leyland steamer *Californian* was less than 20 miles from the *Titanic* when the latter foundered," the story began. "Captain Lord of the *Californian* said tonight that had he only known of the *Titanic*'s plight, all the passengers could have been saved. That his ship was the steamer reported to have passed within five miles of the sinking, Captain Lord denied emphatically." The reporter next had him saying, "I figure that we were from 17 to 19 miles distant from the *Titanic* that night," which is unlikely to have been an accurate quote but accurately represented Lord's stance. If the reporter had then asked whether Captain Lord or any of the crew had seen any rockets, he would have had a better story, as he no doubt realized the next day when he picked up the Boston *American*.

"FROM *CALIFORNIAN* I SAW *TITANIC* SIGNALS," said the banner headline. "MAN OF *CALIFORNIAN* CREW SAYS WAS NEAR THE *TITANIC*" read a headline underneath. A picture showed a man in a cloth cap looking to his left, with dark eyebrows and a luxuriant handlebar moustache. The paper was so pleased with the scoop that it encircled the photo with a sinuous art nouveau capital G. Over the picture a line read, "Ernest Gill, who says he saw *Titanic* rockets" ("rockets" was the word that should have been in the main headline). The caption read: "Gill was donkeyman on the Leyland liner *Californian* and says his captain paid no attention to signals from the doomed vessel."

The main text of the story consisted of an affidavit sworn by Gill in the presence of a named notary public and, said the paper, four members of the crew, who were not named. It was a lengthy statement. Gill said he had been on duty in the *Californian*'s engine room during the first watch on April 14 and had come up on deck at four minutes to midnight. He looked over the starboard rail and "saw the lights of a very large steamer about 10 miles away." A few minutes later he went to his cabin and woke his mate William Thomas. Thomas heard the ice crunching on the side of the ship and asked, "Are we in ice?" Gill said, "Yes, but we must be clear off to the starboard for I saw a big vessel going along at full speed. She looked as if she might be a big German." Gill then turned in.

Half an hour later, unable to sleep, he went back on deck for a smoke. After ten minutes he saw rockets going up about ten miles away, saying to himself, "That must be a vessel in distress." It was not his business to notify the bridge or lookout, but he was certain that they must have seen the rockets, he stated, as they must earlier have seen the very large steamer. He turned in again and knew nothing more until the chief engineer woke him at 6:40 a.m. with the news that the *Titanic* had gone down and that he was needed to lend a hand; the *Californian* by this time was under way.

In the engine room, Gill overheard the second and fourth engineers talking about rockets seen during the night, and about the captain being notified by the apprentice, Gibson. The captain had given orders for Morse signals to be sent, but there had been no reply. Then Gill had heard the second engineer exclaiming, "Why the devil didn't they wake up the wireless man?"

Gill ended his statement by saying he was quite sure the *Titanic* was closer than the twenty miles claimed by his officers, since he could not have seen her at twenty miles and he had seen her plainly. He had no ill will toward Captain Lord or any other officer, and he was losing a profitable berth by making his statement; but he was "actuated by the desire that no captain who refuses or neglects to give aid to a vessel in distress should be able to hush up the men."

The story caused a sensation. Captain Lord issued a strong denial. Gill, it soon came out, had been paid $500 by the Boston *American:* more than a year's wages at his rate of £6 a month. Thomas, named in Gill's affidavit, said Gill had not consulted him before swearing it. He was evidently not one of the four unnamed crew members present, according to the Boston *American,* at the signing. Thomas told a rival paper, the Boston *Herald,* that he remembered asking about the ice but was positive Gill had said nothing about any steamer; nor had Gill mentioned rockets. The *Herald* quoted Thomas as saying that Gill was engaged to a girl in England, and "I could see where the offer of a sum as large as reported in the forecastle would greatly tempt him." Thomas thought Gill could buy a small shop with that amount of money.

Gill returned to England and faded from sight, but only after he had repeated his story to the American and British inquiries. He was not cross-examined with any rigor. He claimed in his affidavit to have seen "a big vessel going along at full speed" and was very precise about the time— 11:56 p.m. But even if the clocks on the *Californian* and the *Titanic* were keeping the same time, Gill's alleged sighting occurred sixteen minutes after the time the *Titanic* hit the iceberg. He was not pressed on this point. Nor was he required to explain how he had been able to see so clearly a vessel ten miles away.

It scarcely mattered. What mattered was that Gill said he had seen rockets, which compelled Captain Lord, appearing before the Senate inquiry the day after Gill's revelations, to admit for the first time that "flashes or rockets" had been seen from the *Californian*. Lord had not said anything about rockets when talking to reporters. He told the senators that he had been informed about the first rocket but had not taken in Gibson's message about the other rockets because he was half asleep. He admitted that "flashes or rockets" had been seen from his ship, that these "flashes or rockets" might have been distress signals, and that the ship he captained had done nothing—except to try to raise the other vessel with a Morse lamp.

These admissions formed the bedrock of the case against Lord. It was central to his defense that the ship seen from the *Californian* was not the *Titanic*, and that the ship seen from the *Titanic* was not the *Californian*. But no other ship could be found. The Senate inquiry called for an expert opinion from the United States Hydrographics Office as to whether a third vessel might have been between the two; the expert thought not. The British Board of Trade tried to find a third vessel and failed.

The written verdict of the Senate committee was harsh, especially since it condemned, and could be expected to ruin, a foreign national. It censured Captain Lord for his failure to respond to distress signals "in accordance with the dictates of humanity, international usage, and with the requirements of the law."

Lord Mersey's verdict was harsher still, and forcefully argued. After setting out the reasons why the *Californian* had stopped, he turned to the problem of where she had stopped. The master (Captain Lord) had told the court that he made her position to be 42 degrees 5 minutes N., 50 degrees 7 minutes W. This position—reached by dead reckoning and verified by observation—was recorded in the log; it was about nineteen miles north by east away from that of the *Titanic* when she foundered. But, Lord Mersey wrote, "I am satisfied that this position is not accurate."

He then rehearsed the evidence about the steamer first sighted from the *Californian* at about 11:00 p.m. The master himself stated that he had seen the steamer approaching, that he saw more lights as she got nearer, and that she was about five miles off when she hove to. In deciding what sort of steamer had been seen, Lord Mersey laid emphasis on the evidence of Third Officer Groves. "Mr. Groves never appears to have had any doubt on this subject; in answer to a question during his examination, 'Had she much light?' he said, 'Yes, a lot of light. There was absolutely no doubt of her being a passenger steamer, at least in my mind.' " Lord Mersey also quoted Gill, who had said, "It could not have been anything but a passenger boat, she was too large."

Lord Mersey then drew attention to a conflict of evidence between Groves and Lord. Groves had said that he had made a remark to the captain about the way the steamer's deck lights seemed to go out when she stopped. Captain Lord stated that Groves made no observation to him about the steamer's deck lights going out.

Lord Mersey next quoted an exchange between himself and Groves.

LORD MERSEY: Speaking as an experienced seaman and knowing what you do know now, do you think that steamer that you know was throwing up rockets, and that you say was a passenger steamer, was the *Titanic*?
A: Do I think it? Yes. From what I have heard subsequently? Yes. Most decidedly I do, but I do not put myself as being an experienced man.
Q: But that is your opinion as far as your experience goes?
A: Yes, it is, my lord.

Lord Mersey moved on to the rockets. Gill had stated that at some time after 12:30 p.m. he had seen two rockets fired from the ship he had been observing. At about 1:10 a.m. Stone (who relieved Groves on watch) reported to the captain by voice pipe that he had seen five rockets coming from the direction of the steamer. Stone said that the master had asked him, "Are they company's signals?" and he replied, "I do not know, but they appear to me to be white rockets." Stone and the apprentice Gibson then saw the vessel firing three more rockets.

"Between one o'clock and 1:40 a.m. some conversation passed between them. Mr. Stone remarked to Gibson, 'Look at her now, she looks very queer out of the water, her lights look queer.' He also is said by Gibson to have remarked, 'A ship is not going to fire rockets at sea for nothing,' and admits himself that he may possibly have used that expression."

Next Lord Mersey described the episode of Gibson's visit to the chart room at five past two to tell the master, on Stone's instructions—"and be sure and wake him"—that the pair of them had now seen altogether eight "white lights like white rockets" and that the steamer was disappearing. At about 2:40 a.m. Stone had again called up the master by voice pipe and told him that the ship from which he had seen the rockets come had disappeared bearing southwest. Stone again assured the master that the rockets "were all white, just white rockets."

Lord Mersey wrote:

There is considerable discrepancy between the evidence of Mr. Stone and that of the Master. The latter states that he went to the voice pipe at about 1:15 but was told then of a white rocket (not five white rockets). Moreover between 1:30 and 4:30 when he was called by the chief officer, he had no recollection of anything being reported to him at all, although he remembered Gibson opening and closing the chart room door.

He concluded:

There are contradictions and inconsistencies in the story as told by the different witnesses. But the truth of the matter is plain. The *Titanic* collided with the berg at 11:40. The vessel seen by the *Californian* stopped at this time. The rockets sent up from the *Titanic* were distress signals. The *Californian* saw distress signals. The number sent up by the *Titanic* was about eight. The *Californian* saw eight. The time over which the rockets from the *Titanic* were sent up was from about 12:45 to 1:45 o'clock. It was about this time that the *Californian* saw the rockets. At 2:40 Mr. Stone called to the Master that the ship from which he had seen the rockets had disappeared. At 2:20 a.m. the *Titanic* had foundered. It was suggested that the rockets seen by the *Californian* were from some other ship not the *Titanic*. But no other ship to fit this theory has ever been heard of.
These circumstances convince me that the ship seen by the *Californian* was the *Titanic* and if so, according to Captain Lord, the two vessels were about five miles apart at the time of the disaster. The evidence from the *Titanic* corroborates this estimate but I am advised that the distance was probably greater though not more than eight to ten miles. The ice by which the *Californian* was surrounded was loose ice extending for a distance of not more than two or three miles in the direction of the *Titanic*. The night was clear and the sea was smooth. When she first saw the rockets the *Californian* could have pushed through the ice to the open water without any serious risk and so have come to the

assistance of the *Titanic*. Had she done so she might have saved many if not all of the lives that were lost.

Odd circumstances surrounded the case, though Lord Mersey either omitted or did not stress them. The *Californian*'s scrap log had vanished. This was the rough log in which (following the practice of all ships) the officer of the watch noted wind and weather, speed, changes of course, and any events or sightings occurring during his watch. Later, the entries in the scrap log were copied neatly into a fair log. But the *Californian*'s scrap log had disappeared and, equally curious, the fair log that survived contained no mention of any of the rockets that had preoccupied Stone and Gibson during the middle watch. The log had been written up from the scrap log by the chief officer. He had, he said, noticed early on Monday morning that there was nothing in the scrap log about what had happened between midnight and four o'clock; he conceded that there should have been; but nevertheless he had not spoken to anyone, not to Stone and not to the captain, about the gaps.

Another unusual circumstance was that on the voyage to Boston, after abandoning the search for bodies, Captain Lord asked both Stone and Gibson to make written statements about what they had seen and done between midnight and 4:00 a.m. Perhaps pointedly, both statements make it plain that they have been asked for by Captain Lord. "At your request . . . ," Stone's letter begins. Gibson's begins, "In compliance with your wishes. . . ." There are no discrepancies between these statements, made three days after the night in question, and their evidence to the British inquiry a month later. Why did Lord take the unusual step of asking for them? It can only have been because he thought he might at some stage be required to account for his own actions or lack of action. If he had not found out from questioning Stone and Gibson, he would have found out from their statements that he was highly vulnerable; and the most damaging testimony was that of Gibson, who reported telling him face to face that he and Stone between them had seen eight white rockets, and that he, Lord, had questioned him and asked him the time.

Lord had a month to think about this episode and to rehearse the explanation he would offer the British court of inquiry to account for his inactivity. Yet his answers to the attorney general's questions were bafflingly inadequate.

ATTORNEY GENERAL: Gibson did come down?
A: So I understand.
Q: But you know perfectly well that he came?
A: I know now.
Q: Did you know then?
A: I did not.
Q: I think you told us you heard Gibson open and close the door?
A: Yes.
Q: And you said, "What is it?"
A: Yes.
Q: And he said nothing?
A: He did not say anything.
Q: And you were expecting him to come down and tell you what the meaning of the rocket was?
A: But in the meantime I was asleep.
LORD MERSEY: Yes, but you were not asleep—at least I suppose not—when you said to the boy, "What is it?"
A: I was wakened up by the opening of the door—the banging of the door.

Later Lord said he had also asked Gibson the time; and he thought he asked him whether there were any colors in the light. But he continued to maintain that he had "no recollection of this apprentice saying anything to me at all that morning." When examined as to why he had asked about the colors in the signals if not in order to know whether they were distress signals, he said, "I really do not know what was the object of my question." Of all the ninety-four appearances before the court, Captain Lord's was the most contradictory and inept.

What happened next to Captain Lord is surprising. One might expect that, having been roundly condemned for incompetence, inhumanity, and law breaking—both in the United States and Britain there were demands that he should face criminal prosecution—Lord would never again have found employment. Shortly after Lord Mersey handed down his verdict Lord was indeed forced to resign from the Leyland Line. But he was soon re-employed. He was taken on by a Scottish shipowner named John Latta, a partner in Lowther, Latta & Co., and chairman of the Nitrate Producers Steamship Company. Latta was a man of some reputation. He had been received by Edward VII for the help his ships had given during the Boer War; and he was later to be made a baronet, though at a period when baronetcies were not hard to come by for a man of means. According to Captain Lord's son, Mr. S. T. Lord, Latta told his father that if he had been employed by a Latta enterprise, instead of Leyland, he would not have been so ill-treated. Captain Lord evidently acquired and retained the confidence of his new employers, who took a risk in hiring him, since before long he was appointed captain of the newest and largest ship in the Nitrate Producers Steamship Company fleet. He retired with an immaculate record—apart from the *Californian* incident—in 1927.

It is difficult to imagine that Lord could have served a further fifteen years at sea, much of the time as a ship's captain, if he had himself believed that while in command of the *Californian* he had failed, through negligence or cowardice, to save 1,500 men and women from a terrible death. At all events, he behaved after 1912 like a man who thinks he has been treated badly, not like a criminal.

Ten days after the report of the British inquiry was published, he wrote from his home in Liscard, Cheshire, to the assistant secretary of the Marine Department at the Board of Trade. The letter was handwritten, with no corrections, and dated August 10.

Dear Sir,

With reference to Lord Mersey's report on the *Titanic* disaster, he states the *Californian* was 8 to 10 miles from the scene of the disaster. I respectfully request you will allow me as Master of the *Californian* to give you a few facts which prove she was the distance away that I gave viz 17 to 19 miles. [On] Apl. 14th [at] 6:30 p.m. I sent my position to the *Antillian* and *Titanic,* this gives me 17 miles away, and you see it was sent some hours before the disaster. Apl. 15th about 5:30 p.m. gave my position to S. S. *Virginian* before I heard where the *Titanic* sunk, that also gave me 17 miles away. I understand the original Marconigrams were in Court.

The evidence of Mr. Boxhall of the *Titanic* who was watching the steamer they had in view, states she *approached* them between one and two a.m., the *Californian* was stopped from 10:30 p.m. to 5:15 a.m. next day.

The steamer seen from the *Californian* was plainly in view from 11:30 p.m., the one seen by the *Titanic* was not, according to the lookout men seen until 0:30 a.m.

Capt Rostron of the *Carpathia* states "When at the scene

of the disaster, it was daylight at 4:30 a.m. I could see all around the horizon, about 8 miles North of me [this was the direction the *Californian* was] there were two steamers, neither of these was the *Californian*." Had the *Californian* been within 10 miles from the *Titanic* she would have been in sight at this time from the *Carpathia,* as she was in the same position as when stopped at 10:30 p.m. the previous evening.

With regard to my own conduct on the night in question, I should like to add a little more. I had taken every precaution for the safety of my own ship, and left her in charge of a responsible officer at 0:40 a.m., with instructions to call me if he wanted anything, and I lay down fully dressed. At 1:15 a.m. (25 minutes after he had seen the first signal), the officer on watch reported the steamer we had in sight was altering her bearing, in other words was steaming away, and had fired a rocket. I did not anticipate any disaster to a vessel that had been stopped nearly for an hour, and had ignored my Morse signals, and was then steaming away, I asked him was it a Co's [company's] signal, and to signal her and let me know the result. It is a matter of great regret to me that I did not go on deck myself at this time, but I didn't think it possible for any seaman to mistake a Co's signal for a distress signal, so I relied on the officer on watch.

Altho further signals were seen between 1:15 a.m. and 2:00 a.m. I was not notified until 2:00 a.m., and then I had fallen into a sound sleep, and whatever message was sent to me then, I was not sufficiently awake to understand, and it was sufficient indication to anyone that I had not realised the message, by the fact that I still remained below, curiosity to see a vessel pushing through the ice would have taken me on deck. The message sent to me at 2:00 a.m. was I heard later, to the effect that the steamer we had in sight at 11:30 p.m. had altered her bearing from S.S.E. to S.W.½W. (to do this she must have steamed at least 8 miles, the *Titanic* did not move after midnight) and had fired 8 rockets, and was then out of sight.

The question of "drink" has been raised as the reason I could not be roused, I don't drink, and never have done.

Further signals were seen after 2:00 a.m. but the officer was so little concerned about them, that he did not think it necessary to notify me. I was called by the Chief Officer at 4:30 a.m., and in conversation he referred to the rockets seen by the second officer. I immediately had the wireless operator called, heard of the disaster, and proceeded at once, pushing through field ice to the scene, and I would have done the same had I understood, as I had everything to gain and nothing to lose.

There is the conversation between the second officer and the apprentice whilst watching the vessel, that they thought she was a tramp steamer, this is their opinion at the time, which is most likely the correct one.

My employers, the Leyland Line, altho their nautical advisers are convinced we did not see the *Titanic,* or the *Titanic* see the *Californian,* say they have the utmost confidence in me, and do not blame me in any way, but owing to Lord Mersey's decision and public opinion caused by this report, they are reluctantly compelled to ask for my resignation, after 14½ years service without a hitch of any description, and if I could clear myself of this charge, would willingly reconsider their decision.

If you consider there was any laxity aboard the *Californian* the night in question, I respectfully draw your attention to the information given here, which was given in evidence, which also proves [it] was not on my part.

I am told that at the inquiry I was a very poor witness, this I don't dispute, but I fail to see why I should have to put up with all this public odium, through no fault or neglect on my part; and I respectfully request you will be able to do something to put my conduct on the night in question in a more favourable light to my employers and the general public.

I am Sir
Your Obedient Servant
Stanley Lord.

At the British inquiry, the attorney general told Lord with exasperation, as he stumbled over his replies, that he was not doing himself justice. His letter did not do him justice either. Clearly he had not asked a lawyer to help him make his case. But the ill-expressed arguments and poor punctuation at least show that the letter was all Lord's own work and, to that extent, is more revealing than a legal document. No matter how cogently Lord had stated his arguments, the Board of Trade would have been deeply reluctant to order the case to be reheard. To do so would have been to repudiate Lord Mersey, for Lord had no new evidence to produce. He asked the board to "do some thing"; but even had the board been willing, what could it do? It could scarcely have been expected to issue a public statement saying that Lord's conduct should be seen in a more favorable light by the public than it had been by Lord Mersey, even if the board believed any such thing. The board declined to take action, and there the matter rested until 1958.

In that year, when he was over eighty, Lord believed he was libeled in the successful film about the *Titanic* based on the book *A Night to Remember*, by his American namesake Walter Lord. He at once approached the Mercantile Marine Service Association, the British shipmasters' professional organization, of which he had been a member for sixty-one years. The association took up his case, but the idea of suing for libel, which they thought the best way of resolving the matter, was ruled out by Captain Lord's age and poor health. Instead, the association attempted to awaken public interest in his cause by issuing statements in his support, but with little effect. Lord died in 1962, on the eve of the fiftieth anniversary of the disaster. Three years later, the association submitted a petition to the president of the Board of Trade, Mr. Douglas Jay, M.P., asking for the 1912 inquiry to be re-opened and detailing what were claimed to be "gross technical inconsistencies" in the case against the *Californian*. The board, however, declined to answer these points and rejected the petition.

In 1968, refusing to give up, the association presented another petition to the board. "New evidence of the utmost importance supporting Captain Lord's case" was in their possession, the association said. The new evidence was a statutory declaration by the Dulwich schoolmaster, Lawrence Beesley, who had died aged eighty-nine the year before. Once again, however, the Board of Trade was unmoved.

After the discovery of the *Titanic*'s remains in 1985, Leslie Harrison, of the Mercantile Marine Service Association, persuaded the Marine Accident Investigation Branch of Britain's Department of Transport to reconsider Captain Lord's actions in the light of new evidence. The resulting report was published in 1992. The two captains who made the investigation disagreed on some points, most notably the distance between the *Californian* and the sinking *Titanic*. They agreed on vital points, stating that distress signals were seen from the *Californian* and appropriate action was not taken. Herbert Stone was severely criticized for his failure to properly inform Captain Lord of the signals he observed. However, the report also states, "Captain Lord was told that rockets had been seen." The report speculates on the reason for the Board of Trade's failure to prosecute Captain Lord after the findings of Lord Mersey's inquiry, saying, "the conduct of his ship, as found by the Court, seems clearly to call for inquiry into his fitness to continue to hold a Certificate of Competency."

The report, which shows signs of haste and inadequate research, was not satisfactory to Leslie Harrison and Captain Lord's other apologists. The dispute has outlived the twentieth century and looks likely to survive the twenty-first.

What, then, are the main arguments of the Lordites?

1. The *Californian*'s position, worked out by dead reckoning and later by observation, was seventeen or nineteen miles away from the position of the *Titanic*. This argument, which was the first point in Lord's letter of 1912, has been eroded by time. Lord thought that he and his officers knew exactly where the *Californian* was stopped. Lord Mersey, supported by experts, concluded that the *Californian*'s position was not what Lord said it was. But the exact whereabouts of the *Californian* is of significance only if it can be related with confidence to the position of the *Titanic*. From 1912 until 1985 almost everyone accepted the accuracy of the *Titanic*'s amended position as worked out by Fourth Officer Boxhall and broadcast in the wireless distress call of 12:25 a.m. Captain Rostron of the *Carpathia* congratulated Boxhall on the "splendid" position he provided, which enabled Rostron to take the *Carpathia* at full speed for fifty-eight miles and at once find the *Titanic*'s lifeboats. Boxhall never had any doubts about it: he asked toward the end of his life for his ashes to be scattered on the Atlantic, over the *Titanic*'s wreck, at 41 degrees 46

minutes N., 50 degrees 14 minutes W.; and on a fine June morning in 1967 the master and crew of the Cunard liner *Scotia* duly carried out his request. But Dr. Robert Ballard, who discovered the wreck in 1985 only after a long search, and after others had failed to find it, has revealed that the *Titanic* was a long way from where she was supposed to be—as much as ten miles. If the *Titanic*'s calculations were inaccurate—despite Rostron's tribute, and despite Boxhall's reputation as an outstanding navigator—why should those of the *Californian* have been accurate?

2. The ship seen from the *Titanic* cannot have been the *Californian* because that ship was moving whereas the *Californian* was stopped. Boxhall indeed testified that the ship he and his fellow officers saw was approaching. He told the British inquiry that he was "watching this steamer . . . and watching this steamer approach us." At that time the *Californian* was, undeniably, stopped.

3. The ship seen by the *Titanic* cannot have been the *Californian* because the *Titanic*'s lifeboats could not find her. Captain Smith told more than one lifeboat to row toward the lights and then return to the *Titanic* to pick up more people. But if the ship was the stationary *Californian*, why did the lifeboats that rowed toward her lights fail to find her? Where had she gone? She might have drifted, but not far enough to have put her out of reach and out of sight of the lifeboats.

The reliable and level-headed Boxhall—after he got into his lifeboat—thought the lights of the ship he had been watching moved away to the west.

SENATOR FLETCHER: Apparently that ship came within four or five miles of the *Titanic,* and then turned and went away in what direction, westward or southward?

A: I do not know whether it was southwestward. I should say it was westerly.

Q: In a westerly direction; almost in the direction in which she had come?

A: Yes, sir.

If Boxhall was right, then the ship cannot have been the *Californian*.

4. If the ship sighted by the *Titanic* was the *Californian*, and vice versa, then the times of the sightings should more or less coincide. But they do not.

The *Californian* saw the lights of another ship at about 11:00 p.m. Boxhall's evidence, however, was that the *Titanic* made her sighting only after he had handed in his Marconigram to the wireless room at 12:25 a.m. Throughout this period lookouts were on duty in the *Titanic*'s crow's nest; they were the first to sight the other ship and alerted the bridge by ringing the lookout bell. How is this long interval between mutual sightings to be explained?

5. If the *Californian* was as close to the *Titanic* as Lord Mersey said she was, why did nobody on board hear the rockets exploding?

6. The times that the rockets were being fired from the *Titanic* do not match the times that rockets were seen from the *Californian*.

This is where the Beesley evidence comes in. To explain its importance, the Mercantile Marine Service Association gives the times of lifeboat launchings and rocket firings the paramount role in the mystery that Freeman Wills Croft, the old detective-story writer, used to give railway timetables.

When were the *Titanic*'s distress rockets fired? The first

rocket (the association maintains) was fired before 12:35 a.m.
By that time, the *Carpathia,* another ship called the *Ypiranga,* and the shore station at Cape Race had all received
the *Titanic's* amended position, as worked out by Boxhall.
But Boxhall gave the wireless room the amended position
after he had started to send off rockets.

This timing is confirmed by others. Third Officer Pitman saw rockets fired "shortly after" he left the *Titanic* in
No. 5 boat "at about 12:30." Fifth Officer Lowe heard the
first rocket go off as he turned from filling No. 5 boat to
No. 3. Quartermaster Rowe said he was ordered to bring
"detonators, which are used in firing distress signals" to the
bridge at 12:25 a.m.; he gave them to Boxhall.

When was the last rocket fired? The evidence about
the rate of firing is conflicting. Lightoller thought "somewhere about eight rockets" were fired "at intervals of a
few minutes—five or six minutes, or something like that."
Boxhall thought the interval was "probably five minutes."
Quartermaster Bright thought only six rockets were fired
"at intervals." Symons the lookout thought they were fired
"every minute, minute intervals."

The significance of Beesley's evidence is that it can be
taken to resolve the question of when the last rocket was
fired. He says in his statutory declaration, "While still on
board the *Titanic* I saw about eight distress rockets fired
from her. I left the ship in Number Thirteen lifeboat and I
am quite confident that the last of these rockets had been
fired *before* this lifeboat cleared the *Titanic's* side after being
lowered into the water."

Beesley in his book of 1912 set out to record the history
of the disaster "as correctly as possible." He made a point
of stating the time of events. He was on the top deck "at
about 12:20 a.m." He saw the musician running down the

deck with the spike of his cello dragging on the floor at "about 12:40 a.m." He was in No. 13 lifeboat being lowered down the *Titanic*'s side at 12:45 a.m.

If the *Californian* was the ship seen from the *Titanic,* then the times the rockets were fired and the times they were seen from the *Californian* must coincide. But in comparing events, it is essential—the association says—to do what both the American and British courts failed to do: to take into account the fact that the times indicated by the clocks in the *Californian* were twelve minutes behind those in the *Titanic.* Here is a masterstroke worthy of Freeman Wills Croft himself. "The reason for this important difference is that the *Californian*'s clocks had been adjusted at noon on Sunday, 14 April, to conform to the apparent time of her then calculated longitude of 47 degrees 30 minutes West, or one hour and fifty minutes in advance of New York Time. Similarly, the *Titanic*'s clocks had been set to an apparent time based on her noon longitude of 44½ West, or two hours and two minutes ahead of New York Time." It is consequently necessary to add twelve minutes to all times noted in the *Californian* before they can be accurately compared with times observed by those in the *Titanic.*

The first rocket seen by the *Californian* was at about 12:45 a.m., which was 12:57 *Titanic* time. But the first rocket was fired before 12:23 a.m. (12:35 a.m. *Titanic* time).

Stone and Gibson saw the last of the eight rockets shortly before 2:00 a.m. Gibson then went down to the chart room to report these eight rockets to Captain Lord. When the captain asked him the time, he said it was five past two. But no rocket was fired, according to Beesley, after 12:45 a.m. *Titanic* time (12:33 *Californian* time): a discrepancy of at least an hour.

Half asleep, Captain Lord had no reason to suppose that

the rockets or flares were necessarily distress rockets. Even if they were white, they could have been part of a private recognition signal.

These are the bare bones of the association's case. They and other Lordites also expound a complex argument about the direction the *Titanic* faced while sinking, and the way the *Californian*'s head swung to starboard during the night; these relative movements do not fit the starboard and port lights seen, it is claimed.

The Lordites complain, besides, about the inquiries' procedures. The senators questioned Lord only briefly, because he said he was due to sail back to England. In London, Lord and the other *Californian*s who gave evidence were in court merely as witnesses; thus the counsel representing them and the Leyland Line had no opportunity to expose the weak links in the deceptively strong-looking chain of argument subsequently deployed by Lord Mersey in his report.

How is one to reach a conclusion about such a controversial matter? Those who condemn Captain Lord have one especially powerful argument on their side. Quite apart from the complex dispute about whether or not the rockets came from the *Titanic,* the simple fact remains that signals that could only have been distress signals were seen coming from somewhere. Yet the *Californian* did nothing; and the captain remained in his cabin from 12:40 a.m. until 4:30 a.m. The point affects officers of the *Californian* besides the captain. Suppose that every word that Captain Lord said in his own defense was true. Suppose he understood nothing of what he was told because he was only half awake. This still does not explain or excuse the apathy of the officer of the watch. If he was in awe of Captain Lord, as has been suggested, he could have shaken the first officer. He could have aroused the wireless operator. But there is no evidence that he even discussed what should be done; he seems to have regarded himself purely as a spectator.

If Captain Lord did indeed understand what the apprentice was telling him, his behavior seems inexplicable. As he said in his letter, he had everything to gain and nothing to lose by action. Captain Rostron thereby won international renown. It has been proposed, as a general though cynical explanation of Lord's failure to act, that he might have been afraid that if he took the distress signals seriously he would be required to risk the safety of his ship; he therefore pretended not to realize what they were, both at the time and later. But he at once got moving through the ice next morning when news of the sinking finally reached him.

However, he did not behave immediately afterward like a man with an entirely clear conscience. It can have only been from motives of self-protection that he told Stone and Gibson to write down their version of what happened. After he reached Boston and was questioned about the voyage, he dissembled—presumably because he hoped nothing further would be heard of the matter. This was not merely unadmirable but foolish, since, as he should have been aware, the entire ship's company as well as the donkeyman Gill knew roughly what had happened.

Even if the Lordites are correct in maintaining that the *Californian* never saw the *Titanic,* and no convincing candidate for the "third ship" has ever been found, it is thus not wholly unjust that Lord should have been one of the disaster's scapegoats. The disaster was a shocking event; and the public, and perhaps not only the public, was looking for someone to blame. The balance of probability is still against Lord, though he had the right to feel aggrieved that his case never received a thorough hearing.

The other scapegoat, who suffered even more "public odium" than Captain Lord, was J. Bruce Ismay.

6

J. "BRUTE" ISMAY

The *Titanic* disaster changed the lives of many of the survivors, and one man was broken by it: J. Bruce Ismay. During the night of April 14–15, 1912, he took a step that transformed—indeed blighted—his whole life; the reasons why it had such a profound, permanent effect on his self-esteem may lie in the familiar problem of a son finding himself unable to follow in the footsteps of a self-made and dominating father. His fall was all the more dramatic because until the crisis came, on the eve of his fiftieth birthday, he had seemed his father's apt successor.

At the time J. Bruce Ismay was born, in 1862—the J. stood for Joseph, after his grandfather the Cumberland boatbuilder—his father was at the beginning of his outstanding career as one of the great Victorian figures of Liverpool, and therefore British, shipbuilding. Thomas Ismay started work in the shipyards at the age of sixteen. His son was given a very different upbringing. Moving up a step in the social ladder, Bruce Ismay was educated not in the north of England at all, but first at a leading boys' private school at Elstree run by a celebrated headmaster, the Rev. Lancelot Sanderson, M.A. (known to the boys as the "Guv"), and then at Harrow, with which Elstree was closely connected. Both schools in that era produced a succession of fine games players. Ismay was one of them; he had an outstanding physique and excelled at all forms of sport. He was a good soccer player at school and won prizes for lawn tennis. Later he took to field sports, becoming one of the finest shots in the country, especially at high pheasants, and a first-class fisherman. He was six foot four: a man with an imposing presence.

On leaving school, he was sent for a year with a tutor to Dinard in France, and then around the world. At home his father, by now a rich man, was building a vast new house eleven miles outside Liverpool on the banks of the River Dee. The architect was the fashionable Norman Shaw, who designed the house in the style of an Elizabethan mansion; the cost was a prodigious £50,000. All nails were of brass, and the indoor servants numbered twenty-two. The choice of Norman Shaw was important. The new mansion had one of the imposing high entrance halls that were a Shaw specialty. When Ismay came to build the *Oceanic*, he was dissatisfied by the original decor and brought in Norman Shaw to redo it. The ideas of the *Oceanic* were developed and enlarged for the *Olympic* and *Titanic;* but the amphitheaters of the new leviathans were recognizably the entrance hall of Dorwell, the new Ismay mansion, on a larger scale.

On his world tour, Bruce Ismay played tennis in Australia and umpired tournaments. On his return, he went into his father's shipping office to learn the business. A revealing story is told of his introduction there. On his first day at work, young Bruce left his hat and coat in his father's private room. When Thomas Ismay arrived, he told a subordinate, in the hearing of the whole staff, including his son, to instruct the new office boy to leave his hat and

coat somewhere else. Having served a brief apprenticeship in Liverpool, he was appointed the firm's representative in New York. In 1888 he married an American, Julia
Schieffelin, who was herself the heiress to a pharmaceutical
fortune. Their prospects were brilliant and assured. Bruce
Ismay returned to England as a director and in 1899, at the
age of thirty-seven, when his father died, inherited control
of the White Star Line.

Even his father would have had difficulties in beating
off the American pressure that soon developed. Certainly
Bruce Ismay was not capable of doing so, especially as he
was dependent on advice and support from his father's old
associate, Pirrie of Harland & Wolff, and Pirrie favored the
sale of White Star to the J. P. Morgan combine. Besides,
Morgan's terms to the shareholders were generous, based
on White Star's earnings in 1900—a particularly profitable
year because of the Boer War. In December 1902, Ismay
gave in. His mother saw it as the end of an era.

Outwardly, his dignity was preserved. He remained
chairman of White Star. Within a year, after prolonged
negotiations, Morgan persuaded him to become president
and managing director of the new combine, International
Mercantile Marine. At first, Ismay was reluctant. Morgan
wanted him to live in New York, which Ismay was not
inclined to do. But Morgan was a persuasive man; he told
Ismay he would give him "entire control" over everything to do with all the shipping lines in the combine,
except finance; and if Ismay took the job, Morgan in person would make available a substantial private line of cash,
which would be greatly to the advantage of both White
Star and Harland & Wolff. Ismay asked his mother's advice.
The new post gave him real power; but there was no dis-
guising the fact that, only three years after he took over
White Star, he had been unable to prevent the great firm

built by his father from passing into the hands of American financiers and railroad magnates, and that he had become one of J. P. Morgan's salaried employees.

It was Ismay and Pirrie—more Pirrie than Ismay, one suspects—who conceived the grandiose idea of the *Olympic* and the *Titanic,* but the idea had to be approved by Morgan. Ismay's relatively subordinate role became plain when he sailed on the *Olympic*'s maiden voyage. He made a number of detailed observations and enthusiastic suggestions for improvements, but all were trivial by comparison with the scale of the enterprise: the reception room was the most popular space in the first class; the after-companionway was not used; the deck space was excessive; a potato peeler was needed in the crew's galley; steam ovens were wanted in the bakehouse; holders for cigarettes and cigars should be supplied to the lavatories; the springs in the beds were too springy. More important defects, such as the inadequate access from steerage to the upper decks   a defect that Lightoller spotted as soon as he joined and explored the *Titanic*—escaped him, unfortunately; nor was he enough of a shipbuilder to be able to form his own opinion about the structural merits of the two new giants. He relied instead on the unrivaled experience of Pirrie and Harland & Wolff, which, admittedly, neither he nor anyone else at that stage had any reason to doubt.

A photograph exists of Ismay walking with Pirrie beside the towering hull of the *Titanic:* Ismay in his bowler hat, the picture of a confident shipowner, and Pirrie in a peaked cap, the picture of a shrewd shipbuilder. Ismay's reputation in shipping circles at that time was high; he had started the cadet ship *Mersey* for training mercantile marine officers, helped to make Southampton the main port for transatlantic travel, and shown his public spirit by supporting a scheme for exchange visits between British and American teachers. But as a man he was regarded as taciturn and austere. After his death, an anonymous correspondent wrote an appreciation in *The Times* saying that his outward appearance had been misleading. "Of a reserved and extremely sensitive nature," the correspondent wrote, "he shrank from exposing to the world the kindness and sympathy which were in him, and no one but those very close to him was permitted to be aware of his innumerable kindly and generous actions." He was also a man who detested personal publicity. These characteristics had a bearing on his fate.

He attended the launch of the *Titanic* but was evidently not excited enough by the mechanics of the biggest and most luxurious liner afloat to go on her trials. He joined her instead in Southampton, accompanied by a secretary and a valet. From the accounts of first-class passengers, we learn that he chatted to them during the first few days about the progress of the voyage, and we learn from his answers to questions put to him at the inquiries—though he did not express it like this—that he was still so incurious about the way the ship worked that he never once visited the bridge.

On the "very fateful night," as the attorney general called it, he invited the ship's doctor, Dr. O'Loughlin, to dine with him in the restaurant at half past seven; he had lunched alone. The meal was not prolonged, and Ismay soon turned in. He was awakened by what he supposed later must have been the collision. For a few moments he remained in bed, speculating that the ship had perhaps lost the blade off a propeller, but then he stirred himself and went out into the passageway. There he saw a steward and asked if he knew what was wrong. The steward could not tell him, so he returned to his stateroom, donned a coat over his pyjamas, and paid his first visit to the bridge, where he found Captain Smith. "We have struck ice," said Smith. Ismay asked, "Do you think the ship is seriously damaged?" Smith answered, "I am afraid so." Ismay then started to go back to his cabin to get dressed but met on the way Chief Engineer Bell. Like Captain Smith, Bell told Ismay that the damage was serious but that he was "quite satisfied"—or "hoped" or "thought" (Ismay was not sure of Bell's exact words)—that the pumps would keep her afloat. Ismay dressed and returned to the bridge, where he was in time to hear Smith give the order to prepare the lifeboats for lowering. He then went to the starboard boat deck and for the next hour and a half, or "perhaps longer," helped to put women and children into the boats.

A ship was sinking fast when Ismay took the step that caused his ruin. He had been putting women aboard what he believed to be the last boat. He told the Senate inquiry: "The boat was there. There was a certain number of men in the boat, and the officer called out asking if there were any more women, and there were no passengers on the deck." He was asked, "There were no passengers on the deck?" and he replied, "No, sir; and as the boat was in the act of being lowered away, I got into it."

A ship's barber said he had seen Mr. Ismay getting into the boat "because there were no women in the vicinity of that boat. . . . The boat was the last to leave to my knowledge." (The barber himself was washed overboard very shortly afterward and climbed on a bundle of floating deck chairs; he was only a hundred feet away from the ship when she sank.) Lightoller said he had been told aboard the *Carpathia* after the rescue, he could not remember by whom, that Chief Officer Wilde, a physically powerful man, "simply bundled him [Ismay] into the boat." Ismay made no attempt to hide behind these alibis. No passengers were on deck; the boat he had been helping to fill was, he thought,

the last one (it was in fact the penultimate); it was "practically" full; men were in it already; it was being lowered; he
got into it.

It is clear that in the hour and a half after the collision Ismay did his best to be helpful. However, glimpses
of him and his curious conduct subsequently reported
by passengers and crew indicate that some kind of mental breakdown—which has been surprisingly little com-
mented on—began immediately after the impact. Martha
Stevenson, who herself had dressed carefully and, like her
sister, done her hair, noticed when she came up on deck
that Ismay must have dressed very hurriedly, "as his pyjamas were below his trousers." Colonel Gracie saw him
soon after the accident. "He wore a day suit"—Gracie was
not as observant as Martha Stevenson—"and, as usual, was
hatless. He seemed too much preoccupied to notice anyone." Accounts by other people do not contradict Ismay,
but show his behavior, after the impact, as ineffectual and,
in one account, hysterical. Fifth Officer Lowe was loading
one of the boats when an unknown man suddenly appeared
shouting, "Lower away! Lower away! Lower away! Lower
away!" Lowe thought this person was "over-anxious" and
"getting a trifle over-excited," since he (Lowe) was already
"on the floor" lowering away. "If you will get the hell
out of that," Lowe shouted back, "I shall be able to do
something." The man made no reply. Lowe said, "Do you
want me to lower away quickly? You'll have me drown the
whole lot of them!" The man still did not explain why he
was shouting or who he was. Indeed Lowe only realized
that he had been swearing at the owner when a steward
identified him to Lowe at the Senate hearings. Ismay was
present when Lowe described the incident from the witness stand and did not contradict him; on the contrary, he

urged Lowe to tell the senators the rough words ("get the hell out of that") he had used.

Boxhall told a similar story. He too was busy getting boats away when a stranger approached and started telling him what to do. Boxhall took no notice, and the stranger, who turned out later to have been Ismay, made no attempt to press his point or to identify himself. Still more strange, although he was the titular owner of the ship, Ismay at no point, during the hour and a half that elapsed after he learned that the damage was serious, made any attempt to speak to the principal authorities on board: the captain, the chief engineer, and the leader of the team from Harland & Wolff.

The lifeboat containing Ismay got away only with difficulty. The *Titanic* by this time had developed a pronounced list, so that the boat's rubbing strake kept catching on the rivets, and everyone, women included, had to help fend the boat from the ship's side. Once the boat was in the water, Ismay took one of the oars, but because he had been rowing with his back to the *Titanic*—the oars were manned by more than one person, and the rowers were not all facing the same way—he had not seen her go down and had not looked over his shoulder. "I am glad I did not," he said later. At the London inquiry, Ismay caused some confusion when he explained that they had for some considerable time rowed in the direction of a light, until the sea got up and they felt they were making no progress, adding that he was sure the light did not belong to the *Californian*. The attorney general and Lord Mersey thought Ismay was denying that the ship's lights seen from the *Titanic* were those of the *Californian,* but Ismay eventually explained that he was talking about a quite different light coming from another quarter; his light belonged, he thought, to a sailing ship. The attorney general and Lord Mersey were glad to have cleared up the confusion, but did not then or later address themselves to the mystery of the sailing ship's identity. If she existed—and Quartermaster Rowe saw the light also—those on board must have been close enough to have watched the *Titanic* go down. Perhaps the light was an illusion, a star.

When rescue arrived with the dawn, Ismay was in good enough shape to climb aboard the *Carpathia* by Jacob's ladder. Two weeks later, at the Senate inquiry in Washington, he gave a rambling, inconsequential account of what happened next. Senator Smith asked a straightforward question about the *Carpathia;* Ismay replied with his longest statement of the whole inquiry:

> I understand that my behavior on board the *Titanic* and subsequently on board the *Carpathia* has been very severely criticized [a woman had complained that he appropriated one of the best cabins]. I want to court the fullest inquiry, and I place myself unreservedly in the hands of yourself and of your colleagues, to ask any questions in regard to my conduct; so please do not hesitate to do so, and I will answer to the best of my ability. So far as the *Carpathia* is concerned, sir, when I got on board the ship I stood with my back against the bulkhead, and somebody came up and said, "Will you not go into the saloon and get some soup or something to drink?" "No," I said, "I really do not want anything at all." He said, "Do go and get something." I said, "No. If you will leave me alone I will be very much happier here." I said, "If you will get me in some room where I can be quiet, I wish you would." He said, "Please go into the saloon and get something hot." I said, "I would rather not." Then he took me and put me

into a room. I did not know whose the room was, at all. This man proved to be the doctor of the *Carpathia*. I was in that room until I left the ship. I was never outside the door of that room. During the whole of the time I was in this room, I never had anything of a solid nature. I lived on soup. I did not want very much of anything. The room was constantly being entered by people asking for the doctor. The doctor slept in the room the other nights that I was on board that ship. Mr. Jack Thayer was brought into the room the morning we got on board the *Carpathia*. He stayed in the room some little time, and the doctor came in after he had been in, I should think, about a quarter of an hour, and he said to this young boy, "Would you not like something to eat?" He said, "I would like some bacon and eggs," which he had. The doctor did not have a suite of rooms on the ship. He simply had this small room, which he himself occupied and dressed in every night and morning.

It was the doctor who asked John Thayer to visit Ismay, hoping it might relieve his "terribly nervous condition" if he could be persuaded to talk to someone he knew. Thayer wrote later:

I immediately went down and as there was no answer to my knock, I went right in. He was seated, in his pyjamas, on his bunk, staring straight ahead, shaking all over like a leaf.

My entrance apparently did not dawn on his consciousness. Even when I spoke to him and tried to engage him in conversation, telling him he had a perfect right to take the last boat, he paid absolutely no attention and continued to look ahead with his fixed stare.

I am almost certain that on the *Titanic* his hair had been
black with slight tinges of gray, but now his hair was virtually snow white.

I have never seen a man so completely wrecked. Nothing I could do or say brought any response.
As I closed the door, he was still looking fixedly ahead.

Immobilized by guilt or shame in the doctor's cabin,
Ismay did nothing for three days except scribble Marconigrams. It was Captain Rostron who persuaded him to
send the first of the series, all of which were addressed
to P. A. S. Franklin, vice president of the International
Mercantile Marine Company, at the White Star offices on
Broadway, New York. It read: "Deeply regret advise you
Titanic sank this morning after collision iceberg, resulting
serious loss life. Full particulars later. Bruce Ismay."* The
full particulars, however, were not sent, possibly because
Ismay's mind became preoccupied with the problem of
getting himself and his employees back home as quickly
as possible. It was Lightoller who persuaded him that he
must give orders for the immediate return to England of
the surviving crew. Lightoller's explanation of his motives,
as given to the American inquiry, is confused. He said he
thought it desirable to keep the crew together. Left to their
own devices, he said, they would not have hung around
New York, but would have quickly found new jobs, particularly with the owners of private yachts, with the result
that "we would have lost a number of them, probably very
important witnesses." The pronoun cannot have embraced
the senators. Had Lightoller's plan succeeded, they would
have had no crew to examine, since they would all, includ-

---

*For reasons never satisfactorily explained, this message was not sent until April 17, by
which time it was old news.—DG

ing Lightoller, have been on their way back to England
before the Senate inquiry opened; and so would Ismay.

Lightoller explained with candor why he had felt it necessary to tell Ismay what to do. Another White Star liner,
the *Cedric,* was in New York and preparing to sail. Lightoller told Ismay, "You ought to telegraph and insist on
their holding her." Lightoller added, "I may say that at that
time Mr. Ismay did not seem to me to be in a mental condition to finally decide anything. . . . He was obsessed with
the idea, and kept repeating, that he ought to have gone
down with the ship because he found that some women
had gone down. I told him there was no such reason; I told
him a very great deal; I tried to get the idea out of his head,
but he was taken with it."

So, instructed by Lightoller, Ismay sent a message to
Franklin signed with the transparently disguised name he
used for confidential communications: "Very important
you should hold *Cedric* daylight Friday for *Titanic* crew.
Answer. Yamsi."

Franklin did not at once reply to this demand. Instead,
he forwarded Ismay a message from his wife in England.
"So thankful you are saved but grieving with you over
terrible calamity. Shall sail Saturday to return with you."
Franklin added: "Accept my deepest sympathy horrible
catastrophe. Will meet you aboard *Carpathia* after docking.
Is Widener aboard? Franklin."

Ismay tried again: "Most desirable *Titanic* crew aboard
Carpathia should be sent home earliest moment possible. Suggest you hold *Cedric,* sailing her daylight Friday
unless you see any reason contrary. Propose returning in
her myself. Please send outfit of clothes, including shoes,
for me to *Cedric.* Have nothing of my own. Please reply.
Yamsi."

Franklin received this message at 5:20 p.m. on Wednesday and sent a reply within three hours rejecting Ismay's request: "Have arranged forward crew *Lapland* sailing Saturday, calling Plymouth. We all consider most unwise delay *Cedric* considering all circumstances. Franklin."

The next Marconigram from Ismay was sent on behalf of Rostron, who wanted the *Titanic*'s lifeboats removed from the deck of the *Carpathia* before he docked. "Send responsible ship's officer and fourteen White Star sailors in two tugboats to take charge of thirteen *Titanic* lifeboats, at quarantine. Yamsi." Ismay added on his own behalf: "Please join *Carpathia* at quarantine if possible." Then he sent two more Marconigrams about the *Cedric*. "Very important you should hold *Cedric* daylight Friday for *Titanic* crew. Reply. Yamsi." Franklin received this injunction at 8:23 a.m. on Thursday, April 18. Eleven minutes later he got a second: "Unless you have good and sufficient reason for not holding *Cedric,* please arrange do so. Most undesirable have crew New York so long. Yamsi."

Ismay's final message shows him still clinging to the hope of returning home at once in the *Cedric:* "Widener not aboard. Hope see you quarantine. Please cable wife am returning *Cedric*. Yamsi." Franklin's last message to Ismay was delivered only after the *Carpathia* was alongside in New York: "Concise Marconigram account of actual accident greatly needed for enlightenment public and ourselves. This most important. Franklin."

Given the scale of the event, it was an unimpressive exchange. Ismay, although he had had three days in which to do so, failed to supply even his own office, let alone the waiting world, with more than the barest facts about the disaster. He provided no news about the morale or physical condition of the survivors aboard the *Carpathia*. He gave no instructions about what arrangements should be made for them. The notion that some *ex gratia* payment should be made to the crew of the *Titanic,* whose wages had automatically ceased as soon as the ship went down, did not occur to him. He sent no message of condolence. Yet he worried about his shoes.*

After the *Carpathia* docked, Franklin was quickly aboard, to be followed in a few minutes by Senator Smith, who told Ismay that the Senate proposed to conduct an inquiry into the disaster and that he, Ismay, would be required to appear before it. Meanwhile, none of the *Titanic*'s crew must leave the United States. The senators suspected that Ismay might be planning to remove himself from American soil as rapidly as possible in order to avoid awkward questions; and their suspicions were increased when they learned the content of the messages that Ismay had sent from the ship. Ismay protested that the senators were mistaken. He had "not the faintest idea" there would be an inquiry until Senator Smith had told him so. Still, however pure his motives in trying to arrange an immediate passage to Liverpool, the head of the White Star Line might have been expected to think it seemly, at the very least, to stay in New York in order to ensure that everything possible was done for the relief and comfort of the survivors and their relations, and to supervise the recovery of the many hundreds of bodies—White Star passengers and White Star employees—still floating in the North Atlantic.

Perhaps the mounting urgency of his Marconigrams to Franklin reflected Ismay's apprehension about the opprobrium awaiting him. From the beginning, the sinking was a huge newspaper story, filling the front pages. The papers carried drawings, tables of other disasters, photographs of the *Titanic*'s lavish interiors, imaginary reconstructions of

---

*Ismay, after pressure from the seamen's unions, agreed to pay the surviving crew for the time they spent away from England. Most received pay for thirteen additional days.

the collision, and, as lists of those drowned filtered through, columns of obituaries. Ismay was a prominent part of the story from the time it broke. On the morning after the news of the sinking was confirmed, he was the first person named in *The New York Times*'s seven-column headline: "*TITANIC* SINKS FOUR HOURS AFTER HITTING ICEBERG; 866 RESCUED BY *CARPATHIA;* PROBABLY 1,250 PERISH; ISMAY SAFE, MRS. ASTOR MAYBE, NOTED NAMES MISSING."

For the next three days, the newspapers had little hard news to go on, as rumors about rescue missions by ships other than the *Carpathia* flickered and died. The arrival of the *Carpathia* in New York was a news editors' field day. She docked at 9:35 p.m. The next morning, in the best-organized piece of mass reporting in journalistic history, *The New York Times* achieved what one of its historians has called, with reason, "the ultimate in disaster news coverage": fifteen out of twenty-four pages were given to the disaster, mainly to stories told by the survivors. Other papers trailed, but not for want of trying. One survivor told her story to the Associated Press, the wire service, which distributed it nationwide. It was published in one of Senator Smith's hometown papers, the *Evening Press* of Grand Rapids, Michigan, under the headline, which was not in quotation marks: "ISMAY TOOK CARE TO SAVE OWN LIFE." The supporting headlines read: "Stories of Survivors Severe on White Star Managing Director; Helped into a Boat; and Selected Men Who Were to Row It; On Board the *Carpathia* He Shut Himself Up, with a Sign on Door that He Was Not to be Disturbed."

Underneath, Mrs. W. J. Cardeza of Philadelphia was reported as saying, after she had arrived at the Ritz-Carlton (one of the city's best hotels), that Ismay was not only seated safely in a lifeboat before it was filled but also selected the crew that rowed the boat. "According to Mrs.

Cardeza, Mr. Ismay knew that Mr. Cardeza was an expert oarsman and he beckoned him into the boat; Mr. Cardeza manned an oar until Mr. Ismay's boat was picked up about two hours later." Mrs. William Bucknell, who had rowed "until her hands were blistered," said that aboard the *Carpathia* Ismay had refused to come out of his cabin until a committee of survivors had demanded that he see them. They wanted to know what White Star would do for them in the way of reparations, but Ismay had said merely that it would do all in its power to make "a partial repayment for their suffering" and had then retired back into his cabin.

Afternoon papers the same day carried a story from Washington reporting a statement by Senator Rayner of Maryland. It was headlined by the Arkansas *Democrat:* "SENATOR RAYNER SAYS ISMAY IS RESPONSIBLE FOR THE DISASTER." Underneath, the senator was quoted as saying, "The captain of the *Titanic* undoubtedly acted under the orders of Mr. Ismay who risked the life of the entire ship to make a speedy passage across the sea." The senator added that Mr. Ismay should be held responsible for the disaster, and that the civilized nations would applaud criminal prosecution of the management of the White Star Line.

Neither the newspapers nor the senator were prepared to wait for evidence before putting a noose round Ismay's neck. Very soon after the *Carpathia* docked it was announced that Ismay and the surviving officers of the *Titanic* had agreed to appear before a Senate subcommittee hastily appointed to investigate the disaster, and that the hearings would start at once in New York. But the newspapers' verdict was already being delivered. The heroes were nominated overnight—Captain Smith, Mr. and Mrs. Straus, the musicians—and so was the villain. He was "J. Brute Ismay."

The allegations were uninhibited, and so were the cartoons. Ismay was reported by the Associated Press to be worth $40 million; one cartoon portrayed an overweight capitalist in a top hat, smoking a cigar, alone in a lifeboat while the *Titanic* went down in the background. But the most telling shaft was fired by Ben Hecht, later a coauthor of the play *The Front Page*. He contributed the following poisoned dart to the Chicago *Journal:*

> News Item—Mr. Bruce Ismay's name appears among those of the "women and children saved." Mr. Ismay is one of the owners of the White Star Line.

> The Captain stood where a Captain should,
> For the law of the sea is grim;
> The Owner romped ere his ship was swamped
> And no law bothers him.

> The Captain stood where the Captain should,
> When a captain's boat goes down;
> But the Owner led when the women fled,
> For an Owner must not drown.

> The Captain sank as a man of Rank,
> While his Owner turned away,
> The Captain's grave was his bridge and, brave,
> He earned his seaman's pay.

> To hold your place in the ghastly face
> Of death on the sea at night,
> Is a seaman's job, but to flee with the mob
> Is an Owner's noble right.

Nor was it only newspapers and politicians who were damning. Rear Admiral A. T. Mahan, the great naval his-

J. Bruce Ismay, hand to moustache, giving evidence to the Senate inquiry in the Waldorf-Astoria Hotel, New York. *Inset:* Senator William Alden Smith, chairman of the U.S. Senate inquiry.

Lady Duff Gordon.

Captain Lord.

Guglielmo Marconi (*right*) with Godfrey Isaacs.

Harold Bride being carried off the *Carpathia* in New York.

Below: All these Southampton children lost a father, brother, uncle, or cousin on the *Titanic*.

Top inset: Outside the White Star offices in Southampton; drawn for the *Sphere* by H. M. Paget. *Bottom inset:* Artist's impression of Quartermaster Hichens giving evidence to the British inquiry.

J. Bruce Ismay giving evidence to the British inquiry.

Opposite above left: Lord Mersey (*right*) and his son, the Hon. Clive Bigham, arriving at the British inquiry.

Opposite above right: Embalming a corpse aboard the *Mackay-Bennett*.

Opposite below: Undertakers and coffins on the jetty in Halifax, Nova Scotia, awaiting bodies picked up by the *Mackay-Bennett*.

Left: Dr. Robert Ballard.

Below: Members of the Franco-American team that found the *Titanic*. Standing in front of *Argo* (*from left to right*): Jean-Louis Michel; Lieutenant George Rey, U.S. Navy; Jean Jarry; Dr. Robert Ballard; and Bernard Pillaud.

Top: The research vessel *Knorr* returning to Woods Hole in September 1985.

Above: Two cranes, still locked into position on the deck of the *Titanic* on the seabed.

Right: Bottles of wine, including French Bordeaux, are scattered over the ocean floor around the wreck. A photograph taken by the Woods Hole expedition of 1985.

torian, wrote to the New York *Evening Post* saying, "I hold that, under these conditions, so long as there was a soul that could be saved, the obligation lay upon Mr. Ismay that that one person and not he should be on the boat." Currents of private opinion were running in the same direction. Brooks Adams, the brother of Henry Adams and not much less distinguished, wrote a private letter along the same lines to a senator, urging Ismay's condemnation.

In this atmosphere of intense hostility and curiosity, Ismay's public ordeal began. He was the first witness put on the stand before the Senate inquiry the morning after the *Carpathia* docked. By then he had acquired some clothes, and he arrived at the Waldorf-Astoria looking slim and elegant in a double-breasted suit, high collar, and bowler hat, carrying an immaculately furled umbrella, and wearing a gleaming pair of shoes. Eleven days later he appeared before the inquiry again after it moved to Washington. He was then allowed to return to England. On June 4 he appeared before the Board of Trade inquiry, and if he expected to be treated more gently by his fellow countrymen than by Americans his hopes were not fulfilled, for in London he was subjected to cross-examination that was as ruthlessly to the point as that of the senators, and more carefully planned.

He resented the way he was treated, especially in the United States. He wrote a captious private letter to Senator Smith during the Washington hearings, pointing out that he had been under "severe mental and physical strain," and asking if he might now be released, "in order that I may go home to my family." Smith at once sent back an irritated reply: Ismay could certainly not leave before there had been the fullest inquiry into the circumstances of the accident, and he should "continue to help me instead of annoying me and delaying my work by your personal importunities." Ismay's feelings of persecution boiled over in public. The inquiry, he told reporters, was "brutally unfair. They are going about it in a manner that seems unjust, and the injustice lies heaviest upon me. Why, I cannot even protect myself by having my counsel ask questions."

Not everyone was against him, however. The correspondent of a Canadian paper, the *Morning Chronicle* of Halifax, wrote: "And J. Bruce Ismay, the man whom a certain class of New York papers prefer to call 'J. Brute Ismay,' 'coward,' 'white-livered,' 'the man who came home with the women and children.' What of him? It is he who is the center of attraction. It is to him that every eye constantly returns. He doesn't look [a coward] and his conduct does not show it. Ismay looks like a strong man. There is real power in the sun-tanned face and the square head with the crisp black curls." The reporter noted Ismay's "red eyes, with deep lines below them." When a witness described the death cries of the *Titanic*, "Ismay closed his eyes and gnawed his upturned black moustache." Sometimes he put "the middle joint of his finger between his teeth." The reporter's last paragraph summed up his impressions: "He seldom smiles, he shows no interest, no matter what the evidence may be. He shows every mark of great suffering."

Ismay may have looked like a strong man, but he was a lackluster witness. The most striking feature of all his appearances was the way he repeatedly countered questions by appeals to his own ignorance. His father had been one of the great shipowners of his time. He himself had been in the business for a quarter of a century. Although, as we have seen, his titular power was in practice severely circumscribed, he was nevertheless chairman of the company that owned the *Titanic* and president of a huge American trust that controlled five British and two American shipping lines. Ships were the source of his fortune, his reputation, and his career.

Yet he seemed to wish to present himself as an amateur who had strayed aboard the *Titanic* almost by mistake. In London he described himself as a "passenger" until the attorney general asked him whether he had paid for his accommodation. In the United States he said he was "not a navigator." He was not a ship construction expert. He was "not a sailor." He repeated certain phrases: "I saw none"; "I could not tell you, sir"; "That I could not answer, sir"; "I really do not remember." Senator Smith asked, "What was the full equipment of lifeboats for a ship of this size?" "I could not tell you that, sir," Ismay replied. Smith also asked, "What proportion of women and children were saved?" to which Ismay replied, "I have no idea." He did not know the full number of the crew. He presumed there were two wireless operators but did not know. He did not know about the boiler construction on the *Titanic*. It was "not possible" for him to judge the time it took to lower a lifeboat. He did not see the ship go down and "really could not say" when he last saw her: "It might have been ten minutes after we left her. It is impossible for me to give any judgement of the time. I could not do it." He did not observe any confusion. He did not see any passengers on deck when he entered the lifeboat. He did not hear an explosion. He did not look to see if there was a panic. He could not put a name to any of the passengers he saw aboard the *Titanic* during the hour and a half before she sank. He did not know whether the *Titanic* broke in two. At one extravagant moment in the British inquiry he went so far as to suggest that he did not understand longitude and latitude, which brought a sharp, incredulous rebuke from the attorney general. He told the American inquiry that the number of his stateroom had been B52. Then, when an English businessman said that he had occupied B52, Ismay thought he must have been in B56. Three weeks later in London he was still confused about the number. He believed it must have been B52 after all, though he could not be sure; most remarkably, he was not certain whether his stateroom was on the port or the starboard side.

Did Ismay truly not know the many things he said he did not know? Had he decided that the less said the better? Or was he throughout the two inquiries in a state of nervous shock bordering on amnesia? (Before the disaster he was noted in shipping circles for his extraordinary memory.) Possibly his performance was a mixture of all three. He does not seem to have set out to be obstructive. He combined professions of ignorance with assurances that he would do all he could to acquire from other sources the information sought from himself.

The Senate committee wanted answers to two questions above all, if only because they had been fastened on by the press and politicians. Why had he, the owner, been saved when the captain and many of the passengers for whose safety his company was responsible had been drowned? How far was he—as Senator Rayner of Maryland alleged—personally to blame for the high speed at which the *Titanic* had headed into a region of ice—perhaps looking for a record crossing?

Given the public uproar about Ismay's failure to do his duty by going down with his ship, the senators made surprisingly little attempt to investigate his conduct in detail. They did not, for instance, call another first-class male passenger who had got into the same boat as Ismay. This was the wealthy Mr. William Carter from Philadelphia, whose beautiful and fashionable wife was a former

Miss Polk, a member of the Scottish-Irish family that gave
the United States its eleventh president. The Carters had
two children at school in England—Lucille at Wycombe
Abbey and William, Jr., at a prep school in Rugby—and
the Carters had been spending a year in a manor house
they had leased in Leicestershire so that Mr. Carter could
hunt. All the family had been saved, and when Mr. Carter
reached New York he innocently explained that he and
Ismay had been advised to get into the lifeboat by Chief
Officer Wilde because they were recognized as first-class
passengers. Carter, who unlike Ismay escaped all criticism,
evidently thought this preferential treatment entirely reasonable. Whether Wilde gave any such advice, however, is
doubtful, although the senators might have been expected
to show an interest in the point. They must have been
convinced that Ismay's simple account of his action was
truthful, as it probably was.

Both inquiries cross-questioned him much more closely
about whether or not he had as owner influenced the
Titanic's speed. He flatly denied any such influence. He
had never discussed the matter with Captain Smith. The
only conversation he had had with any officer about it had
been with the chief engineer before the ship left Ireland.
They had agreed that the *Titanic* should at some stage be
tried at full speed, but that was routine practice for any
ship on her first crossing. Of course the ultimate decision
would have remained with the captain. It was true that on
Sunday he had spoken to passengers and mentioned the
plan to go at full speed on Monday; but there was no question of his having either ordered or influenced the captain
in this regard.

Captain Rostron gave Ismay useful support. It would
be unthinkable, said Rostron, for any self-respecting
captain—least of all Captain Smith—to take orders from

anybody while at sea. The captain was supreme. Nor did Ismay have any difficulty in dismissing ill-informed talk about the *Titanic* trying to set a transatlantic record.

The Marconigram that Ismay pocketed was more troublesome. Captain Smith before lunch on Sunday had given him, without comment, the message from the *Baltic* saying that a Greek steamer had reported icebergs and field ice. He, Ismay, had not really understood it, he said; he had "attributed no special importance" to it. He was asked by the attorney general in London, "Had you no curiosity to ascertain whether or not you would be travelling in the region in which ice was reported?" Ismay replied, "I had not." So he had put the Marconigram in his pocket as he went to lunch alone, and returned it to Captain Smith in the smoking room at ten past seven, before dinner, because the captain wanted to put it up in the chart room.

The attorney general slowly pushed Ismay into a corner. Ismay had seen a Marconigram warning of ice. He expected the *Titanic* to enter a region of ice that night— because of the Marconigram, he eventually conceded. How then could Ismay justify her speed?

Q: If you were approaching ice in the night it would be desirable, would it not, to slow down?
A: I am not a navigator.
LORD MERSEY: Answer the question.
ISMAY: I say no. I am not a navigator.

But the only reason for going fast in a region of ice, the attorney general suggested, would be to get out of danger as fast as possible. Ismay agreed; to get out of the region before, for instance, fog came down. Then it was Ismay's admitted view, said the attorney general, closing in, that it would be best for a ship's captain to go as fast as he could

through an ice region at night? Ismay was in a hopeless
tangle. He feebly replied, "I say he was justified in going
fast to get out of it if the conditions were suitable and right
and the weather clear." "I think we understand," said the
attorney general.

Ismay was made to appear ridiculous over the ice warning; but nobody suggested that he personally was responsible for the *Titanic*'s failure to slow down as a result. The
inadequate number of lifeboats showed Ismay in a more
questionable light. The subject came up after the *Daily
Mail* published an interview with the Rt. Hon. Alexander
Carlisle, one of the *Titanic*'s principal designers from Harland & Wolff. Carlisle told the paper he had recommended
the provision of forty lifeboats, but his proposal had been
turned down. Called before the London inquiry, he said
that he had put his ideas, accompanied by designs, to two
White Star directors. They had discussed the idea briefly
before rejecting it. Who were these two directors? One of
them was Ismay.

Ismay said he had never heard any mention of forty
lifeboats. Yet even Ismay, with his professed ignorance of
almost everything about ships, must have known that the
modern and much discussed Wellin davit, as installed in
the *Titanic*, was able to carry four lifeboats; he must also
have been aware that the original plan was for each *Titanic*
davit to carry two lifeboats. Besides, Carlisle's account of
the way his suggestion was dismissed fits in with Ismay's
apologia to the inquiry. The reason why the *Titanic* had not
carried more lifeboats, Ismay said, was partly that she was
not required to do so by Board of Trade regulations, but
also because she was thought to be practically unsinkable
and was thus a gigantic lifeboat herself. She was given lifeboats not so much because anyone believed that her own
passengers and crew might need them, but because they

might be needed to rescue passengers and crew from other ships. This was the one shipping subject on which Ismay freely gave his views. His sudden articulateness suggests that it was indeed he who decided that more deck space for passengers was preferable to unnecessary lifeboats.

Ismay was cleared by both investigations; Lord Mersey noted briskly that if he had gone down with the ship he would merely have lengthened the casualty list. Two footnotes to the inquiry may be added. Three years after Ismay's death, John Thayer privately published his short account of his experiences. He wrote of Ismay:

> There was some disturbance in loading the last two for-
> ward starboard boats. A large crowd of men was pressing
> to get into them. No women were around as far as I could
> see. I saw Ismay, who had been assisting in the loading of
> the last boat, push his way into it. It was really every man
> for himself. Many of the crew and men from the stokehole
> were lined up, with apparently not a thought of attempt-
> ing to get away without orders. Purser H. W. McElroy, as
> brave and as fine a man as ever lived, was standing up in
> the next to last boat loading it. . . . McElroy did not take a
> boat and was not saved.

This is a very different version of events from Ismay's, who gave the impression that the decks were deserted when he got into the boat. Ismay said repeatedly that there were no passengers on deck; but if there was "a large crowd of men," would Ismay have known which were crew and which were passengers? Thayer's word "push" is damag-ing. He knew Ismay well enough to recognize him. How-ever, he was writing twenty-eight years after the event.

The other footnote comes from the third wife of Colo-nel J. J. Astor's son Vincent. In her autobiography, Brooke

Astor describes a trip across the Atlantic in 1958 aboard the *United States,* in which her husband Vincent owned a large stake:

> It was during the trip that I really saw Vincent in action. It was soon after the *Queen Elizabeth II* had been put in service, and it was said in the papers that she would break the Atlantic speed record for Atlantic crossing, thereby relegating the *United States* to a back seat. We were having a leisurely lunch in the upper deck dining room of the *United States* when a smiling waiter came up and said, "If you look out of the window, sir, you will see the *Queen Elizabeth* just behind us." Vincent took one look over his shoulder at the *Queen Elizabeth* looming over the horizon, and saying to me, "I am going to the bridge," threw down his napkin, and dashed out of the dining room.
>
> Within five minutes as I was sipping my coffee, the whole ship began to shake, and the passengers, bewildered, jumped up to see what was happening. I went out on deck, and hanging onto the rail, watched as the *Queen Elizabeth* disappeared below the horizon behind us. Eventually, I went down to our suite, where Vincent appeared, beaming from ear to ear. "Miss *United States* kicked up her heels, Pookie," he said. "She wants to keep her record, and we will dock hours before the *Elizabeth.*"

Considering Vincent Astor's ancestry, this incident throws an interesting light on Captain Rostron's blanket denial at the *Titanic* inquiry that owners ever intervened with their captains.

Ismay soon resigned the presidency of the International Mercantile Marine Company and the chairmanship of White Star. But his public ordeal was not yet over. Two years later a long-deferred court case opened in New York to settle compensation claims against his old company. The hearings ranged over the whole question of White Star's incompetence and failures; but since it was part of the claimants' argument that the company's direct responsibility was proved by the part its chief executive had played in the disaster, Ismay's personal conduct repeatedly came up for blame and criticism.

The case centered on a $30,000 claim from Mrs. William Renouf of Elizabeth, New Jersey, for the loss of her husband and two brothers. Total claims amounted to $16,804,112. Some of them were large. The Straus and Astor families did not sue, but Mrs. H. B. Harris, the wife of a prominent theatrical producer, estimated her damages at a million dollars. The company submitted that its liability was limited to $97,972 and 12 cents, a ridiculously precise figure worked out by its lawyers and accountants when Ismay was still chairman.*

So on June 23, 1915, at the U.S. District Court in the Woolworth building, Charles Burlingham, proctor in Admiralty for White Star, who had attended all the Senate hearings, opened proceedings by arguing that White Star had taken every possible precaution for the *Titanic*'s safety, and that the line was therefore responsible only for the loss of freight and the passengers' financial losses. He gave as one example of White Star's prudence the doubling of lookouts when ice was reported, a precaution he had thought up himself.

A lawyer for the claimants, George Betts, at once introduced the name of Ismay. The company's chief executive, said Betts, had been "practically allowed to captain the ship." The *Titanic* had been going too fast; no prac-

---

*Under American law, White Star's liability was limited to the value of the salvaged lifeboats, unless it could be proved that Captain Smith was negligent *and the company knew of his negligence and connived at it.* Hence the claimants' pursuit of Ismay.—DG tice lifeboat muster had ever been held; the lifeboats had not been properly manned. To underline the irresponsibility of sending the boats away half full, Betts produced Captain A. T. Lundin of the Wellin Marine Equipment Company, suppliers of the davits, who said—as was already well known—that each davit was capable of picking up and lowering four lifeboats one after the other and strong enough to swing four times the weight of a single full lifeboat. This evidence was introduced to counter the excuse for the half-full boats that had been put forward by *Titanic* officers during the Senate inquiry; they had assumed that the number of people that could be safely put into a boat being lowered was a matter of personal judgment.

Then came the young John Thayer. He said that he and his father had been constantly in the company of Ismay during the first few days of the run. He recalled a conversation on the Sunday of the sinking. The three of them had been chatting about the ship's speed and the time they would reach New York, and Mr. Ismay had said, "Two more boilers are to be opened up today"—evidence of Ismay's interest in speed. Thayer added that he and his father (who, it will be remembered, was drowned) went to "about eight boats" and asked which would take first-class passengers and each officer sent them to another boat, "so we gave it up."

Next came three women who had lost relatives. Mrs. Renouf said her brothers could not get into one boat because it was being so badly lowered; it was "almost vertical." Mrs. Kenyon from Connecticut, a first-class passenger whose husband drowned, said, "No one warned us of the danger. It wasn't until my husband went up and spoke to Captain Smith that we knew the truth." Her boat had contained only twenty-eight people, and the one person in it who knew how to row was not any member of the crew but the Countess of Rothes (this stalwart woman was on her way to join her fruit-farming husband in Canada). Mrs. Horace de Camp (Mary Marvin in 1912) said that there were only thirteen in her boat, yet her husband was not allowed in, and he had been drowned.

A well-known tennis player, Karl H. Behr, said it was not until forty or fifty minutes after the collision that the passengers were given any warning of danger. He said Ismay had been giving orders in his shirtsleeves; Ismay had told the boat Behr was in to lower away although it contained only forty or fifty and could have taken fifteen or twenty more. Mrs. Futrelle, the wife of an American writer, confirmed Behr's account of the delay before the officers warned the passengers; her husband had been assured by one officer that there was absolutely no danger at all. The Futrelles' first intimation that anything untoward had occurred came not from any information they were given by the ship's authorities but from going on deck and finding that men were being separated from women by stewards.

Eugene Daly of Newark developed the theme of casualness and muddle. He had been told to go on deck by a steward, and when he got there had found a group of stewards smoking and laughing. He tried to get into a lifeboat and was threatened by an officer with a gun. He saw two men lying on deck and was told they had been shot (nobody else claimed to have seen these bodies). He had finally jumped into the sea and had been picked up by the very boat he had been refused permission to get into.

William Mellors from England told further stories of half-filled lifeboats, overexcited crew stopping people from getting into boats, and officers threatening male passengers with revolvers.

Then came the professionals. Captain Robert Niss of the *Bohemia* testified about ice conditions. He took the

position that the International Ice Patrol takes today. Even
on a clear starlit night, you could not guarantee to see
ice far enough ahead to avoid striking it, he said. Even in
moonlight you could miss it, unless the moon was behind
the ice. Had he, like the captain of the *Titanic,* entered an
ice zone, he would have slowed down to a speed that he
was sure would give him room to stop in an emergency.

Captain Henry Meyerdierks, the captain of the Hamburg-
Amerika Line steamship *President Grant,* said that if he had
had the same warnings as the *Titanic,* he would have gone
at least fifty miles south. Later Captain Niss took the stand
again, this time carrying the 1912 logbook of the *Pisa,*
which had preceded the *Titanic* by thirty hours. The log
showed that on April 13 the *Pisa* had encountered a large
icefield, had sighted seven large icebergs, and had promptly
sent ice warnings to all quarters. Niss, like Meyerdierks,
spoke of the difficulty of seeing icebergs at night.

The indictment continued with the former chief of
naval construction to the United States Navy saying that
the *Titanic* had been built on traditional principles but represented such an unusual increase in size that her builders should have produced a new theory of construction.
There should have been an increase in transverse bulkheads
to ensure reasonable safety. Rear Admiral Richard M.
Watt, another U.S. Navy construction expert, said that
"side rips" like the one that sank the *Titanic* were unknown
in the U.S. Navy, but they had had "bottom rips" from
submerged reefs. If the *Titanic* had had a watertight deck
extending to the top of her bulkheads, she would still be
afloat. Longitudinal bulkheads would have increased buoy-
ancy.

Twelve days after the case opened, the lawyer Roger
Foster summed up for the claimants. "BLAMES ISMAY FOR
WRECK" was the headline the next day in *The New York*

Times. Foster said the question of White Star's liability was to be determined by "whether the company had knowledge that the *Titanic* was going at high speed knowingly, having been warned that there was obstruction ahead." In answering that question, he continued, it must be remembered that Mr. Ismay, the chief executive of the line, had spoken to the engineer about the speed, had told passengers about the two additional boilers to be opened up, and had carried in his pocket all day a Marconigram warning the *Titanic* of ice. The Marconigram should have been sent to the chart room and the position of the ice marked on the chart. "It has been said that the captain is the supreme being on his ship, but this is not the case. The owner could dismiss him in mid-ocean."

The case was settled out of court. On December 17, 1915, it was announced that claims against White Star had been reduced to $2,500,000. White Star had expressed a willingness to pay $550,000, plus legal costs, without an admission of liability. A few claimants still held out, in the hope that the court would rule that White Star's liability was unlimited. On July 28, 1916, Judge Julius M. Mayer signed a decree by which the claimants received $665,000, divided between them and the lawyers according to a formula biased in favor of the needier dependents. The claimants agreed to hold Oceanic Steam Navigation Company "guiltless of any privity or knowledge such as were charged in the complaints" and "not liable to any extent for any loss, damage, injuries, destructions and fatalities or for any claim whatever in any way resulting or arising from or growing out of said collision." All further action was barred.

The largest sum allowed for a death claim was $50,000, as against, for instance, the million dollars claimed by Mrs. Harris. Smaller claims were not reduced by anything like the same proportion. Death claims for the immigrants had been filed at $1,500; they were scaled down to $1,000 each. These sums were not inconsiderable: on the day the settlement was announced, the "oldest tea rooms in New York" on Fifth Avenue advertised breakfast for thirty-five cents; and Thomas Cook offered a five-day steamship tour to Bermuda for twenty-eight dollars.

Ismay had been trying to keep out of sight. While the British inquiry was still in progress, he bought a retreat in Ireland, in County Galway, without seeing it. It was a sporting estate on the Atlantic, with a lodge, private boats, and three lakes, and when there was no salmon fishing there was fishing in the sea. He spent more and more time on the estate; when it burned down in 1927 he had it entirely rebuilt. It was remarkable in that part of Ireland for the number of its bathrooms.

The Ismays had four children, two of them boys. One of them, George, used to recall in later life how he and his brother had been made to have cold baths every morning, even in winter. He also remembered how the children's part of the house was separated from their parents' not by one but by two green baize doors. George worked for Cunard; one of the daughters married a Scotsman and retired to Mull. Ismay's wife lived until she was over ninety, active to the end, giving bridge parties and concealing her age. She was a woman of strong character. It is said by descendants that she would never allow her husband to talk about the *Titanic*.

He had sought in vain, after the disaster, to hold on to the chairmanship of White Star, but the Morgans—J. P. Morgan, now at the end of his life, and his son—were adamant that he could not do so. In any case, Ismay had been going to retire from the presidency of International Mercantile Marine in the summer of 1913; the *Titanic* was to have been a final triumph. But he retained a few directorships, one of them with the London, Midland and Scottish Railway. Although he spent more and more time in Ireland, he kept a house in Mayfair. His natural shyness became more marked. He enjoyed music; when he went alone to a concert, he bought two seats, one for himself and one for his hat and coat. When he traveled to Liverpool from London for a board meeting, he would reserve a whole compartment and be provided with a cold hamper, so that he did not have to enter the restaurant car. In Liverpool he never revisited the White Star offices. Shortly before he died, he had a leg amputated and rigged up a series of pulleys over his bath so that he could get in and out without help. He died in 1937 and was buried in Putney. His entry in the *Dictionary of National Biography,* written by the former editor of a shipping journal, does not mention the *Titanic.* Ismay would have welcomed that omission.

7

THE CURIOUS BEHAVIOR
OF MARCONI

One of the fascinations of the *Titanic* disaster is that more clearly than any other event, it reveals the modern world just starting to burst out of its Victorian chrysalis, so that the old world and the new can be seen almost simultaneously.

Ismay was the victim of a vicious assault by the new mass circulation press, led by William Randolph Hearst. Hearst's papers and their competitors were merely looking for stories and a target. At the same time, Ismay was judged and condemned by the moral standards of the old school; Admiral Mahan thought he should have behaved with "a particularity of conduct" because of his station in life—a very Victorian notion that Hearst, for one, would not have dreamed of applying either to Ismay or to himself.

Technology was also in transition; the motorcar coexisted in New York with three million horses. The same was true of communications. Carrying out his constitutional duty to keep the sovereign informed, Prime Minister H. H. Asquith wrote officially to King George V after every Cabinet meeting by hand—as he did after the Cabinet discussed the *Titanic*. To keep the Foreign Office and the Board of Trade (the Archbishop of Canterbury was still one of its ex-officio members) in touch with the Senate hearings, the British Embassy in Washington could find no quicker way of doing so than by sending newspaper clippings and the daily transcripts of the U.S. inquiry to London by mail steamer. Two years earlier, however, Crippen the murderer had been unmasked as a result of wireless messages exchanged between the liner on which he and his mistress were traveling and Scotland Yard. Guglielmo Marconi, the pioneer of wireless communication, was one of the new men emerging from the chrysalis.

During the three and a half days that elapsed between the sinking of the *Titanic* and the arrival of the *Carpathia* in New York, nobody's fortunes dipped as low as Ismay's, and nobody's rose higher than Marconi's, as if they were two men on opposite ends of a seesaw. The more it became plain that the shipbuilding technology of the *Titanic* had failed—the double bottom, the watertight compartments—the more successful seemed the miraculous new technology of wireless telegraphy. Were it not for Marconi and his invention, another seven hundred lives would have been lost.

Marconi companies boomed. Looking back now, though, it is hard to avoid the conclusion that Marconi came out of the *Titanic* disaster better than he deserved. The Senate inquired into the part he played in it—he happened to be in New York on business—but he escaped virtually unscathed. So did Marconi employees, one or two of whom behaved as ambiguously as their chairman.

Marconi was an undoubted genius who at a very early age captured the imagination of the western world. He was one of the scientists named by Henry Adams as having called into existence an invisible new universe whose infinite complexities someone with Adams's education could not begin to grasp; even though Adams "wrapped himself in vibrations and rays," he achieved only "a paradise of ignorance." Before Marconi, the advances in communications since the middle of the nineteenth century had been more or less comprehensible to the educated mind. The first electric telegraph had been laid along the Great Western Railway between Paddington and West Drayton in 1843, making it possible for the first time in history to send a detailed message faster than the man who carried it. Eight years later England and France were joined by submarine cable; another cable was laid under the Atlantic in 1865; a link with India followed in 1870. The telegraph transmitted messages by code, usually Morse. Then came Alexander Graham Bell, who discovered a way of sending the human voice down wires; Britain's first telephone exchange opened in 1879. The next giant step was Marconi's invention of wireless telegraphy.

The history of the new communications vocabulary is instructive. The term "telegraph" was first applied in 1792 to a simple device constructed by a Frenchman, a M. Chappe: an upright post with mobile arms that sent messages in accordance with a prearranged code. By 1805 the word was being used by cricketers to denote a scoreboard. "Telegram" was an American coinage of 1857, a replacement for the clumsy "telegraphic dispatch."

A wholly new word was needed to describe Marconi's achievement. In 1887 the German physicist Hertz had found a way of generating radio waves by electrical spark discharges. Marconi (1874–1937) discovered how to send messages down these waves; hence, used for the first time in 1894, "wireless" ("wire sb, + less," as the *Oxford English Dictionary* explains). Marconi was shrewd as well as brilliant. He was barely out of his teens when he invented his apparatus. His father was a comfortably-off Italian and his mother a member of the Jameson Irish whisky family. A Jameson cousin persuaded Marconi to move from Bologna to London in order to exploit his revolutionary device, and he had a well-publicized success in 1896 when, to the wonder of all, he sent a message, without benefit of wires, from the roof of the post office in St. Martin's Lane to another roof in Queen Victoria Street, near St. Paul's. Two years later he helped reporters covering Gladstone's last illness to send news from Bournemouth to Fleet Street; he always kept in with the press. The United States Navy invited him in 1899 to send messages between battleships, which he did, over a distance of twenty-five miles. Marconi apparatus was used in the Boer War. Skeptics maintained that radio waves traveled in a straight line and that the range of the apparatus would be limited by the curvature of the earth. Marconi solved that problem by bridging the Atlantic: he set up a transmitting station in Cornwall, arranged for the letter "S" to be sent in Morse code, and picked up the signal on an aerial supported by kites and balloons in Newfoundland. No wonder Henry Adams's head spun. The dapper young Marconi became a popular hero. He was photographed with a strange twenty-foot-high cylinder erected on top of a steam bus; here was the first mobile wireless. The cylinder was an "aerial" (a word first used to describe a wire for receiving or radiating the waves of wireless telegraphy in 1904).

The first British vessel to use Marconi's apparatus was the royal yacht, in 1898. By 1912, besides the *Titanic,* hundreds of British ships were carrying Marconi's machines, and only a very few, fewer than a dozen, the machines of his competitors. By then he had an exclusive contract with the Italian government, had equipped German lightships, and had built a ring of stations on the North American coast, with a particularly important one at Cape Race, on the eastern tip of Newfoundland, to serve the ships using the St. Lawrence Seaway and to provide information about snow and ice to shipping in the North Atlantic. He had also landed a contract to construct a chain of wireless stations across the world to link up the British Empire, won a Nobel Prize for physics, and married the daughter of an Irish peer. As well as "wireless" and "aerial," another new word had had to be coined to describe his work: Marconigram, first used in 1902.

The invention had spread rapidly to ships but was not properly adjusted to ships' needs. Marconi companies fitted the apparatus and supplied, with the shipping company's agreement, an operator, or, as was usual in the case of big ships, two operators. These men were trained and paid by Marconi, and it was their responsibility to maintain a commercial telegraphic service on board their ship. But they served two masters, since their hours of work were determined by the captain. In practice, since most captains were unable to judge, for instance, whether it would be better for the apparatus to be worked in the day, when its range might be five hundred miles, or at night, when the range might double, the operators tended to decide their own duties. Thus it was sheer bad luck that the *Californian* operator had finished work for the night before the *Titanic* began to send distress signals; had he been at his machine, all those aboard the *Titanic* might have been saved. And it was sheer good luck that the operator on the *Carpathia,* who had already taken his coat off before turning in, decided as an afterthought to check an earlier message and, returning to his apparatus, picked up the *Titanic*'s call for help.

The chief operator of the *Titanic* who sent out that call at once became one of the heroes of the disaster. Memorials commemorating his heroism survive on both sides of the Atlantic, one in Battery Park, New York, and another in Godalming, Surrey. It was his twenty-two-year-old junior colleague who created his posthumous fame. Of all the survivors' stories told immediately, Harold Bride's was by far the most arresting.

The arrival of the *Carpathia* in New York was chaotic. Since White Star officially admitted the sinking, the world had been three days without news. Nobody was quite sure who was alive and who was drowned. Thursday night began with rain and thunder. Morning-paper reporters (sixteen from *The New York Times* alone) were hard pressed. It was already ten to eight when the *Carpathia,* trailed and occasionally illuminated by photographers taking flashlight pictures from a tug, passed the Statue of Liberty; twenty-five to ten before she tied up at the Cunard pier. Reporters and curious crowds were kept well away by police. When the survivors eventually came ashore, most of those who spoke English were swept up by weeping friends and relations.

Accurate reporting, under these circumstances, was not easy. News editors were clamoring for copy; some survivors were hysterical, or wishing to make a splash. Besides, as with most disaster stories, the less scrupulous reporters knew that what they wrote could never be checked. Friday morning's papers thus released a flood of unreliable information on the world.

"We had been crunching through ice all day," Mr. C. H. Romsacue (actually Charles Hollace Romaine) of Georgetown, Kentucky, was reported as saying. A woman survivor claimed that "everyone rushed on deck and made for the same lifeboat. Many men made for the boats and were shot down by Captain Smith. Several fell to the decks mortally wounded before there was a semblance of order or discipline." This fantasy was credited to Lady Duff Gordon.

John Thayer was quoted as saying that he and his father had jumped overboard together. An Italian told an exciting tale of saving himself by clinging to "a cake of ice."

Some of the alleged quotes printed the next day read as if they were spoken by rewrite men. The Grand Rapids *Herald* quoted Quartermaster Moody, "helmsman on the night of the disaster," on the dramatic moment when an officer had suddenly shouted at him, "Port your helm!"— too late for the *Titanic* to avoid the "submerged portion" of an iceberg. That a British sailor would have talked about the "submerged portion" of anything is unlikely, and further doubt is thrown on the authenticity of the quote because the helmsman was actually named Hichens, not Moody, and the order given was not "port your helm" but "hard-a-starboard."

Among the dozens of survivors' stories, though, Harold Bride's stood out, both for its intrinsic interest and for its ring of truth. It was published on the front page by *The New York Times* under the headline "THRILLING STORY BY TITANIC'S SURVIVING WIRELESS MAN." A precede explained that the account had been dictated the night before to a *Times* reporter. It reads like it. The reporter, concealing his trade, had managed to cross the police lines and board the *Carpathia* under the wing of Guglielmo Marconi himself, while all other reporters were being held back. Marconi and the reporter, Jim Speers, made their way to the tiny wireless cabin where Bride, his feet swathed in bandages, was still at work. Marconi was a famous man; he was also Bride's employer. The story Bride told was as follows:

> In the first place, the public should not blame anybody because more wireless messages about the disaster to the *Titanic* did not reach shore from the *Carpathia*. I positively

refused to send [answer] press dispatches because the bulk of personal messages with touching words of grief was so large. The wireless operators aboard the *Chester* got all they asked for. And they were wretched operators.★

They knew American Morse but not Continental Morse sufficiently to be worthwhile. They taxed our endurance to the limit.

I had to cut them out at last, they were so insufferably slow, and go ahead with our messages of grief to relatives. We sent 119 personal messages today, and 50 yesterday.

When I was dragged aboard the *Carpathia* I went to the hospital at first. I stayed there for ten hours. Then somebody brought word that the *Carpathia*'s wireless operator was "getting queer" from the work.

They asked me if I could go up and help. I could not walk. Both my feet were broken or something. I don't know what. I went up on crutches with somebody helping me.

I took the key and I never left the wireless cabin after that. Our meals were brought to us. We kept the wireless working all the time. The navy operators were a great nuisance. I advise them all to learn the Continental Morse and learn to speed up with it if they ever expect to be worth their salt. The *Chester*'s man thought he knew it but he was as slow as Christmas coming.

We worked all the time. Nothing went wrong. Sometimes the *Carpathia* man and sometimes I sent. There was a bed in the wireless cabin. I could sit on it and rest my feet while sending sometimes.

★The *Chester* was one of two United States Navy vessels sent by President Taft to give any help they could; he was privately anxious, besides, to learn the fate of his trusted aide, Archie Butt, who had been aboard the *Titanic*. But the *Chester* operators had been unable to extract any information at all from the *Carpathia,* although their calls were acknowledged.

At this point it sounds as if the *Times* reporter was worried that Bride would never get around to the *Titanic* and asked him to start further back.

> To begin at the beginning. I joined the *Titanic* at Belfast. I was born at Nunhead, England, 22 years ago, and joined the Marconi forces last July. I first worked on the *Hoverford* [*Haverford*] and then on the *Lusitania*. I joined the *Titanic* at Belfast.
>
> I didn't have much to do aboard the *Titanic* except to relieve Phillips from midnight until some time in the morning, when he should be through sleeping [the reporter's shorthand must have failed him here]. On the night of the accident, I was not sending, but was asleep. I was due to be up and relieve Phillips earlier than usual. And that reminds me—if it hadn't been for a lucky thing, we never could have sent any call for help.
>
> The lucky thing was that the wireless broke down early enough for us to fix it before the accident. We noticed something wrong on Sunday and Phillips and I worked seven hours to find it. We found a "secretary" burned out, at last, and repaired it just a few hours before the iceberg was struck.
>
> Phillips said to me as he took the night-shift, "You turn in, boy, and get some sleep, and go [get?] up as soon as you can and give me a chance. I'm all done for with this work of making repairs."
>
> There were three rooms in the wireless cabin. One was a sleeping room, one a dynamo room, and one an operating room. I took off my clothes and went to sleep in bed. Then I was conscious of waking up and hearing Phillips sending off to Cape Race. I read what he was sending. It was traffic matter.
>
> I remembered how tired he was and I got out of bed

without my clothes on to relieve him. I didn't even feel
the shock. I hardly knew it had happened [until] after the
Captain had come to us. There was no jolt whatever.

I was standing by Phillips telling him to go to bed when
the Captain put his head in the cabin. "We've struck an
iceberg," the Captain said, "and I'm having an inspection
made to tell what it has done for us. You better get ready
to send out a call for assistance. But don't send it until I
tell you."

The Captain went away and in 10 minutes, I should
estimate the time, he came back. We could hear a terrible confusion outside, but there was not the least thing to
indicate there was any trouble. The wireless was working
perfectly.

"Send the call for assistance," ordered the Captain,
barely putting his head in the door.

"What call should I send?" Phillips asked.

"The regulation international call for help. Just that."

Then the Captain was gone. Phillips began to send
"C Q D." He flashed away at it and we joked while he did
so. All of us made light of the disaster.

We joked that way while he made signals for about five
minutes. Then the Captain came back.

"What are you sending?" he asked.

"C Q D," Phillips replied.

The humor of the situation appealed to me. I cut in
with a little remark that made us all laugh, including the
Captain.

"Send S O S," I said. "It's the new call, and it may be
your last chance to send it."

Phillips with a laugh changed the signal to S O S. The
Captain told us we had been struck amidships, or just back
of amidships. It was ten minutes, Phillips told me, after he

had noticed the iceberg, that the slight jolt that was the collision's only signal to us occurred. We thought we were a good distance away.

We said lots of funny things to each other in the next few minutes. We picked up first the steamship *Frankfurt*. We gave her our position and said we had struck an iceberg and needed assistance. The *Frankfurt* operator went away to tell his captain.

He came back and we told him we were sinking by the head. By that time we could observe a distinct list forward.

The *Carpathia* answered our signal. We told her our position and said we were sinking by the head. The operator went to tell the Captain, and in five minutes returned and told us that the Captain of the *Carpathia* was putting about and heading for us.

Our Captain had left us at this time and Phillips told me to run and tell him what the *Carpathia* had answered. I did so and I went through an awful mass of people to his cabin. The decks were full of scrambling men and women. I saw no fighting, but I heard tell of it.

I came back and heard Phillips giving the *Carpathia* fuller directions. Phillips told me to put on my clothes. Until that moment I forgot that I was not dressed.

I went to my cabin and dressed. I brought an overcoat to Phillips. It was very cold. I slipped the overcoat upon him while he worked.

Every few minutes Phillips would send me to the Captain with little messages. They were merely telling how the *Carpathia* was coming our way and gave her speed.

I noticed as I was coming back from one trip that they were putting off women and children in lifeboats. I noticed that the list forward was increasing.

Phillips told me the wireless was growing weaker. The

Captain came and told us our engine rooms were taking
in water and that the dynamos might not last much longer.
We sent that word to the *Carpathia*.

I went out on deck and looked around. The water was
pretty close up to the boat deck. There was a great scramble aft, and how poor Phillips worked through it I don't
know.

He was a brave man. I learned to love him that night
and I suddenly felt for him a great reverence to see him
standing there sticking to his work while everyone else was
raging about. I will never live to forget the work of Phillips
for the last awful fifteen minutes.

I thought it was about time to look about and see if
there was anything detached that would float. I remembered that every member of the crew had a special lifebelt
and ought to know where it was. I remembered mine was
under my bunk. I went and got it. Then I thought how
cold the water was.

I remembered I had some boots and I put these on, and
an extra jacket and I put that on. I saw Phillips standing out
there still sending away, giving the *Carpathia* details of just
how we were doing.

We picked up the *Olympic* and told her we were sinking by the head and were about all down [presumably,
"done"]. As Phillips was sending the message I strapped
his lifebelt to his back. I had already put on his overcoat.

I wondered if I could get him into his boots. He suggested with a sort of laugh that I look out and see if all the
people were off in the boats, or if any boats were left, or
how things were.

I saw a collapsible boat near a funnel and went over to
it. Twelve men were trying to boost it down to the boat
deck. They were having an awful time. It was the last boat
left. I looked at it longingly a few minutes. Then I gave

them a hand, and over she went. They all started to scramble in on the boat deck, and I walked back to Phillips. I said the last raft had gone.

Then came the Captain's voice: "Men, you have done your full duty. You can do no more. Abandon your cabin. Now it's every man for himself. You look out for yourselves. I release you. That's the way of it at this kind of a time. Every man for himself."

I looked out. The boat deck was awash. Phillips clung on sending and sending. He clung on for about ten minutes or maybe fifteen minutes after the Captain had released him. The water was then coming into our cabin.

While he worked something happened I hate to tell about. I was back in my room getting Phillips's money for him, and as I looked out the door I saw a stoker, or somebody from below decks, leaning over Phillips from behind. He was too busy to notice what the man was doing. The man was slipping the lifebelt off Phillips's back.

He was a big man, too. As you can see, I am very small. I don't know what it was I got hold of. I remembered in a flash the way Phillips had clung on —how I had to fix that lifebelt in place because he was too busy to do it.

I knew that man from below decks had his own lifebelt and should have known where to get it.

I suddenly felt a passion not to let that man die a decent sailor's death. I wished he might have stretched rope or walked a plank. I did my duty. I hope I finished him. I don't know. We left him on the cabin floor of the wireless room and he was not moving.

From aft came the tunes of the band. It was a ragtime tune. I don't know what. Then there was "Autumn." Phillips ran aft and that was the last I ever saw of him alive.

I went to the place I had seen the collapsible boat on the boat deck, and to my surprise I saw the boat and the men still trying to push it off. I guess there wasn't a sailor in the crowd. They couldn't do it. I went up to them and was just lending a hand when a large wave came awash of the deck.

The big wave carried the boat off. I had hold of an oarlock and I went off with it. The next I knew I was in the boat.

But that was not all. I was in the boat and the boat was upside down and I was under it. And I remember realizing I was wet through, and that whatever happened I must not breathe, for I was under water.

I knew I had to fight for it and I did. How I got out from under the boat I do not know, but I felt a breath of air at last.

There were men all around me—hundreds of them. The sea was dotted with them, all depending on their life-belts. I felt I simply had to get away from the ship. She was a beautiful sight then.

Smoke and sparks were rushing out of her funnel. There must have been an explosion but we had heard none. We only saw the stream of sparks. The ship was gradually turning on her nose—just like a duck does that goes down for a dive. I had only one thing on my mind—to get away from the suction. The band was still playing. I guess all the band went down.

They were playing "Autumn" then. I swam with all my might. I suppose I was 150 feet away when the *Titanic,* on her nose, with her after-quarter sticking straight up in the air, began to settle—slowly.

When at last the waves washed over her rudder there wasn't the least bit of suction I could feel. She must have kept going just as slowly as she had been.

I forgot to mention that, besides the *Olympic* and *Carpathia,* we spoke [to] some German boat, I don't know which, and told them how we were. We also spoke [to] the

Baltic. I remembered those things as I began to figure what ships would be coming towards us.

I felt, after a little while, like sinking. It was very cold. I saw a boat of some kind near me and put all my strength into an effort to swim to it. It was hard work. I was all done when a hand reached out and pulled me aboard. It was our same collapsible. The same crowd was on it.

There was just room for me to roll on the edge. I lay there not caring what was happening. Somebody sat on my legs. They were wedged in between slats and were being wrenched. I had not the heart left to ask the man to move. It was a terrible sight all around—men swimming and sinking.

I lay where I was, letting the man wrench my feet out of shape. Others came near. Nobody gave them a hand. The bottom-up boat already had more men than it would hold and it was sinking.

At first the larger waves splashed over my clothing. Then they began to splash over my head and I had to breathe when I could.

As we floated around on our capsized boat and I kept straining my eyes for a ship's lights, somebody said, "Don't you think we ought to pray?" The man who made the suggestion asked what the religion of the others was. Each man called out his religion. One was a Catholic, one a Methodist, one a Presbyterian.

It was decided the most appropriate prayer for all was the Lord's Prayer. We spoke it over in chorus with the man who first suggested that we pray as the leader.

Some splendid people saved us. They had a right-side-up boat, and it was full to its capacity. Yet they came to us and loaded us all into it. I saw some lights off in the distance and knew a steamship was coming to our aid.

I didn't care what happened. I just lay and gasped when

I could and felt the pain in my feet. At last the *Carpathia* was alongside and the people were being taken up a rope ladder. Our boat drew near and one by one the men were taken off.

One man was dead. I passed him and went to the ladder, although my feet pained terribly. The dead man was Phillips. He had died on the raft from exposure and cold, I guess. He had been all in from work before the wreck came. He stood his ground until the crisis had passed, and then he had collapsed, I guess.

But I hardly thought that then. I didn't think much of anything. I tried the rope ladder. My feet pained terribly, but I got to the top and felt hands reaching out to me. The next I knew a woman was leaning over me in a cabin and I felt her hand waving back my hair and rubbing my face.

I felt somebody at my feet and felt the warmth of a jolt of liquor. Somebody got me under the arms. Then I was bustled down below to the hospital. That was early in the day, I guess. I lay in the hospital until near night and they told me the *Carpathia*'s wireless man was getting "queer" and would I help.

After that I was never out of the wireless room, so I don't know what happened among the passengers. I saw nothing of Mrs. Astor or any of them. I just worked wireless. The splutter never died down. I knew it soothed the hurt and felt like a tie to the world of friends and home.

How then could I take news queries? Sometimes I let a newspaper ask a question and get a long string of stuff asking for full particulars about everything. Whenever I started to take such a message I thought of the poor people waiting for their messages to go—hoping for answers to them.

I shut off the inquirers, and sent my personal messages. And I feel I did the white [*sic*] thing.

If the *Chester* had a decent operator I could have worked with him longer but he got terribly on my nerves with his insufferable incompetence. I was still sending my personal messages when Mr. Marconi and the *Times* reporter arrived to ask that I prepare this statement.

There were, maybe, 100 left. I would like to send them all, because I could rest easier if I knew all those messages had gone to the friends waiting for them. But an ambulance man is waiting with a stretcher, and I guess I have got to go with him. I hope my legs get better soon.

The way the band kept playing was a noble thing. I heard it first while still we were working wireless, when there was a ragtime tune for us, and the last I saw of the band, when I was floating out in the sea with my lifebelt on, it was still on deck, playing "Autumn." How they ever did it I cannot imagine.

That and the way Phillips kept sending after the Captain told him his life was his own, and to look out for himself, are two things that stand out in my mind over all the rest.

It was a magnificent story, but was it accurate? It is disconcerting to find that Bride, when he appeared before the inquiries, somewhat changed his tune. One should perhaps bear in mind that he was only twenty-two (Phillips was twenty-four), and that his experience of the world was confined to three trips to Brazil and three to New York. He had been a Marconi operator for only nine months.

In the interview, he said he saw the dead body of Phillips in the lifeboat as he was boarding the *Carpathia*. Under oath, he said he had "heard" that Phillips had been seen in one of the boats. Again, in the interview he clearly implies that he alone, with murderous intent, knocked out the stoker who was stealing Phillips's lifebelt. Under oath, he said first that Phillips had held the man while he, Bride, struck him; but he later changed that account, too, saying that "I held him and Phillips hit him."

There are other, minor, inconsistencies. In the interview, describing his last sight of Phillips alive, he is quoted as saying that Phillips "ran" aft; later, he said Phillips "walked." More puzzling, he said in the interview that he became impatient with the U.S. Navy wireless operators because they did not know Continental Morse; but Continental Morse was the system that the U.S. Navy employed.

When Bride appeared before the Senate committee his feet were still in bandages, and he was in and out of hospital. Many papers had published a photograph of him being carried down the *Carpathia*'s gangway, his arms around the shoulders of two helpers and his feet in the air. In court, he looked pale and ill, with black rings under his eyes. The senators did not press him.

Why did he change his story? It sounds as if the passage in the interview when he recognizes the dead body of Phillips was Jim Speers stretching a point for dramatic effect. If Bride really saw the body, or at the time thought he saw the body, he would have had no reason to change his story later. Perhaps he told Speers that Phillips might have been in the boat, and Speers could not resist firming the story up a bit. Who would ever know? On the other hand it seems likely that the original account of the attack on the stoker and the revision both came from Bride. He might have thought on reflection that it was imprudent to admit to an attempted—possibly a successful—murder. "Ran" might again be the reporter.

Despite these changes, Bride's interview established two enduring *Titanic* legends: the heroism of Phillips, and the band that played on as the ship went down. Others testified about the band, and some said it was playing the hymn "Nearer, My God, to Thee." Colonel Gracie was sure it was not. "If 'Nearer, My God, to Thee' had been one of the selections," he wrote, "I assuredly should have noticed it as a tactless warning of imminent death." The "Nearer, My God, to Thee" report seems to have come first from a story written by Charles F. Hurd, a staff correspondent of the New York *Evening World* who happened to be traveling in the *Carpathia* and was thus in a position to question survivors at leisure before they got back to New York. He sounds like an honest reporter. At first he was evidently skeptical about the hymn, but was convinced by the evidence. He wrote, "To relate that the ship's string band gathered into the saloon* near the end and played 'Nearer, My God, To Thee' sounds like an attempt to give an added solemn color to a scene which was in itself the climax of solemnity. But various passengers and survivors of the crew agree in the declaration that they heard this music." Much argument has centered around this episode. The "Nearer, My God, to Thee" school of thought was persuasively opposed by those who considered Bride to be the best witness and believed that the "Autumn" he mentioned in his interview must refer to the musical setting of an entirely different hymn. However, the latest discovery, endorsed by Walter Lord in a recent essay, is that "Autumn" was also the name often given to a popular waltz of the day called "Songe d'Automne." Bride did not say that "Autumn" was a hymn.

But the interesting fact about Bride at the time had nothing to do with Phillips or hymns. It was that he had spent a large part of the voyage in the wireless room of the *Carpathia,* together with the *Carpathia*'s own operator, Harold Cottam. Between them, this pair had controlled

---

*There was no "saloon." He was probably referring to the smoking room on the promenade (or A) deck.

the access of the outside world to news of the disaster; and they had kept it to themselves.

"WATCHERS ANGERED BY *CARPATHIA*'S SILENCE," said the New York *Evening News.* "FOUR DAYS OF TERRIBLE SUSPENSE BREED WILD RUMORS," said the seven-column headline over a feature in the Springfield *Sunday Union* a week after the disaster. "ENTIRE WORLD'S THIRST FOR NEWS ONLY ASSUAGED WHEN RESCUE SHIP CREPT INTO PORT THROUGH FOG AND DARKNESS" read a second headline. The headlines were true. The Associated Press had tried every possible means to find out what had happened to the *Titanic,* beyond the bare fact of the sinking. So had the United States Navy, acting on behalf of the president of the United States. So had Marconi himself, who sent two messages to ask why the *Carpathia*'s captain did not supply some news. But the *Carpathia* refused to reply. She transmitted partial lists of survivors and the private messages of survivors, nothing else.

Why? Perhaps the first point to note is that Bride and Cottam were not only young (Cottam was twenty-one), but ill-paid. The British Marconi company claimed to start its operators at thirty shillings a week, rising to two pounds—half the American rate for the job. But in practice it sometimes paid less: after three years with the company Cottam was drawing £4.10s. a month; Bride was on £4. A second pertinent point is that both men would have been aware of the history of Jack Binns.

Three years earlier, Binns had been the Marconi operator aboard another White Star liner, the *Republic,* when she was in a serious collision off Nantucket. The wireless apparatus had been badly damaged, but Binns had contrived to repair it and send out distress signals. As a result, nearly all hands aboard the *Republic* had been rescued before the ship sank, and Binns had become a celebrity. Shortly afterward, he resigned his job with the Marconi company and turned himself into a popular and well-paid writer on maritime topics.

The behavior of Cottam and Bride required an explanation, to say the least. Ismay's Marconigram with the message that the *Titanic* had struck an iceberg and sunk did not reach the White Star office in New York for two days. The Senate committee was so astounded by this dilatoriness that they cabled Captain Rostron, of whom with good reason they had formed a high opinion, and asked if he could account for it. Rostron by this time was in Gibraltar. He cabled back to say that the message was given to the purser on the afternoon of the fifteenth, and that the purser had taken it to operator Cottam personally. He, Rostron, had particularly mentioned that everything possible must be done to get official messages away by the most convenient means; yet he now discovered that the Ismay message, which could and should have been passed to another ship for onward relay, had not been transmitted until the seventeenth, when the *Carpathia* was within range of the Marconi shore station on Sable Island, south of Nova Scotia. So Cottam and Bride had not only ignored requests for information from the head of their company, the United States Navy, the White Star Line, the Associated Press, and the president of the United States, but had declined to follow the instructions of the captain of the ship.

They gave three reasons for their conduct. First, the American operators were incompetent and ignorant of Continental Morse; to have dealt with their inquiries would have slowed up other traffic. Second, it was Marconi company practice not to send messages to shore stations via other ships; that was why, Cottam said, he had held back Ismay's message. Third, Captain Rostron had told them, given the pressure they were under, to deal only with official traffic and messages of survivors. That was why they had not answered queries from the press or Mr. Marconi.

These reasons are unconvincing. The American operators knew Continental Morse. Marconi policy did not forbid operators to send messages via other ships, and in any case Rostron had told Cottam to use any means possible. The pressure was not so unrelenting that neither of them had time, in three or four days, to alert Rostron to what the Springfield *Sunday Union* described, accurately, as "the entire world's thirst for news," of which both men were certainly aware. Neither of them lacked initiative. They slipped between the authority of the captain and the authority of their employers. Like Binns, they were at the center of a marine drama that had attracted the world's attention, but they were much better placed to turn it to immediate advantage.

At the Senate inquiry, Senator Smith in particular tried hard, and with some success, to disentangle the nature of Marconi's relations with *The New York Times* after the disaster. How was it that the news for which the world had been waiting had not come from the *Carpathia* and had emerged only after the *Carpathia* reached New York in the form of two exclusive interviews, with Bride and Cottam, in *The New York Times*?

The fact was that *The New York Times* for seven years had had a commercial arrangement with Marconi about transatlantic news. The paper had given a banquet in his honor a month before. Marconi and the *Times* managing editor, Carr Van Anda, knew each other. The *Times* historian, Meyer Berger, has described how, as the *Carpathia* approached New York, the *Times* day editor told his assembled news staff that the Associated Press had just sent the paper a note saying that the *Carpathia* "studiously refuses to answer all queries." It was therefore up to the reporters.

Around the same time, according to Marconi's chief engineer in New York, Frederick M. Sammis, *The New York Times* rang the Marconi office saying they wanted to interview any Marconi operators aboard the *Carpathia* and would pay. Sammis thought this a good idea and undertook to get word to Cottam. So he telephoned, he told the Senate inquiry, a fellow at the Seagate shore station near New York, a temporary operator hired for the crisis, and told him to try to get a message through. The temporary was a wit and can scarcely have expected that his four cheerful Marconigrams would be intercepted by the United States warship *Florida,* passed on by her commanding officer to the secretary of the Navy, and finally be read out before delighted reporters and a less delighted Senate committee.

"Say old man Marconi Company taking good care of you. Keep your mouth shut and hold your story. It is fixed for you so you will get big money," said the first Marconigram, in part. The second said, "Arranged for your exclusive story for dollars in four figures. Mr. Marconi agreeing. Say nothing until you see me"—"me" was Sammis. Cottam was told to go to the Strand Hotel as soon as the ship docked.

Sammis insisted that he had had nothing to do with the phrasing of these messages. He realized that they were not "gems of English literature." But he defended their general sentiments. Their phraseology, he considered, was designed "to spruce the boys up a little," and he saw no reason to be ashamed of the part he had played in their inspiration. His superior, Mr. Bottomley, knew of the exchanges, and he believed that Mr. Marconi did also. "I am proud of the fact," he said, "that being an employer of labor and being

the superior of poorly paid men, or mediumly paid men—
men who do not see much of this world's goods—I will do
them a good turn honestly if I can."

Cottam at first tried to pretend to the senators that he
had been off duty when the messages came in and had not
read them properly. Then he admitted he had seen two.

As soon as the *Carpathia* was tied up, Cottam made off
to the Strand Hotel. He was interviewed by *The New York
Times*. Mention was made of a four-figure fee—nearly four
years' wages. Cottam was not paid on the spot, but he got
his money, $750, before the month was out. So did Bride,
although the size of Bride's fee is not clear. He told the
Senate inquiry it was $1,000 but wrote to his boss in Lon-
don saying it was $500.*

But what was the role of Marconi? Senator Smith was
out to discredit him. His organization had possessed almost
exclusive control over information about the catastrophe.
That information should have been made immediately
available as of right to everyone, especially the distraught
relations of the victims. Instead, Smith felt, it had been
held back for the benefit of a single business partner,
namely *The New York Times*. Here was an issue that went
far beyond a journalistic scoop or rivalry between newspapers; the conduct of Marconi and his employees raised the
whole question of the malign grip exerted by the spread-
ing tentacles of business monopolies.

Marconi said that he too wished that Cottam and Bride
had said something "more explanatory" before reaching
New York. He had been "exceedingly surprised" by the
Carpathia's silence, "as everyone else was." That was why
he had sent two messages—never answered—to ask why
the captain did not put out some news.

The New York Times paid Bride $500. Admirers added a further $500.

As for *The New York Times,* said Marconi, there had been no deal. He had had no knowledge whatever of the Marconigrams sent to Cottam about keeping his mouth shut. He disapproved of them. Cottam had telephoned him after the *Carpathia* arrived, saying that "a journalist wanted a story" and wanting to know if it was all right to accept money for it. Marconi had said that was all right so far as the British Marconi company was concerned. But he had certainly not known that the interviews with Cottam and Bride were to be exclusive. He regretted that they had been exclusive: "There was no idea of an exclusive story in my mind." That had been his position all along.

Marconi's testimony cannot all have been truthful. On the evening the *Carpathia* docked, Marconi dined with the managing director of the American Marconi Company, John Bottomley, on the Upper West Side. During dinner, a reporter, Jim Speers, arrived from *The New York Times,* sent by Carr Van Anda. Marconi intended to drive down to the *Carpathia* later on to see the operators, after the survivors were ashore. Van Anda on the telephone from the *Times* office persuaded him to go at once and take Speers with him. Van Anda knew that no reporters were being allowed on board but thought Speers might have a chance if he accompanied Marconi.

It was first expected that the *Carpathia* would arrive at one or two in the morning. The ship's position was unknown even to shore-based Marconi operators; the wit who telegraphed Cottam about the money ended one message, "Where are you now?" When news spread that the ship would dock much earlier, a rush to the pier began. Seventh Avenue, asphalted for its whole length, was the main route downtown. By 8:15 p.m., as one paper reported, the street was jammed with "racing autoists" in "limousines, touring cars, smaller autos, and taxicabs." Van Anda advised Marconi to avoid the roads and take the Ninth Avenue Elevated Railway to Fourteenth Street. Marconi abandoned his dinner and followed Van Anda's advice. At Fourteenth Street, he, Bottomley, and Speers were met by a taxicab ordered by the *Times* that took them as close as possible to Pier 54.

Estimates of the size of the crowd vary, but the figure of thirty thousand recurs. Many were sightseers. Two thousand people secured pier passes; the rest of the mob was kept back by several hundred police. Apart from friends and relations, those present on the pier included city officials, representatives of the Coroner's Office, doctors in white jackets, nurses in uniform, stretcher bearers, the immigration commissioner and members of his staff, ambulance men with twenty or more ambulances, the drivers of fifteen trucks containing three nurses each and two hundred blankets supplied by a department store, Miss Eva Booth of the Salvation Army supported by a team ready to put up male passengers at their headquarters in Chatham Square and female passengers at the Women's Hotel on West Fifteenth Street, Monsignor Lavelle with ten Sisters of Mercy, and a committee from the New York Stock Exchange with $20,000 in cash to be distributed among the needy; the money had been raised on the Exchange by popular subscription and was carried by the president of the Stock Exchange in a big oblong box.

At the gates of the pier, Bottomley was kept back by the police, but Marconi and Speers were allowed through.

Now the obvious question arises: why did Marconi think the managing editor of *The New York Times* was so keen for him to fight his way downtown and covertly escort a *New York Times* reporter into the presence of the Marconi operators? Can he really have supposed that Van Anda wanted interviews with his employees so that *The*

New York Times could distribute them to its rivals? Marconi had dined in Bottomley's company and traveled downtown with him. Bottomley, according to the unchallenged evidence later given to the Senate committee by Sammis, knew *The New York Times* was ready to pay for interviews with Cottam and Bride; he had sanctioned the approach to Cottam. Even if Marconi, with uncharacteristic obtuseness, had failed to understand why Van Anda so urgently sought his help, Bottomley would have enlightened him. Marconi was sophisticated and worldly wise. He had been dealing with newspapers since the death of Gladstone fourteen years earlier. He and his apparatus had been commissioned by the New York *Herald* to cover (exclusively) America's Cup races, and the triumphant return to New York of Admiral Dewey, the hero of Manila. He knew how newspapers worked. He was present at the interview with Bride.

Later that night, Marconi went to *The New York Times* office. Van Anda was there, directing the paper's fifteen-page coverage of the *Carpathia*'s arrival. The first edition went out at 12:30 a.m., with the Bride interview on the front page. The precede under the headline and above the opening paragraph read: "This statement was dictated by Mr. Bride to a reporter for *The New York Times*, who visited him with Mr. Marconi in the wireless cabin of the *Carpathia* a few minutes after the steamship touched her pier." Then came the italic line: "Copyright, 1912, by The New York Times Company."

It was after Marconi had returned to his hotel, the Holland House, that he was telephoned by Cottam. Marconi told the Senate committee that Cottam had asked if it would be all right to give an account of his experiences. Marconi had urged him "to disclose anything he knew." He also told Cottam that he could accept payment for the interview. Cottam had telephoned very late, Marconi said, "about two o'clock in the morning."

Something is wrong about the timing here. When Marconi and Speers reached the *Carpathia*'s wireless cabin, Cottam had already left for the Strand Hotel nearby. Even allowing for the crowds, he cannot have arrived much later than ten o'clock. He told the inquiry he waited at the hotel for "an hour or an hour and a half" to be interviewed, which is hard to credit, since *The New York Times* had hired a suite as a *Carpathia* news base and Cottam was one of the paper's main targets. But say the interview did not begin until 11:00 or 11:30 p.m. The reporter would have been in a hurry. Cottam must have finished his interview before he phoned Marconi. He said he thought it was over by midnight. Why then did he telephone at such an ungodly hour? He cannot have been seeking permission to give an interview he had already given. Perhaps the four figures "talked of" again in the Strand Hotel made him think he had better get Marconi's personal approval for the deal.

But whatever the substance and purpose of that call, it is clear that Marconi knew that Cottam, like Bride, was being paid by *The New York Times* in return for an interview. In both cases, Marconi personally acted as a go-between. What did Marconi think *The New York Times* was paying money for, if not for exclusivity?

The conclusion is inescapable. Marconi lied to the Senate committee when he said he did not intend the interviews to be exclusive.

The researches of the Michigan psychologist Wyn Craig Wade into Senator Smith's papers have shown that the senator considered Marconi's dealings with *The New York Times* to be anything but a trivial matter. A presidential election campaign was starting. The power of the big American trusts and monopolies was a prime issue; the trustbusters, of whom Smith was one, were keenly interested in the way the monopolies used their monopoly power. Marconi had a news monopoly over the *Titanic* and had abused it, Smith strongly suspected.

The senator was usually an obstinate and persistent interrogator, but he let Marconi off the hook. He failed to expose, or to try to expose, Marconi's pretenses. The reason may have been, as Wade suggests, that Smith's fellow senators on the committee were reluctant to support him, fearful of the political unpopularity they might incur by attacking Marconi too roughly. His invention, after all, had just saved seven hundred lives.

Honors continued to be showered on Marconi. He concluded a deal with the Western Union cable company that marked another step toward his ambition of covering the world with a communications system. Later he became an Italian senator and an enthusiastic supporter of Mussolini. In Marconi House in the Strand, his behavior became increasingly odd. He refused to share the lift with any employee he did not know personally. He died in 1937—wireless stations everywhere closed down for two minutes—at a moment when his political sympathies were beginning to put his English connections under strain.

Cottam remained in the Marconi service. Harold Bride recovered from his injuries and returned to sea, serving as a radio operator until 1919. He then retired to Scotland and became a traveling salesman. He died on April 29, 1956.

8

SENATOR SMITH
AND HIS "FARCE"

Like a murder that lifts the lid off a secret corner of society, the *Titanic* deaths suddenly exposed the hidden attitudes and tension of the Anglo-American world of 1912. Power was crossing the Atlantic from east to west and was causing strains. The American Civil War had left the United States momentarily the greatest military power on earth; Henry Adams, then at the legation in Grosvenor Square, observed that the unexpected display of American might left Londoners "stupid with unbelief." By the turn of the century, America had achieved great power status as it dismembered the old Spanish empire, establishing a protectorate over Cuba and annexing Puerto Rico and the Philippines. The half century before the *Titanic* disaster had seen also a vast explosion of industrial energy and the creation of immense financial trusts and monopolies to exploit the continent's resources:

> The great metallic beast
> Expanding West and East.

The *Titanic* millionaires—Morgan, Guggenheim, Astor, Widener, Straus, Thayer—were beneficiaries of this unparalleled expansion.

As the balance tilted, the tensions began to show. The venom of the American attacks on Ismay cannot be explained by the objective facts about his conduct. He was vilified because he was a convenient symbol of the moral corruption of the old world, an effete aristocrat who seemed, with his disdainful and withdrawn British manner, to be looking down on the inhabitants of the new. Similarly, the British seized on Senator Smith, the inspirer and leader of the American inquiry into the disaster, as an example of an American who was too big for his boots, a man whose ignorance made him entirely unfit to exercise power—particularly over the British. In self-defense, the British turned him into a joke, a figure so comical that the London Hippodrome, with malice aforethought, invited him at the height of the inquiry to appear on stage and lecture on any maritime subject of his choice. When Smith declined, the manager said regretfully that he could have named his own price.

Outwardly, Anglo-American relations had never been closer, especially among the upper crust. They were helped by the new ease and speed of transatlantic travel. The liners carried Americans to Europe in search of pleasure, culture, health cures, and titled husbands, and Britons to the United States in search of business, relatives who had emigrated and prospered, and fees from lecture tours. At the top, neither society was difficult to penetrate. Visiting the United States on a lecture tour, John Morley found himself staying with President Theodore Roosevelt, who explained that the United States had moved into the Panama Canal because it was "mush," and then with Andrew Carnegie, who arranged for Morley to visit his steelworks but did not accompany him because, the manager explained, he hated the place.

The new American wealth enabled Americans to establish prominent social bridgeheads in England. One leading London hostess in 1912 was the former Maud Burke from California, Lady Cunard, who was renting the house of the prime minister, H. H. Asquith, in Cavendish Square. A second social magnet was Nancy Astor from Virginia, a close friend of the prime minister's wife. A third was the divorced first wife of Colonel J. J. Astor (and soon to become Lady Ribblesdale); she was credited with introducing a new fashion for breakfast parties. The elderly J. P. Morgan and his son were both well known at London dinner tables. The Strauses of Macy's knew the Burbages of Harrods. Henry James was not the only American who sought an ideal world in the "well-appointed, well-administered" English country house; Lady Cunard's husband, Sir Bache, a direct descendant of the Samuel Cunard who founded the shipping line, converted himself entirely into an English country gentleman, with a great house in Leicestershire and his own pack of hounds. Sport was an important link. The Carters came for the hunting. John Thayer came from Philadelphia to England to play cricket, which was also the favorite game of Colonel Archibald Gracie. The amateur lawn tennis and rackets players knew one another.

The English kept an eye open for the new American money, selling off their daughters, or paintings, or shipping lines. But there was often an undercurrent of disdain. Asquith as prime minister could scarcely conceal his boredom with the American politicians he was compelled to meet. What could have been less interesting, he complained in a letter to Venetia Stanley, than a memorial service for poor Lady Hardinge followed by lunch with "an American Senator Lodge"? If Asquith could find nothing in common with Lodge, as much a scholar and a lawyer as Asquith, there was not much hope that he would be interested by any other American politician. Lloyd George described the frostiness when Teddy Roosevelt visited London and was a guest at the same table as Asquith: "When R. declaimed trite statements, such as 'I believe in liberty, but liberty with order,' the PM glowered at him with a look of curiosity. I think Roosevelt saw it." Asquith wrote to Venetia Stanley: "Roosevelt held the floor practically the whole time, and talked to & at us as tho' we had been a public meeting or (occasionally) a Sunday school. What is it that makes all Americans so intolerably long-winded, and so prone to platitude?" English and Americans found it hard to appreciate one another's virtues. Asquith judged Roosevelt "second-rate," though probably *au fond* a good fellow, with a passable sense of humor. Roosevelt judged Asquith second-rate too, describing him dismissively as "able," in the limited sense that Woodrow Wilson and Taft were "able."

Over the *Titanic,* many British resented being called to account by Americans. The *Titanic* was a British-built ship, with a British crew; and the Atlantic was much more British than anyone else's. Their resentment was not allayed as they learned more about the man chosen to sit in judgment.

Senator William Alden Smith came from a poor family in Dowagiac, Michigan. He sold newspapers and popcorn as a boy to help the family finances, managed to become a lawyer in Grand Rapids, and despite the opposition of the moneyed power brokers got himself elected as a congressman in 1895 and as a senator in 1906, when he was forty-seven. He was a Republican, but of a rather unorthodox kind. Like Roosevelt and Taft, he was antitrust and had worked in the Senate against the J. P. Morgan interests well before the *Titanic* went down; his general political stance was in favor of "the little man." But when the Republican

Party split between the old guard under President Taft and the progressives under Teddy Roosevelt—Roosevelt made his famous announcement, "My hat is in the ring," three weeks before the *Titanic* went down—Smith declined to join either group. In character, he could readily be made to fit the British stereotype of the sort of Americans who were wielding the new American power: bumptious, self-important, uninformed, provincial, and full of zeal.

The trusts had reason to be wary of Smith. So had the British. The British ambassador in Washington when the *Titanic* went down was the formidable and learned James Bryce, for twenty years the Regius Professor of Civil Law at Oxford, and a former president of the Board of Trade and chief secretary for Ireland. After five years as ambassador, Bryce knew more than any Briton and as much as most Americans about America, especially American politics. He was seventy-two; however, as Asquith said, he might look like Father Time but could still climb mountains (he had a peak named after him in the Canadian Rockies) and "discourse at a moment's notice and at any required length on any topic, human or divine." Bryce had had trouble with Smith. Twice Smith had frustrated him: once when he was trying to negotiate a trade treaty between Canada and the United States that Smith, with others, claimed would hurt midwestern farmers and lumbermen; and again over a bilateral treaty between Britain and the United States on which Bryce had set his heart. The treaty was designed to show that Anglo-Saxons were uniquely able to settle their differences in a civilized manner by decreeing that all maritime disputes between the two countries should be settled by the arbitration court at The Hague. Smith was suspicious. Were the British trying to entangle the United States in their disreputable European struggles with Germany for naval supremacy? If the treaty was merely concerned, as the British claimed, with the peaceful resolution of international maritime disputes, then Germany should be included. The treaty foundered. Smith later opposed United States entry into World War I, declaring that Woodrow Wilson was in Britain's pocket.

Smith was put in charge of the Senate inquiry largely because it was he who inspired it. On Wednesday, April 17, as soon as the scale of the disaster was known, Smith, as a member of the Senate Commerce Committee, introduced a resolution into a worried Senate directing that a subcommittee of Commerce should at once begin to investigate the causes of the wreck. His resolution was adopted unanimously. Before the day was out Smith was appointed chairman of the inquiry and had assembled a carefully balanced committee of Republicans and Democrats. Smith's motives in pressing for the inquiry do not seem to have been primarily inspired by a desire to win popularity among voters in his home state, since he was confident of being reelected by the state legislature, as was the practice in Michigan at the time. He appears to have been genuinely stirred, even outraged, by the disaster; besides, it created a rare opportunity of marshaling public opinion behind an investigation into the way the shipping trusts operated. Legislation would follow.

Once his committee was appointed and its considerable powers agreed upon, Smith set to work with tremendous energy. The U.S. Navy had intercepted Ismay's Marconigrams urging the White Star office in New York to hold the *Cedric* so that Ismay and the *Titanic* crew could at once return to England. Smith went to see President Taft. Could a Treasury revenue cutter be sent to intercept the *Carpathia* before she docked, to ensure that witnesses the Senate wanted to question could not escape? Taft arranged it. Barely ten minutes after the *Carpathia* tied up, Smith,

Senator Francis Newlands (a Democrat from Nevada), the Senate master-of-arms (who had powers to issue subpoenas), a sheriff, and Smith's private secretary hurried up the gangway and asked the whereabouts of J. Bruce Ismay.

In Ismay's cabin, Smith found P. A. S. Franklin, the White Star manager in New York. Franklin was ten minutes ahead of Smith, and it is easy to imagine the exchanges that took place between Ismay and Franklin in that time. Ismay still did not know why Franklin had failed to hold the *Cedric*. Franklin would have told him, as he later told Senator Smith's committee, that it would have been disastrous to hurry the crew out of New York or agree to Ismay's sailing in the *Cedric:* "We were here, and we were hearing the criticism." Ismay had no choice but to make the best of it. When Smith came off the ship, he told reporters that he found no disposition in the White Star management to hinder the subcommittee's inquiry; on the contrary, he was sure that they would do everything they could to cooperate. Smith had secured his star witness.

Then and later, Smith showed how nimble footed and decisive he could be, and he was unafraid of using his powers to the full. The inquiry had scarcely started, in the gilded surroundings of the Waldorf-Astoria Hotel—senators, witnesses, reporters, and spectators crammed into the East Room, later into the ballroom—before the White Star lawyer, Mr. Burlingham, followed by Franklin, complained about the number of the company's employees being detained in New York. On a ship, a crew could be controlled, but once they were living ashore the line was virtually helpless. "They get into endless troubles," said Franklin. That was why all shipping lines made it a policy to get crews home again as fast as possible. Was it really necessary to hold two hundred of the *Titanic*'s crew? Smith was unmoved. "We are not at all concerned," he said.

What mattered was not the convenience of the White Star Line but the thoroughness of the inquiry.

In London, when news of these events arrived, the British government reacted with alarm, for the alacrity with which the Americans had acted had taken it entirely by surprise. Agitated messages were sent from the Foreign Office to the Washington embassy saying that the Board of Trade urgently wanted to know whether the United States Senate had the power to investigate an accident to what was, after all, a British-registered ship. Cold comfort was sent back by Bryce. There was nothing to stop the Senate conducting an inquiry, and nothing to be done to keep it in check. On April 22 Bryce explained in a letter to the foreign secretary, Sir Edward Grey, that the inquiry was quite different "of course" from the projected inquiry by the British Board of Trade. Formally, the aim of the Senate was to inquire into the causes of the wreck; but in truth it was merely responding to the press and public opinion, and those senators conducting the inquiry were doing so because they sought the limelight. Bryce explained the influence of the American press, especially the Hearst press, the New York *American,* the New York *Journal,* the Boston *American,* etc.: "However much may have been written about this school of journalism, it is difficult for any person not residing in this country to realize to what extent their influence over the less well-educated classes is pernicious in its heartless exploitation of every calamity that has ever saddened, and of every scandal that has ever attracted attention in, this country."

On April 24 Bryce advised London that he had discussed the Senate inquiry with the President. Taft had said that it had nothing to do with him or his administration; it was entirely the initiative of the Senate. Bryce asked Taft how long he thought the inquiry would last. The ambassador, like the Board of Trade, was worried that the British inquiry would be hampered because its witnesses were still being held in the United States. "The President was of the opinion that as long as the Chairman of the Committee thought it would keep him in the headlines the enquiry would go on." Bryce two days later called on the secretary of state. He agreed with the President and Bryce: the proceedings were "mere self-advertisement."

Bryce was wholly dismissive of Senator Smith. The ambassador was annoyed from the beginning by Smith's failure to inform the British of his motives and intentions, even though he was investigating an accident to a British ship. "It might have been more courteous," Bryce wrote to Grey, "if some communication had been addressed to this embassy, though from persons so ignorant of the usages of international relations as most members of the Senate are no such action need have been expected." Bryce referred to Smith's "singular incompetence," then to his "conspicuous incompetence," and, in case Sir Edward had failed to grasp his meaning, ended by saying it was "generally admitted that Senator Smith is one of the most unsuitable persons who could have been charged with an investigation of this nature." He was "a person always anxious to put himself forward where any passing notoriety can be achieved." By the time the inquiry had been in progress for ten days, Bryce was so indignant about what he thought was the irresponsible and time-consuming way Smith was conducting himself that he advised London to make a formal protest. "The chairman," he wrote "is now generally ridiculed," and his committee "now altogether abusing its powers."

Bryce's general attitude was mirrored in London. "I am told," a Foreign Office official minuted, that "the whole business has been engineered by Senator Smith of Michigan who is very hostile to the U.K. and Canada. The only upshot, I imagine, will be to discredit the U.S. Senate." However, the Foreign Office did not agree with Bryce that His Majesty's government should make a formal protest. Nothing would be gained and much might be lost by complaining. Left alone, the committee would surely discredit itself more and more in American eyes; whereas if the British objected American opinion might well rally to the senators on the ground that the British were trying to interfere. "It can be left as it is," Sir Edward Grey decided, in red ink. The prime minister agreed. He wrote to George V after a Cabinet meeting on April 25 to say that "however ill-judged in some of its methods" the Senate committee might be, it was acting within its legal powers, and that was that.

The government resigned itself to watching the Senate's follies in a mood of intense irritation, almost contempt. But it presented an undisturbed face to the outside world, as represented by the House of Commons. M.P.s asked if British citizens were not being held against their will? No, the ministers replied, no suggestion of that kind had reached London; Foreign Office information was that all British witnesses had freely consented to help the U.S. inquiry. But was the government aware that the senator conducting the inquiry had asked whether the purpose of watertight compartments was to provide a safe refuge for passengers at times of danger? The Hon. Member asking the question was advised not to depend too heavily on incomplete reports of the inquiry in the newspapers.

Smith was fully conscious of British suspicions and disapproval. He put his star witnesses on the stand immediately—Ismay, Rostron, Harold Bride—thus attracting maximum publicity before moving to Washington at the weekend. To ensure that his key witnesses moved with him, his committee issued subpoenas to Ismay, Franklin, all surviving *Titanic* officers, and twenty-nine members of the crew, instructing them to be on hand in the Senate when hearings resumed on Monday. Five more crew members who should have been subpoenaed sailed from New York in the *Lapland*. Smith sent a vessel to bring them back.

As an interrogator, Smith could be faulted. He had a long-winded habit of repeating witnesses' replies that Asquith would have found painful to listen to. Sometimes he got himself into a muddle, unable to remember who was who, confusing the officers of the watch on the *Titanic* with those on the *Carpathia*. He argued about marine terminology, as in this characteristic exchange with Major Arthur Peuchen, a Canadian in the chemical business who was an experienced amateur yachtsman:

SMITH: Did she [the *Titanic*] go down by the bow or by the head?
PEUCHEN: Eventually, you mean?
SMITH: Yes.
PEUCHEN: She was down by the bow. You mean "the head" by the bow do you not?
SMITH: Exactly.
PEUCHEN: It is the same thing.
SMITH: No; not exactly the same thing.

But Smith had many virtues. He was convinced that he was a standard-bearer for the common man against the trusts, which made him impervious to outside pressures. He cut himself off from press criticism by ceasing to read the newspapers. He was indifferent to the insults from both sides of the Atlantic about his lack of expertise and his unfitness to be in charge of an investigation that required it. "Energy is often more desirable than learning," he said in his speech to the Senate after the inquiry was over (again, not a maxim likely to appeal to Asquith). He was above all dogged, with a sound instinct for where the bones were buried. He unearthed in the engine room of the *Olympic* a stoker formerly of the *Titanic* who supplied him with valuable evidence about the speed of the *Titanic* before she struck. He required Marconi and Franklin to produce all wireless messages.

Nor was the inquiry as amateurish as the British especially liked to pretend; it was regularly attended and assisted by experts from the U.S. Navy and the U.S. steamship inspectorate. In any case, the much-despised amateurism in some respects produced more interesting results than the professionalism of the British inquiry The senators felt at liberty to investigate any aspect of the disaster that they chose—the behavior in the boats, the last moments of Captain Smith, allegations of drinking among the crew—and their informal procedures allowed them to invite witnesses to describe their experiences at length in their own words. In London, the format of the inquiry, the judge, the distinguished lawyers, the conventions and rules of the courts of law meant that every scrap of testimony had to be extracted piecemeal. Lord Mersey was conducting a much more technical inquiry than the Americans, with a long list of precise questions to be answered; and he was impatient with diversions.

The advantages of the American method over the British, not in determining the causes of the wreck but in illuminating the nature of the disaster, are well illustrated by the record of testimony taken separately on the twelfth day of the hearings, when the indefatigable Smith interviewed a Mrs. J. Stuart White. One of the themes that comes out of the American inquiry, here stated with particular candor by Mrs. White, was the resentment felt by some first-class passengers over the way that lower-class riffraff had managed to survive, while more upstanding males had drowned. Mrs. White also exploded the notion, which still persists, that everyone aboard the *Titanic* underwent great suffering. As she said, people ashore who could not find out what had happened to their friends and relations experienced more and longer anguish than some of the *Titanic*'s passengers; and Mrs. White's point is not weakened because those kept in suspense, in her case, were resident at the Waldorf-Astoria.

SMITH: Do you make the Waldorf-Astoria your permanent home, Mrs. White?

MRS. WHITE: My home really is Briarcliff Lodge, Briarcliff Manor, N.Y. That is my summer home. When I am in New York, I am always here at the Waldorf-Astoria.

Q: I want to ask one or two questions, Mrs. White, and let you answer them in your own way. You were a passenger on the *Titanic*?

A: Yes.

Q: Where did you get aboard the ship?

A: At Cherbourg.

Q: Where were your apartments on the *Titanic*? What deck were you on?

A: We were on C Deck.

Q: Do you remember the number of the room?

A: I do not believe I could tell you with any degree of certainty, at all. Miss Young and my maid could tell you.

Q: Miss Young or your maid would know the number of your room?

A: Yes. I never went out of my room from the time I went into it. I was never outside of the door until I came off the night of the collision.

Q: That was due, I believe, to a little accident that you had on entering the ship?

A: Yes, sir.

Q: You went directly to your apartment and remained there?

A: Yes; I remained in my room until I came out that night. I never took a step from my bed until that night.

Q: Were you aroused especially by the impact?

A: No; not at all. I was just sitting on the bed, just ready to turn the lights out. It did not seem to me that there was any very great impact at all. It was just as though we went over about a thousand marbles. There was nothing terrifying about it at all.

Q: Were you aroused by any one of the ship's officers or crew?

A: No.

Q: Do you know whether there was any alarm turned in [on] for the passengers?

A: We heard no alarm whatever. We went immediately on deck ourselves.

Q: On the upper deck?

A: Yes, sir.

Q: And Miss Young and your maid were with you?

A: Yes; and my manservant.

Q: What were they doing then?

A: Simply all standing around.

Q: Was anything being done about the lifeboats?

A: No; we were all standing around inside, waiting to know what the result was.

Q: The lifeboats had not then been cleared?

A: Nothing had been said about the lifeboats in any way, when suddenly Captain Smith came down the stairway and ordered us all to put on our life preservers, which we did. We stood around for another twenty minutes, then, I should think.

Q: Still on that deck?

A: No; on deck B.

Q: You went down to deck B?

A: Yes; he said we must go back again, then, to deck A, which we did, to get into the boats.

Q: Where did you enter the lifeboat?

A: I entered the lifeboat from the top deck, where the boats were. We had to enter the boat there. There was no other deck to the steamer except the top deck. It was a perfect rat trap. There was no other deck that was open, at all.

Q: Do you recollect what boat you entered?

A: Boat 8, the second boat off.

Q: On which side of the ship?

A: I could not tell you. It was the side going this way— the left side, as we were going.

Q: That would be the port side?

A: Yes. I got in the second boat that was lowered.

Q: What officer stood there?

A: I could not tell you that; I have no idea.

Q: What officer supervised this work?

A: I have no idea. I could not even tell whether it was an officer or the captain. I know we were told to get into the boat.

Q: Did you have any difficulty in getting into the boat?

A: None whatever. They handled me very carefully because I could hardly step. They lifted me in very carefully and very nicely.

Q: How far out from the side of the ship did the lifeboat hang? Were you able to step into it?

A: Oh, yes.

Q: Or were you passed into it?

A: No; we stepped into it. It did not hang far out.

Q: Did you see how far out it was?

A: No, sir; I have no idea. We got into it very easily. We got into the lifeboat without any inconvenience whatever. As I said, my condition was such that I had to be handled rather carefully, and there was no inconvenience at all.

Q: Did you see anything after the accident bearing upon the discipline of the officers, or crew, or their conduct, which you desire to speak of?

A: Yes; lots about them.

Q: Tell me about them.

A: For instance, before we cut loose from the ship two of the seamen with us—the men, I should say; I do not call them seamen; I think they were dining-room stewards— before we cut loose from the ship they took out cigarettes and lighted them; on an occasion like that! That is one thing we saw. All of those men escaped under the pretense of being oarsmen. The man who rowed me took his oar and rowed all over the boat, in every direction. I said to him, "Why don't you put the oar in the oarlock?" He said, "Do you put it in that hole?" I said, "Certainly." He said, "I never had an oar in my hand before." I spoke to the other man and he said, "I have never had an oar in my hand before, but I think I can row." Those were the men that we were put to sea with at night—with all those magnificent fellows left on board, who would have been such a protection to us. Those were the kind of men with whom we were put out to sea that night.

Q: How many were there in your boat?

A: There were twenty-two women and four men.

Q: None of the men seemed to understand the management of a boat?

A: Yes; there was one there, one who was supposed to be a seaman, up at our end of the boat who gave the orders.

Q: Do you know who he was?

A: No; I do not know. I do not know the names of any of those men. But he seemed to know something about it.

Q: I wish you would describe, as nearly as you can, just what took place after your lifeboat got away from the *Titanic.*

A: What took place between the passengers and the seamen?

Q: Yes.

A: We simply rowed away. We had the order, on leaving the ship, to do that. The officer who put us in the boat—I do not know who he was—gave strict orders to the seamen, or the men, to make for the light opposite and land the passengers and get back just as soon as possible. That was the light that everybody saw in the distance.

Q: Did you see it?

A: Yes; I saw it distinctly.

Q: What was it?

A: It was a boat of some kind.

Q: How far away was it?

A: Oh, it was ten miles away but we could see it distinctly. There was no doubt but that it was a boat. But we rowed and rowed and rowed, and then we all suggested that it was simply impossible for us to get to it; that we never could get to it, and the thing to do was to go back and see what we could do for the others. We only had twenty-two in our boat.

Then we turned and went back, and lingered around there for a long time, trying to locate the other boats, but we could not locate them except by seeing them.

The only way they could locate us was by my electric light. The lamp on the boat was absolutely worth nothing. They tinkered with it all along, but they could not get it into shape. I had an electric cane—a cane with an electric light in it—and that was the only electric light we had. We sat there for a long time, and we saw the ship go down, distinctly.

Q: What was your impression of it as it went down?

A: It was something dreadful.

Nobody ever thought the ship was going down. I do not think there was a man on the boat who thought the ship was going down. They speak of the bravery of the men. I do not think there was any particular bravery, because none of the men thought it was going down. If they had thought the ship was going down, they would not have frivoled as they did about it. Some of them said, "When you come back you will need a pass," and "You can not get on tomorrow morning without a pass." They never would have said those things if anybody had had any idea that the ship was going to sink.

In my opinion the ship when it went down was broken in two. I think it very probably broke in two.

I heard four distinct explosions, which we supposed were the boilers. Of course, we did not know anything about it.

Q: How loud were those explosions?

A: They were tremendous.

We did what we were ordered to do. We went toward the light. That seemed to be the verdict of everybody in the boat. We had strict orders to do that from the officer or whoever started us off—to row as fast as possible for that boat, land the passengers and come right back for the others. We all supposed that boat was coming toward us, on account of the rockets that we had sent up.

Q: Did you urge the man in charge of your lifeboat to go back?

A: One of us did.

Q: Did you urge him to go back to seek to pick up more people?

A: Not until we had gone out for half an hour and found it perfectly useless to attempt to reach that boat or that light. Then everybody suggested going back and we did, too, but we could not get there.

Q: You went back?

A: Yes. The sailor changed our course and tried to go back. That was after trying to reach that light for three-quarters of an hour. It was evidently impossible to reach it. It seemed to be going in the same direction which we were going, and we made no headway toward it at all. Then we turned and tried to go back.

Q: Did anybody try to get in or get out of your boat?

A: No.

Q: Did you land alongside the *Carpathia* with the same party with which you started from the boat deck of the *Titanic*?

A: Exactly.

Q: You all landed safely?

A: We all landed safely. We had a great deal of trouble, but we all landed safely.

Q: How many were there in your party?

A: Three; Miss Young, myself, and my maid. My valet was lost.

Q: Did you make any attempt to communicate with your friends, after you got aboard the *Carpathia,* by wireless or otherwise?

A: That was the first thing we did.

Q: Did you succeed?

A: No; we did not succeed. They never received the

telegram until last Monday night in the hotel. They took our telegram the first thing when we got on board the *Carpathia,* Monday morning. They took our Marconigram. I think the people on land had a much more serious time than we had, so far as real suffering was concerned.

Q: Will you describe what you saw after daybreak, with regard to ice or icebergs?

A: We saw one iceberg in front of us. Of course, I could not see it, because I was standing this way (*indicating*). I did not even see the *Carpathia* until my attention was called to her. I stood up all night long because I could not get up onto the seats, which were very high, on account of my foot being bound up. I had no strength in my foot, and I stood all night long.

After we got on board the *Carpathia,* we could see thirteen icebergs and forty-five [four to five?] miles of floating ice, distinctly, right round us in every direction.

Everybody knew we were in the vicinity of icebergs. Even in our staterooms it was so cold we could not leave the porthole open. It was terribly cold. I made the remark to Miss Young, on Sunday morning: "We must be very near icebergs to have such cold weather as this." It was unusually cold.

It was a careless, reckless thing. It seems almost useless to speak of it.

No one was frightened on the ship. There was no panic. I insisted on Miss Young getting into something warm, and I got into something warm, and we locked our trunks and bags and went on deck.

There was no excitement whatever. Nobody seemed frightened. Nobody was panic-stricken. There was a lot of pathos when husbands and wives kissed each other good-bye of course.

We were the second boat pushed away from the ship, and we saw nothing that happened after that. We were not near enough. We heard the yells of the steerage passengers as they went down, but we saw none of the harrowing part of it at all.

As I have said before, the men in our boat were anything but seamen, with the exception of one man. The women all rowed, every one of them. Miss Young rowed every minute. The men could not row, they did not know the first thing about it. Mrs. Swift, from Brooklyn, rowed every minute from the steamer to the *Carpathia*. Miss Young rowed every minute, also, except when she was throwing up, which she did six or seven times. Countess Rothe [Rothes] stood at the tiller. Where would we have been if it had not been for our women, with such men as that put in charge of the boat? Our head seaman would give an order and those men who knew nothing about the handling of a boat would say, "If you don't stop talking through that hole in your face there will be one less in the boat." We were in the hands of men of that kind. I settled two or three fights between them, and quietened them down. Imagine getting right out there and taking out a pipe and filling it and standing there smoking, with the women rowing, which was most dangerous; we had woollen rugs all around us.

Another thing which I think is a disgraceful point. The men were asked, when they got into our boat, if they could row. Imagine asking men that are supposed to be at the head of lifeboats—imagine asking them if they can row.

There is another point that has never been brought out in regard to this accident and that is that that steamer had no open decks except the top deck. How could they fill the lifeboats properly? They could not lower a lifeboat seventy feet with any degree of safety with more than twenty people in it. Where were they going to get any more people in them on the way down? There were no other open decks.

Just to think that on a beautiful starlit night—you could see the stars reflected in the water—with all those Marconi warnings, that they would allow such an accident to happen, with such a terrible loss of life and property.

It is simply unbearable, I think.

Q: There were no male passengers in your boat?

A: Not one.

Q: Do you know who any of the other women were in your boat?

A: Mrs. Kenyon, Mrs. Dr. Leder [Dr. Alice Farnham Leader], of Brooklyn, Mrs. Swift, and the Countess Rothe [Rothes] who was at the tiller and her maid, and Miss Young, my maid, and myself. I did not know any of the other ladies. Those were the ladies right round me.

I never saw a finer body of men in my life than the men passengers on this trip—athletes and men of sense—and if they had been permitted to enter these lifeboats with their families the boats would have been appropriately manned and many more lives saved, instead of allowing the stewards to get into the boats and save their lives, under the pretense that they could row, when they knew nothing whatever about it.

Q: I am very much obliged to you for your statement, Mrs. White.

By calling so many passengers, Smith constructed a much more detailed and broader picture of the disaster than he could have obtained from the crew alone. Like

Ismay, some of the crew felt that they were on trial; others, like Lightoller, thought it their duty to protect their colleagues and White Star. But the passengers were not on the defensive. Even as the *Carpathia* was making its way through the icebergs toward New York, a group of them led by Lawrence Beesley, the Dulwich schoolmaster, began to draw up a joint statement critical of White Star; on arrival, they issued it to the Associated Press. Lightoller and others might complain about the senators' maritime inexperience; but technical questions about watertight compartments or pumps were not the only points at issue. On these other matters, the senators were well qualified to ask awkward questions, and the passengers—or some of them—were more likely to give candid and independent answers than the crew. The British inquiry called no passengers at all apart from Bruce Ismay. The Duff Gordons appeared at their own request.

Consider the major in the Canadian militia, Major Peuchen. He had left the *Titanic* with honor. The quartermaster in charge of a half-lowered lifeboat sang out to say he needed another hand. Peuchen said to Lightoller, "Can I be of any assistance?" adding that he was a yachtsman and could handle a boat. Lightoller ordered him to get aboard. Captain Smith himself, standing nearby, had told Peuchen, "You had better go down below and break a window and get in through a window, into the boat." Peuchen said he did not think that was feasible and instead swung himself off the ship on a loose rope hanging from the davits and so down into the lifeboat.

He comes out of his testimony as pleased with himself, but he evidently remained calm throughout, and he was curious and observant. He had several fresh points to make. Cabin stewards had given evidence that they had woken up all passengers after the collision; but Peuchen was not so sure. On the *Carpathia* he had talked to two young ladies who claimed to have had a very narrow escape. They had slept through the crash and had not been awakened by their steward; luckily they had been woken up by chance by Mrs. Astor, "who was in rather an excited state." He was "rather surprised" that the sailors were not at their stations by the lifeboats; "they seemed to be short of sailors." He thought Lightoller could and should have allowed more men into the lifeboats instead of sticking rigidly to the "women and children first" principle when there were no more women to be found and there was still room in the boats.

He had been impressed by the behavior of crew and passengers. "I never saw such order. It was perfect order. The discipline was splendid. The officers were carrying out their duty and I think, the passengers behaved splendidly. I did not see a cowardly act by any man." He described how about a hundred stokers carrying their bags suddenly appeared on deck, crowding around in front of the boats, and how one of the officers—"a very powerful one"—probably Wilde—came along and "drove them, every man, like a lot of sheep, right off the deck."

Peuchen was less complimentary about the quartermaster in charge of his lifeboat. This was Hichens, who had been at the wheel when the ship hit the iceberg. Peuchen thought him unfit to be a quartermaster. Hichens was evidently in a panic; before they shoved off he told Peuchen to "get down and get that plug in" and then, when Peuchen fumbled in the dark, came rushing down the boat urging him to hurry up because the ship was going to founder—at least an hour before she did so.

After they pulled away (and after a stowaway, "an Italian by birth, I should think," had mysteriously appeared from under the bow) they heard "a sort of whistle" from the *Titanic*—an officer calling them back. Peuchen and the others thought they should go back, but Hichens refused, saying "It's our lives now, not theirs," and insisted on Peuchen and the one other oarsman (Fleet the lookout) rowing farther away.

Peuchen was plainly frustrated because Hichens was at the tiller, which put him in control. "He was a very talkative man. He had been swearing a good deal and was very disagreeable. I had one row with him. I asked him to come and row, to assist us in the rowing, and let some woman steer the boat, as it was a perfectly calm night. It did not require any skill for steering. The stars were out. He refused to do it, and he told me he was in charge of that boat, and I was to row."

After the ship went down and they heard the cries for help, "moaning and crying," Hichens was urged a second time to go back but again refused, saying offensively that there were "only a lot of stiffs there," an expression the women very much resented. He asked one of the women for brandy "and he also asked for one of her wraps, which he got." He thought he saw a light (Peuchen was sure it was a reflection) and called out to another boat to ask whether they knew of any buoy around there, which "struck me as being perfectly absurd, and showed me the man did not know anything about navigating, expecting to see a buoy in the middle of the Atlantic."

Peuchen remained alert after the rescue. He was astonished that when the *Carpathia* steamed very slowly through the *Titanic*'s wreckage—"something like two islands"—he could not see one body. He had thought a life preserver was supposed to keep a person up, whether alive or dead. He was sure nobody could have lived very long in such cold water. He noted one telling detail: a barber's pole floating among the debris. Since the barber's shop was on C deck, he concluded that the force of the explosions they all heard must have been tremendous, to detach the pole—a deduction that was very probably correct. He also noticed quantities of floating cork, whose significance was, and is, obscure. On the *Carpathia* he had heard talk that there had been no food or water in some of the *Titanic*'s lifeboats, so he had made it his business to inspect one or two of them and had found hardtack in sealed containers and kegs of water.

Hichens the quartermaster asked leave to make a statement about taking the brandy and the woman's wrap, a charge first leveled against him by Mrs. Edgar J. Meyer of New York.

> I was very cold, sir, and I was standing up in the boat. I had no hat on. A lady had a flask of whisky or brandy, or something of that description, given her by some gentleman on the ship before she left, and she pulled it out and gave me about a tablespoonful and I drank it. Another lady, who was lying in the bottom of the boat, in a rather weak condition, gave me a half wet and half dry blanket to try to keep myself a little warm, as I was half frozen. I think it was very unkind of her, sir, to make any statement criticizing me. When we got to the ship I handled everyone as carefully as I could, and I was the last one to leave the boat, and I do not think I deserve anything like that to be put in the papers. That is what upset me and got on my nerves.

Senator Smith did not ask Hichens why, if he was "half frozen," he rejected Peuchen's suggestion that he should share the rowing, which would have warmed him up.

A former naval enlisted man, Edward Buley, in charge of
the last lifeboat to leave, gave more evidence about bodies.
His boat picked up four people alive, but

> all the others were dead. . . . There were a good few dead.
> Of course you could not discern them exactly on account
> of the wreckage; but we turned over several of them to
> see if they were alive. It looked as though none of them
> were drowned. They looked as though they were frozen.
> The lifebelts they had on were that much [*indicating*] out of
> the water, and their heads laid back, with their faces on the
> water, several of them. Their hands were coming up like
> that [*indicating*]. . . . It looked as though they were frozen
> altogether.

Smith's address to the Senate on May 28, after the inquiry
was concluded, is a fine example of senatorial rhetoric, the
prose equivalent of one of the *Titanic*'s baroque staterooms:

> From the builders' hands, she was plunged straightway
> to her fate—and christening salvos acclaimed at once her
> birth and death. Builders of renown had launched her on
> the billows with every assurance of her strength, while
> every port rang with praise for their achievement . . . the
> ship went down carrying as needless a sacrifice of noble
> men and brave women as ever clustered about the Judg-
> ment Seat in any single moment of passing time.

The senator spoke of Captain Smith's "clear eye and
steady hand"; for forty years, "storms sought in vain to vex
him or to menace his craft"; he had been "strong of limb,
intent of purpose, pure in character, dauntless." At the
Titanic's moment of crisis, "the ice, resistless as steel, stole
upon her and struck her in a vital spot." Smith continued:

In our imagination, we can see again the proud ship instinct with life and energy, with active figures again swarming upon her decks—musicians, teachers, artists, and authors; soldiers and sailors and men of large affairs; brave men and noble women of every land. We can see the unpretentious and the lowly progenitors of the great and strong turning their back on the Old World, where endurance is to them no longer a virtue, and looking hopefully to the New. At the very moment of their greatest joy, the ship suddenly reels, mutilated and groaning. With splendid courage the musicians fill the last moments with sympathetic melody. The ship wearily gives up the unequal battle. . . .

It was an emotional occasion, and senators and spectators were duly moved. But besides the rhetoric, Smith's speech contained a series of precise and devastating criticisms:

1. Captain Smith's indifference to danger was a direct cause of the disaster: he was overconfident.

2. The organization of the escape was haphazard.

3. A higher proportion of steerage passengers was lost because they were given no warning before the ship was doomed.

4. Some lifeboats were only partially loaded; none had compasses and only three had lamps. They were so badly manned that if their rescue had been delayed they would have been crushed by the advancing ice floe, "nearly thirty miles in width and rising sixteen feet above the surface of the water. . . . Nearly five hundred people were needlessly sacrificed for want of orderly discipline in loading the few [boats] that were provided."

5. Some crew never reported to their stations and deserted their ship too quickly. Some were shockingly

indifferent to the plight of others, remaining at a safe distance in partially filled boats while others drowned.

6. The use of wireless at sea must be reformed. Wages should go up, to discourage operators from exploiting tragedies. Wireless apparatus should be manned night and day.

7. Captain Lord of the *Californian* deluded himself about the presence of another ship between himself and the *Titanic*. There was no such ship. He bore a heavy responsibility. By contrast, Captain Rostron of the *Carpathia* should be honored throughout the ages.

8. Ismay was not to blame for the *Titanic*'s high speed in a region of danger; but his presence on board, and that of Thomas Andrews from Harland & Wolff, unconsciously stimulated greater speed.

The senator's speech and his committee's simultaneous report were a serious blow to British shipbuilding and the mercantile marine. Smith recommended, and the Congress approved, the award of the Congressional Gold Medal to Captain Rostron (it was later presented to him by President Taft). Tribute was paid to the unselfish men and women and the faithful officers who went down with the ship. But for those who survived, speech and report contained little comfort. Even Lightoller, who might be thought to have conducted himself with exceptional courage and professionalism, was by implication found guilty. He had defended the ship's speed to the inquiry; he had been one of the principal organizers of the manning and loading of the lifeboats—the very points on which the committee was most critical.

What did Smith and his committee achieve in the long run? Some changes had already been made by the time the committee reported. Shipping lanes were moved farther south, away from the ice. The U.S. Navy assigned two scout cruisers to patrol the Grand Banks (one of them was the *Chester,* the ship whose wireless operators had been so scorned by Harold Bride); this was the beginning of the International Ice Patrol. Ismay himself at once decreed that no White Star liner must in future sail without lifeboat accommodation for everyone aboard.

But Smith also did much to prod a reluctant U.S. government into legislative action. The Smith bill laid down new rules about bulkheads, lifesaving equipment, pumps, the number of skilled crewmen for each boat, and the designation of a particular place in each lifeboat for each passenger and member of the crew. The near-anarchy of wireless operation was stopped: all vessels with over fifty passengers must be equipped with a wireless set with a range of at least one hundred miles; all sets must have auxiliary power; direct communication must be provided between wireless operators and the bridge; wireless apparatus must be manned day and night. On rockets, the bill made it a misdemeanor to send up rockets except as distress signals.

Smith also called for new international agreements to regulate sea traffic. The first Safety of Life and Sea conference met in London between November 12, 1913, and January 20, 1914, producing an unprecedented degree of international cooperation. Many of the measures had been prefigured by the Smith bill. Lifeboats must be provided for everybody. Ships approaching ice at night must slow down or alter course. Rockets were officially recognized as international distress signals and banned for any other purpose. All ships were to carry wireless with an auxiliary power source; the power of existing sets was to be increased. The United States agreed to continue and expand its ice patrol, which was to be financed by thirteen nations.

In the United States, Smith's efforts eventually led to new laws about lifeboat drills and the training of seamen assigned to lifeboats. Moreover, Smith's bill took a crack at the trusts; it sought to ensure that all companies carrying passengers in or out of U.S. ports disclose more information than hitherto about their ownership and finances, and brought them under the Sherman Anti-Trust Act, which, in theory at least, outlawed conspiracies in restraint of trade and all monopolies. More generally, the public attention first focused on conditions at sea by the *Titanic* disaster— and deliberately kept on the boil by Smith—helped to produce the LaFollette Seaman's Act of 1915, which gave the oppressed men of the American mercantile marine, largely foreigners, the rights they had long been denied.

The *Titanic* disaster also led to the regulation of wireless. Communication between shore and ships had been seriously compromised by the interference of amateur operators; henceforward, all radio operators in the United States were required to be licensed—the beginnings of the Federal Communications Commission.

This burst of regulation and lawmaking cannot all be ascribed to Senator Smith, but it could not have happened without the climate of opinion he helped to create.

In Britain the reception of his committee's report was mixed. Some of those who had been scornful of the committee's competence changed their tune when they read the sober report. Bryce was one of them. Lightoller was not. Twenty-three years later, he wrote that the only achievement of the inquiry was to "make our seamen, quartermasters, and petty officers look ridiculous." It was a farce, he said, "wherein all the traditions and customs of the sea were continuously and persistently flouted." Lightoller, though a fine seaman and an admirable man, was scarcely impartial. At the very least Smith and his colleagues—who particularly referred to the Board of Trade's "laxity"—produced a weight of embarrassing and even shameful testimony that the board's own simultaneous inquiry and subsequent report would not be able to ignore.

When the U.S. committee started work, the correspondent of the London *Times*—reflecting the attitudes of the British embassy—loftily stated his view that Senator Smith and his colleagues were "not likely to elicit much important or even sensational information." Not for the first time, or the last, British disdain had underestimated American doggedness.

9

LORD MERSEY AND THE WHITEWASH BRUSH

From the beginning, suspicious people thought that the British inquiry into the sinking was bound to be unsatisfactory. The news itself had appalled the nation. For twenty-four hours, in Britain as in the United States, there was a strong disposition to believe that the ship, since she had been called unsinkable, must somehow be safe. In response to an anxious message from the Board of Trade, the White Star office in Liverpool sent back a telegram saying that although the *Titanic* had indeed struck an iceberg, the *Virginian* was standing by and "there is no danger of loss of life." When the truth was known, the shock was all the more devastating. Crowds besieged the White Star offices in Liverpool, Southampton, and London. The lord mayor of London, the *Daily Mail,* and others opened appeals for bereaved families. The bishop of Winchester pronounced what became the commonplace verdict on the disaster, describing the *Titanic* as "a monument to human presumption." The two-hundred-and-fifty-strong choir of the Leeds Orchestra, performing in Paris, opened its concert by singing "Nearer, My God, to Thee." The nation mourned.

The Cabinet met on the morning of April 16. Afterward, Asquith wrote to George V: "Mr. Buxton reported the latest news as to the sinking of the *Titanic*—one of the saddest maritime disasters of our time." Sydney Buxton was president of the Board of Trade, and thus head of the department responsible. An inquiry under Board of Trade auspices would have to be held: two separate shipping acts required it. But there was a difficulty. The Board of Trade had certified as safe a ship that, on its maiden voyage, had proved to be spectacularly unsafe. How then could a Board of Trade inquiry into the causes of the disaster be impartial? Mr. Martin, M.P., put down a question for the prime minister. Since the Board of Trade "must necessarily be itself on trial," he asked, would it not be more appropriate if the inquiry was conducted by a select committee of the House? Asquith's private secretary was Eric Drummond, later the sixteenth earl of Perth and, in the 1930s, ambassador to Rome. He noted in the weary tones of an intelligent man who knows he is stating the obvious: "I suppose the line to take is that the Court of Inquiry though appointed by the Board of Trade will be independent of them, and can report favourably or adversely as they may think fit with regard to Board of Trade regulations and actions." Drummond's grasp of the procedures was imperfect. The inquiry was required to report to the Board of Trade; but the person who presided over the inquiry—a Wreck Commissioner of the United Kingdom, an ancient office seldom revived—was appointed by the lord chancellor; and the five expert assessors appointed to help the commissioner were nominated by the Home Office. This convenient confusion allowed the Home Office to pass on complaints about partiality to the Board of Trade, and the Board of Trade to do the same to the Home Office.

The Bradford and District Trades and Labour Council

soon sent the Home Office a resolution expressing "no confidence in the Court of Inquiry" and describing it as "an attempt to lull public confidence and to whitewash those who are most responsible for the terrible loss of human life." This may have been the first time the word "whitewash" was applied to the inquiry, but it was not the last. Second Officer Lightoller used it in 1935. In 1969 Geoffrey Marcus published *The Maiden Voyage* expressly to expose "the whitewash so liberally applied by Lord Mersey and his assessors." Patrick Stenson, in his biography of Second Officer Lightoller, published in 1984, endorses Lightoller's comments about "the whitewash brush."

The announcement of the name of the wreck commissioner—Lord Mersey—was made on April 27. Almost immediately, the prime minister was having to defend it in the House. Sir Edward Carson asked, "Does the right honourable gentleman imagine that Lord Mersey will be influenced by the Board of Trade?" Asquith replied, "No, sir. It is an insult to Lord Mersey to suggest such a thing."

But who was Lord Mersey, in whose independence Asquith put such trust, and what sort of man was he? The accusation that the report on the *Titanic* was a whitewash can be sensibly examined only in the light of Mersey's background and connections. To begin with, he was not an aristocrat, as some Americans at the time—because of his title—assumed. He was born John Charles Bigham, the second son of a Liverpool merchant. The only distinctive fact in his ancestry was that his great-grandfather, a farmer in Kirkcudbrightshire, was a friend of Robert Burns, who, when he was an excise man at Dumfries, used to ride over and sit by the fire, smoking his pipe and telling stories.

Mersey's own roots were entirely in Liverpool. His father, brought up in what Mersey used to describe as "grinding poverty," started his career very modestly as a clerk in a riverside shipping office. Soon, however, he saved enough money to buy a small schooner, which was stolen by one of his sea-captain brothers-in-law; he chased him to San Francisco, a journey of four months, and arrived in time to see the ship's masts disappearing over the horizon. Back in Liverpool he was declared bankrupt. But he was a strong and industrious character and did not despair. During the American Civil War he cornered the rosin and turpentine market; after the war he dealt successfully in insurance shares. By the time of his death, in 1880, he had become a rich man and a substantial figure—though of lesser standing than the Ismays and Holts—in Liverpool's civic and maritime life.

Mersey had a strict upbringing. He called his parents "sir" and "ma'am" and was forbidden to sit down when he took meals in their company. He was sent to a school in Germany where he acquired a passion for the opera and theater that he never lost; his first ambition was to go on the stage. He had a good baritone voice and in later life would entertain his guests after dinner with old English songs and arias from Verdi and Gounod operas. He was slow in coming to the law. For seven formative years he worked in his father's office, making some money, learning about maritime affairs, and acquiring a strong distaste for business. While reading for the bar he also picked up a degree at the Sorbonne, adding French to his German. He was called to the bar in 1871, married the daughter of a prosperous Liverpool outfitter, and before long, helped by his local connections, was established as one of the leading counsels on the northern circuit, with a large share of the commercial business in Liverpool. Though without physical advantages, being small with a weak voice, he was learned, industrious, and quick witted. A difficult judge said to him one day, "Well, Mr. Bigham, I may be able to teach you law, but I cannot teach you manners." He replied, "My lord, I agree."

He became Queen's counsel in 1883, the beginning of his real success. He became the friend of the lord chief justice, the master of the rolls, and the attorney general. He sent his sons to Eton. Though not particularly interested in politics, he stood as a Liberal—unsuccessfully—for the Toxteth Division of Liverpool in 1885, and successfully for the Exchange Division in 1895. By now he was in the front rank of the bar, with an enormous practice. During the short time he was an M.P., he played a leading part in the House of Commons committee set up to inquire into the Jameson Raid. The question was whether the British had connived at this abortive attempt, inspired by Cecil Rhodes, to instigate an uprising against President Paul Kruger of the Transvaal. The committee cleared the government, but Boers and many British were skeptical. Mersey's role in this inquiry, when he conducted much of the cross-examination, was the reason why some people, when he was put in charge of the *Titanic* inquiry, mistrusted him; they thought that, having helped with what they regarded as one whitewash, he was fully capable of presiding over another.

He went from strength to strength. At the age of fifty-seven, after twenty-six years at the bar, he became a high court judge and traveled to Windsor to be knighted by Queen Victoria. In 1901, he was one of the judges summoned to advise at Lord Russell's trial for bigamy in the House of Lords. He went to South Africa on a royal commission on martial law. In 1909 he was made president of the Probate, Divorce, and Admiralty Division but suffered a series of alarming heart attacks and quickly had to retire. Henceforward, though soon recovered and as industrious as ever, he undertook only *ad hoc* assignments.

Mersey was the obvious choice as *Titanic* wreck commissioner. He was wholly familiar with the shipping business and maritime law; his coat of arms, acquired when he was raised to the peerage in 1910, featured bare-breasted supporters carrying an oar and an anchor. His legal experience included every kind of litigation except murder cases, which he loathed.

In the light of the accusations, it should be noted that although his connections were wide, and although his career had brought him membership in the small circle of the English governing class, he was little interested in politics and did not move in political society. He had an essentially crossbench mind. One of his protégés was Lord Sankey, who went out of his way to thank Mersey for his early encouragement after he was appointed lord chancellor in Ramsay MacDonald's second Labour government. His domestic life was peaceful, with a handsome and cultivated wife and two successful and devoted sons. He had no financial worries; he saved more than he spent. For leisure, he traveled to France or read—his favorite authors were Dickens, Balzac, and Daudet. His friends came from the world of the theater and music—Lillian Bayliss and both Gilbert and Sullivan among them—and above all from the bar. The law and lawyers were his passion. To the end of his life, even as an extremely old man, he would still totter off to dine with the Benchers of the Middle Temple.

Some of Mersey's critics assume or imply that he intended the *Titanic* inquiry to be a whitewash from the start. This is highly improbable. When he was appointed, Mersey was in Newcastle, acting as chairman of a Minimum Wage Committee. His first act was to get hold of his son, invite him to be secretary to the inquiry, and ask him to get on with the preliminaries: to hire a hall, prepare a list of the first witnesses, find a small office, and make arrangements for counsel, shorthand writers, and the press. (The son in turn enlisted the help of his father's clerk, Arthur Donis, always called A. Donis because of his agreeable nature and striking good looks—qualities he transmitted to his two actress daughters, Zena and Phyllis Dare.)

Captain the Hon. Clive Bigham, then aged thirty-nine, was in some ways a more remarkable man than his father. Like his friend Aubrey Herbert, the model for John Buchan's *Greenmantle,* he was stimulated by foreign exploits that served a patriotic need. He was given a conventional education—the Eton connections were useful to him later on—and decided, somewhat against the wishes of his father, who hoped he would choose the law, to become a soldier. For a time he enjoyed the light duties required in those days of an officer in the Grenadier Guards (a captain could expect six months' leave a year) and the opportunity to explore London night life. Then he grew bored. He therefore approached his Etonian friends in the diplomatic service and secured a temporary post as a Queen's Messenger, which enabled him to travel at public expense on the Orient Express to Constantinople.

During the next five years he enjoyed a life of high adventure. He learned the Turkish language and investigated the causes of the Armenian massacres taking place in little-known parts of Asia Minor, reporting his conclusions to the Foreign Office. He covered the Turco-Greek war of 1897 for *The Times.* He traveled unceasingly in the remoter parts of Asia, Russia, and China. A journey of ten thousand miles in the eighteen provinces of China, by river and horseback, was particularly intrepid, since he was often among people who had never before seen a European and whose reactions were unpredictable. His purpose was to make a report on a projected Russian railway through Manchuria. When, after one or two narrow escapes, he

came at the end of this year-long journey to within striking distance of Peking, where he hoped to arrive in time
for a reunion dinner of Old Etonians, he found himself in
the midst of the Boxer Rebellion. He acquitted himself
bravely; at twenty-eight, he became the youngest person
ever to be awarded a CMG.

All members of the governing classes in those days knew
all other members. Back in London, through friends, Bigham found a job in military intelligence. Almost his first
task was to go to Paris to try to stop the attacks of two
low-class newspapers on Queen Victoria; he silenced them
without difficulty, settling up with the editors for a few
five-pound notes. He had already written books about his
travels. He now wrote military handbooks on Abyssinia,
Arabia, and Morocco, three of the few countries he had
never visited. At the general election of 1906, he stood as a
Liberal in Windsor. He was defeated, but with the Liberal
victory, though he was still attached in some obscure fashion to the Grenadier Guards, he began a new career as an
itinerant investigator for the government. He was well read
and a concise writer. He knew everyone. Like his father, he
believed in disposing of the matter in hand as expeditiously
as possible. In a very short time, as if extracting chocolate
bars from a slot machine, he himself or the committees to
which he was secretary had produced reports and sometimes recommendations about freight rates, the regulation
of motorcars, railways, the administration of lighthouses,
vivisection, and the prevalence of alcohol consumption in
Great Britain (less prevalent than it used to be, was his
conclusion).

To round off this sketch of father and son: Lord Mersey
was promoted to viscount in recognition of his services
in World War I, when he had been constantly at work
on shipping claims, or conducting an inquiry into hos-

pital out-patients, or sitting as a lord of appeal; he died in 1937. During the war Bigham served at Gallipoli, made friends with T. E. Lawrence, had four narrow escapes from death—from a bullet through his car, a shell through his tent, a bomb in his room, and a torpedo—but survived to become a member of the British delegation to the peace conference at Versailles. He later wrote several more books, one of them a history of the Roxburghe Club, a select group of scholarly bibliophiles to which he belonged. He died in 1956, leaving a library of ten thousand volumes.

An old photograph shows Lord Mersey and his secretary arriving at the London Scottish Drill Hall, near St. James's Park station, for the first day of the inquiry. Lord Mersey looks confident and well equipped, with top hat, tail coat, umbrella, wing collar, tie pin, eyeglasses, and watch chain. His son, deceptively elegant in top hat and frock coat, looks as though he had never ventured east of the Savoy Hotel, nor encountered any foreigner more outlandish than the Savoy's head waiter, Monsieur Ritz.

They were principals in a considerable event. Under Captain Bigham's supervision, the drill hall had been turned into a makeshift courtroom; long curtains concealed the brickwork; a dais at one end supported Lord Mersey's desk and, at a slightly lower level, the desks of the assessors; a table, chair, and decanter of water for witnesses stood to Lord Mersey's right; and one wall was occupied by a large model of the *Titanic* supplied by White Star and a chart of the North Atlantic.

Facing Lord Mersey were some of the most eminent lawyers in Britain: For the Board of Trade, the attorney general, Sir Rufus Isaacs, K.C.; the solicitor general, Sir John Simon, K.C.; Mr. Butler Aspinall, K.C.; Mr. S. T. Rowlatt; Mr. Raymond Asquith (the prime minister's son); for the

White Star Line, Sir Robert Finlay, K.C.; Frederick N.R. Lang, K.C.; and Maurice Hill, K.C.; Mr. Thomas Scanlan for the National Sailors' and Firemen's Union; Mr. Clement Edwards for the Dockers' Union; Mr. W. D. Harbinson for the third-class passengers; Mr. Henry Duke, K.C., for Sir Cosmo and Lady Duff Gordon; Mr. C. Robertson Dunlop for the owner, master, and officers of the *Californian*. The hall was packed and remained so throughout the hearings.

The attorney general opened with an eloquent statement of sorrow about the disaster, followed by Sir Robert Finlay for White Star. "There is only one thing," said Sir Robert, "that gives some consolation, and to that the Attorney General has alluded, that this disaster has given an opportunity for a display of discipline and of heroism which is worthy of all the best traditions of the marine of this country."

The preliminaries were followed by complaints. Lord Mersey had before him twenty-six precise questions to answer (set by the attorney general and Board of Trade officials), but they had been "very hurriedly typewritten" and the "very few copies" were not enough to go around. Next came complaints about the "great difficulty of hearing. This hall was not built for the purpose of holding inquiries of this kind and its acoustic properties are very bad indeed." The attorney general agreed; it was "most difficult to hear and most inconvenient." Lord Mersey was brisk, as he remained throughout the inquiry. "We must go on here until we find another room," he said, not mentioning that the hall had been chosen by his son. That ended the proceedings for the first day. The second day began with the calling of Archie Jewell, one of the lookout men. He proved to be the first of ninety-four witnesses.

Every word spoken at the inquiry is to be found in the *Evidence, Appendices, and Index of the Formal Investigation into the Loss of the SS Titanic,* published by His Majesty's Stationery Office as a single large volume in 1912. The pages of the copy in the Marine Library of the Department of Transport are crumbling, their corners, unless the reader is careful, liable to break off. A vandal has marked in ink the passages referring to Captain Lord of the *Californian.* But all the spoken evidence on which Mersey based his alleged whitewash is readily available.

Evidence about behind-the-scenes activity at the Board of Trade is less complete. Yet the files kept in cardboard boxes at the Public Records Office tell us something. The first point liable to strike the reader who comes to these yellowing documents after reading contemporary newspapers is that he is now seeing traces of a great government department run by clear-headed bureaucrats expertly preparing to defend its flanks. The writers of these minutes are little concerned with the subjects exciting the newspapers and general public. There is no trace of any departmental interest in the conduct of those on the *Titanic,* or in the *Titanic*'s speed, or in questions of negligence, or in who escaped and why. These are matters for the court or the company. The board's concern is first to examine its own vulnerability. The question of the impartiality of the inquiry can be left to ministers—if necessary the prime minister. The board's main anxiety—and it was already under attack—was to find out whether their Marine Department had been negligent. Were the board's regulations about lifeboats out of date, as seemed to be the case? Had the *Titanic*'s sea trials been properly carried out? Had the *Titanic*'s equipment been properly tested? The court— if not Lord Mersey, then one or other of the phalanx of lawyers—would demand precise answers to these questions, and the department must at once discover where it stood.*

Reading between the lines, it looks as though the civil servants very quickly, and correctly, identified lifeboats as their main weakness. The outside world already knew that more lives would have been saved if the *Titanic* had carried more lifeboats; and the world also knew that the *Titanic* had carried more lifeboats than Board of Trade regulations required. That horse had bolted; but at least the stable door could be shut. Within the week, the board summoned all British shipping lines to a meeting. What action were they taking about lifeboats in the light of the disaster? The White Star representative said that Mr. Ismay, in his capacity as chairman of the International Mercantile Marine, had already publicly announced that all component companies—White Star, Leyland, Atlantic, Red Star, American—must in future ensure that their ships carried enough lifeboats to accommodate all passengers and crew. The representative plainly thought that Ismay had acted precipitately. The chairman had given his order without consulting his nautical advisers, who might raise objections. Nor had he considered the difficulty of obtaining enough boats. Cunard and the other lines said they were reviewing the matter urgently. For the moment, pending the outcome of the inquiry, there was little more the board could do. They would have to be satisfied with a half-shut stable door.

With equal speed they established, at least to their own satisfaction, that they were not vulnerable over the tests and trials carried out by their inspectors. In Belfast, the board's surveyor repeated a test on a lifeboat of the type

---

*Accurate transcripts of the U.S. and British inquiries are now available online at www.titanicinquiry.org.—DG

supplied to the *Titanic;* it was designed and certified to carry sixty-five persons; he had put sixty-six aboard and there was no difficulty in using the oars. Precise details of the materials used in the lifeboats' construction were forwarded to London. Lifebelts had also been correctly tested, he assured the board, with iron attached.

By the time Lord Mersey was appointed, the board had already conducted, by chance, a small-scale inquiry of their own into the fundamental cause of the disaster. Professor J. H. Biles of Glasgow University, a recognized expert on the structure of big ships who had himself designed some of them, was acquainted with Sir Alfred Chalmers, a master mariner who advised the Marine Department of the Board of Trade on nautical technicalities. A week after the *Titanic* sank he wrote to Chalmers: "Does it interest you to know what I think of the *Titanic?* If it does not, don't waste any more time in reading this letter." He went on:

> We have never known of a ship being lost by a collision with an iceberg—some cases of mysterious disappearance have been suspected of having been caused by ice. Many cases of collision with other ships have been known and can be provided against because the amount of *damage* that can be done by collision is limited. The worst is that a ship may be struck on a watertight bulkhead and so flood two compartments. Provision is usually made for safety in such an event.
>
> In the earlier smaller ships it was necessary to carry bulkheads to the upper deck to give the necessary safety. As the size of ship and number of decks increased, the added space above the upper deck was left undivided in order to give greater freedom in arranging passenger quarters. If these spaces had been sub-divided by carrying the bulkheads up through them, more than two compartments could have

been flooded and the *Titanic* would have remained afloat very much longer and probably might have been towed into port. . . .

I think the public outcry about the boats is likely to obscure the real causes of the trouble: the neglect to carry the bulkheads as high as possible.

Why the ship ran into the ice we shall probably never know, but it is obviously the sailor man's business to keep clear. It is the owner's business to make the ship as safe as possible.

Chalmers circulated the letter. "Much in what Professor Biles has written," concluded Captain Young of the board's technical staff. "I agree with his main contention," wrote the principal ship surveyor. Someone at the Board of Trade presumably spoke to someone at the Home Office. A few days later, Professor Biles became one of the Court of Inquiry's assessors. It appears to have been a significant appointment. At the end of July, when after much questioning of ship construction experts by the lawyers, Lord Mersey presented his report, one of his main recommendations concerned the extension of bulkheads to a greater height—essentially the point made by Biles a week after the disaster. In due course, the Biles doctrine led to new regulations, and hence to the reconstruction of many of the passenger ships afloat.

At the time, the board could take some comfort from Biles's opinion that bulkheads, not lifeboats, were the culprits. The board alone was responsible for laying down the number and type of boats carried by liners, but it did not carry sole responsibility for the rules governing bulkheads; these were drawn up by a Bulkhead Committee partly composed of outside experts.

Other problems dealt with by the board during this

period were, by comparison, routine. The Imperial and Royal Austro-Hungarian Consulate-General wanted to know how many of the crew were Austrian or Hungarian nationals; the answer was one, a steward. The Armenian Patriarch solicited assistance for the relatives of four drowned Armenians; they were sent £25 each, pending further inquiries. From Sofia came news of a Royal Ukase that sanctioned a grant of £200 for proceedings against White Star with a view to claiming indemnities for Bulgarians who had perished. New rates of compensatory pay for witnesses attending the inquiry had to be worked out in consultation with the Treasury; alarm was expressed about the large leap, under the revised rates, in the pay of the chief baker. The files contain an acrimonious correspondence with Fourth Officer Boxhall, who complained that he had been underpaid by £3.10s. and that his letters were "utterly ignored" (it was not until September that he was finally told he had been paid the same as the third and fifth officers and had no grounds for complaint). Lists were compiled of those drowned, showing their country of origin: seventy-three Irish had been lost in steerage.

One laborious administrative task, relating to Captain Lord and the *Californian,* concerned a ship with a black funnel and a white band reported to have been seen near the sinking. British representatives all over the world were asked to pursue inquiries with foreign governments, port authorities, and shipping lines. The investigation was meticulous; a British consul suspected that the funnel of one ship might have been repainted, and surreptitiously scratched it with his knife. Although answers to the board's inquiries were still coming in as late as 1913, no ship fitting the description was found.

As the prolonged and scrupulous search for the ship with the black funnel indicates, the inquiry was thorough, within the limits it set itself. During thirty-six days of sittings, the ninety-four witnesses were asked 25,600 questions. The lawyers were efficient, pursuing—unlike Senator Smith—carefully thought-out lines of questioning; Sir Rufus Isaacs was particularly brilliant, demonstrating the advantages of getting up shortly after dawn, his invariable custom, to read briefs.

Lord Mersey liked cases before him to bowl along as fast as possible. He discouraged diversions. His mind was usually a step or two ahead of everyone else's in court, and he was inclined to become restless when he felt he had heard enough evidence to answer one of his twenty-six questions. Captain Lord later complained to the Board of Trade about this characteristic, since he was sure Mersey had decided on his, Lord's, guilt before he had heard all the evidence. When lawyers put blurred questions, Mersey rephrased them, always more concisely. He was sharp from time to time with the third-class passengers' counsel, Harbinson, but never seriously hampered him. With the crew, he was polite: "Thank you, Jewell," he told the first witness, "and if you will allow me to say so, I think you have given your evidence very well indeed."

The report is clear and well-written. Perhaps Clive Bigham had something to do with it; he had a taste for straightforward prose, and it was he, as secretary, who officially sent the finished document to the Board of Trade (who pointed out that he had got the date of a shipping act wrong by forty years on page one). The board made special arrangements to publish the report as quickly as possible, authorizing the printers to pay extra for overtime and work over the bank holiday, and asking for especially large type. These arrangements were made before the board knew the report's contents. By the shipping journals and the serious newspapers, the reception was on the whole favorable. The report recommended many changes: to wireless, to lifeboat regulations, to methods of ship construction. The Board of Trade did not escape censure. The files show, however, that the bureaucrats were relieved to have got off relatively lightly, at least by comparison with the charges of sloth and dereliction of duty that had been leveled at them before the inquiry began.

But the most remarkable point about the report was that it did not find Captain Smith and the White Star Line guilty of negligence. This is where the charges of white-wash come in. The report said that Smith could not be convicted of negligence because in maintaining his ship's speed, despite the presence of ice, he was following the long-established practice of the North Atlantic. What was foolhardiness in Smith's case, however, would be negligence in similar cases in the future. Mersey had said in court that he did not wish to be too hard on a man who could not be present to defend himself. Having let off Smith, the inquiry could scarcely convict the company that employed him; and here the report implicitly accepted the Lightoller theory that the accident had happened only because conditions that night had been exceptional. Mersey and Isaacs had discussed openly in court the question of Lightoller's reliability as a witness; both were skeptical. Mersey wondered whether Lightoller really could remember exactly what Captain Smith had said to him during his watch. Even so, the report took his word for it that the conditions—an exceptionally calm sea, a starry night, an iceberg that was invisible—formed "a combination that would not happen again in a hundred years."

Years later Lightoller wrote of the inquiry: "A washing of dirty linen would help no one. The BOT had passed that ship as in all respects fit for sea, in every sense of the word, with sufficient margin of safety for everyone on board. Now the BOT was holding an inquiry into the loss of that ship—hence the whitewash brush."

The charges of whitewash may be summed up as follows: Smith may indeed have been conforming to the practice of mail steamer captains; several of them had testified to that effect in court. Nevertheless that practice was reckless—as the inquiry report itself stated. That Smith's recklessness imitated that of others was no reason to excuse him from negligence.

As for White Star, its regulations stated that the safety of the ship must always be the captain's prime consideration. Yet the chairman of the line, J. Bruce Ismay, had been handed a Marconigram by the captain which reported the proximity of ice; he knew the ship was traveling at nearly full speed. Ismay could not reasonably claim, though he attempted to do so, that he was a mere passenger. Like Smith, he should have taken steps to ensure the safety of the passengers. But he had done nothing. The company was therefore as negligent as Smith. Unlike the American inquiry, the British inquiry was silent about the subtle pressure that the presence of "the owner" might have exerted on Captain Smith to chalk up an impressive maiden voyage.

A further point made in support of the whitewash charge is that Mersey brushed aside the criticism that there were not enough seamen on the *Titanic* to handle the lifeboats properly. But the evidence pointed to a shortage of seamen: certainly of seamen in the right place at the right time. Lightoller ordered a passenger, Major Peuchen, into a boat because he could not find any member of the crew capable of helping Quartermaster Hichens.

The inquiry had other weaknesses. It blandly concluded

that there had been no discrimination against steerage passengers yet did not examine a single steerage passenger—although here Lord Mersey could point to the fact that Harbinson, the counsel for the third class, agreed that there was no evidence that they had been unfairly treated.★ The inquiry also failed to investigate properly the practices among Marconi operators. Nor did it bring out the very important fact that the officers did not know that the life-saving equipment was strong enough to allow the lifeboats to be filled to capacity at the davits, if necessary.

But was it a whitewash? There is no evidence of collusion between Mersey and the Board of Trade. There is no evidence of the fabrication or suppression of facts. The inquiry was under the close scrutiny of the bar: twenty-eight lawyers were usually in court. Mersey would have been much more alert to what barristers and judges would think of his performance than of what politicians or public or shipowners would think. Even if he had wished, he would not have dared to reach conclusions that would not command general professional support. He also had to get the agreement to his report of the five assessors. He was not the sort of man to risk his standing simply to protect officials in the Board of Trade, or a dead merchant navy captain, or the directors of a shipping line owned by American capital.

Yet he was much too easy on Smith, the builders, the owners, and the Board of Trade. Professor Biles had made the relevant points in his private letter of April 21 to the Board of Trade. It was the sailor's business to steer clear of danger; and it was the owner's business to make the ship as safe as possible. Neither had done so. Why then did Mersey

---

★Harbinson's incompetence is exposed in *Titanic: Monument and Warning.* It was he who failed to call third-class witnesses or place sworn statements before the court.—DG give them the benefit of the doubt? He may have thought that since Captain Smith was dead, there was no point in censuring him too harshly. He may have been influenced in letting off the company by the industrial unrest in the shipping business: White Star faced a virtual mutiny during the inquiry when the crew walked off the *Olympic* as a protest against inadequate lifesaving equipment. He may have said to himself that the object of the inquiry was to find the facts and make recommendations for improved public safety, not to judge people guilty or not guilty. Or he—and the assessors—may consciously or unconsciously have been deterred by the spirit of the times from making unnecessary trouble for members of the governing class; after all, the only person who might have broken the law was Captain Lord, by failing to assist a vessel in distress. But whatever went on in Mersey's mind, and it is not impossible that he thought of nothing except justice, his report reached the very peculiar though unstated conclusion that, despite failures here and there, nobody at all was responsible for the worst maritime disaster in history. It was not a deliberate, conscious, calculated whitewash, but it was a whitewash nevertheless.

In Britain as in the United States the inquiry was sooner or later followed by a string of reforms: to wireless regulations, navigation practices, provision of lifeboats, ship construction. If nobody had been negligent, the reforms would not have been necessary.

But the real proof that Mersey had been too indulgent came sixteen months later. An Irish farmer who had lost a son in the *Titanic* sued White Star for compensation. Some of the same cast of characters reappeared: Scanlan and Duke among the lawyers; Lightoller, Lee, and Fleet of the crew. After much of the ground had been gone over again, the jury found no negligence about lookouts but did find negligence about speed. White Star appealed. In February 1914 the Court of Appeal upheld the jury's verdict. The question was, said Lord Justice Vaughan Williams, whether the danger had been unforeseen and unforeseeable. If so, there could not have been negligence. But the dangers had been foreseen. Lightoller had ordered the lookouts to keep a special eye out for ice; Captain Smith had ordered an alteration of course to the south of the regular shipping lane; both actions showed that danger was foreseen. If danger was foreseen, it was not unforeseeable. The verdict was upheld.

So, having been exonerated by Lord Mersey in 1912, White Star was found guilty by the Court of Appeal in 1913 and settled the American compensation out of court in 1916, which was a tacit admission of guilt. The later events did not confirm the Mersey verdict.

It is clear that one of the most prominent people in the inquiry ought not have been part of it at all. Rufus Isaacs (1860–1935) enjoyed one of the most spectacular careers of the century. The fourth of nine children of a Jewish fruit merchant in Spitalfields, in the East End of London, he finished his schooling before he was fourteen, yet rose to become attorney general, lord chief justice, ambassador to Washington, viceroy of India, foreign secretary, and a marquess.

His early years were uncertain. He signed articles as a ship's boy when he was sixteen for a wage of ten shillings a month. (Charles Booth, in *Life and Labour of the People in London,* published in 1888, drew the "poverty line" at thirty shillings a week.) In Rio, he jumped ship but was caught. Back home, he worked briefly in the drudgery of his father's fruit business before becoming a stock jobber; he next had the disastrous experience of being "hammered" on the Stock Exchange. Then his mother took a hand and made him read for the bar. He had a fine, handsome presence, expressive hands, and "an alert glance," as a contemporary put it. He rapidly made his mark. In 1904 it was Isaacs who prosecuted Whitaker Wright for fraud in a case in which Mersey was criticized for unjudicial bias against the accused. In 1910 he became attorney general and thus official head of the bar. In 1911 he led for the prosecution in a criminal libel case brought as the result of an allegation that George V, then on the eve of his coronation, had been married before he married Queen Mary. In the same year, he was knighted and made a privy councillor.

Now it so happened that around the time Rufus Isaacs became attorney general in 1910, his brother Godfrey became joint managing director of the Marconi Wireless Telegraph Company. The company was famous and making progress, but its performance was not outstanding. But in March 1912 Godfrey Isaacs and Marconi secured an important contract from the British government—the department principally concerned was the Post Office—to construct and operate the ambitious long-distance wireless telegraphy service that would link up the Empire. The law officers were not consulted. The right-wing journal *Eye Witness,* edited by G. K. Chesterton's brother Cecil, alleged, nevertheless, that the monopoly obtained by the Marconi company was due to the influence exerted by the attorney general in favor of his brother. It was said that Rufus Isaacs, as well as Lloyd George, and the Liberal chief whip, the Master of Elibank, were seeking to make money out of the contract.

These allegations, inspired by anti-Semitism, were untrue. What was true, though not publicly known, was that Godfrey Isaacs had acquired a large block of shares in the American Marconi company; and on April 9, 1912, over lunch at the Savoy Hotel, he offered to dispose of some of them to his brothers Rufus and Harry. That was the day before the *Titanic* sailed. Rufus Isaacs declined the offer, on the grounds that he preferred not to have any dealings with a company in commercial relations with the government. Harry Isaacs accepted.

The *Titanic* sank on April 15, and the world, as it waited anxiously for details, realized fully for the first time the revolutionary significance of Marconi's invention. On the morning of April 17, for instance, the paper that W. T. Stead used to edit, the *Northern Echo,* carried a story from its New York correspondent as follows:

> It is more than 36 hours since the greatest disaster in the history of the Atlantic Ocean occurred, and New York has not received a single dispatch from any eyewitness, or any journalist within a thousand miles of the spot off the Newfoundland Banks where the *Titanic* went down.
>
> Every message so far has been by wireless, and has come from some steamship officer or land station officer who has picked up others emitted from the keyboard of the *Carpathia,* the *Olympic,* the *Parisian,* the *Virginian,* the *Baltic,* or the *Californian* and intercepted in their mysterious passage through the air.
>
> The tremendous anxiety of the relatives of the *Titanic*'s 1,400 passengers to ascertain the names of the survivors has found expression in the greatest avalanche of Marconigrams ever dispatched up the Atlantic coast.

That very day, Harry Isaacs offered to sell his brother Rufus some of his share in the American Marconi company. This time, the attorney general accepted. He bought 10,000 shares at £2; a substantial purchase, the equivalent of about £690,000 at today's prices, according to the Central Statistical Office. On the same day he transferred 1,000 of them to each of his ministerial friends, Lloyd George and the Master of Elibank, keeping 8,000 for himself.

The *Titanic* inquiry opened on May 2. The attorney general played a leading part, questioning, among others, Marconi; the Mersey report was duly published at the end of July. But rumors about share dealings persisted. On October 11, the postmaster general, Herbert Samuel, moved in the House of Commons for the establishment of a select committee to investigate the Marconi affair. Then the attorney general spoke. He strongly denied (as did Lloyd George) that he had ever had any interest in the English Marconi company. But he did not think it necessary to refer to his holdings in the American company. "It was a lamentable error of judgement," Lord Simon wrote after Isaacs's death (Simon in 1912 was solicitor general and at Isaacs's side during the *Titanic* inquiry; later he became lord chancellor). Indeed, the information about Isaacs's holdings in the American Marconi company came out only in January 1913, during a libel action against a Paris newspaper, *Le Matin*. The final report of the Commons select committee said that ministers had acted in the sincere belief that their share dealings were not in conflict with their public duty; but it was a majority, not a unanimous report, and it was accepted by the House only after fierce party controversy. On June 18, 1913, Isaacs admitted, "It was a mistake to purchase those shares." The mistake, however, did not interrupt his career; four months later, Asquith after some hesitation appointed him lord chief justice of England.

An outcry followed. Kipling was provoked to write one of the most vitriolic poems in the language, about Gehazi, Elisha's swindling servant in the Old Testament, which opens:

Whence comest thou, Gehazi,
So reverend to behold,
In scarlet and in ermines
And chains of England's gold?

Rupert Brooke on his way to Fiji wrote to a friend in England saying he was thinking of giving up the National Liberal Club "because I hate the Liberal Party and the Marconi affair and Rufus Isaacs as Lord Chief Justice."

In the long run, though, few people held Isaacs's Marconi dealings against him. He had been a friend of Lord Mersey's before the inquiry and the revelations; and he remained so afterward. Mersey was the last person Isaacs visited before he sailed to India as viceroy and the first he visited after he came back. He befriended and helped Mersey's son, Clive Bigham, advising him about his half-hearted attempts to become a Liberal M.P. and speaking for him at elections. Isaacs died, as marquess of Reading, laden with honors, and, wrote Bigham in his diary, "Few people of our day have had, or deserved, more success, respect and affection."

Yet the Marconi affair was discreditable. Isaacs must have thought he had something to hide, or he would have told the House of Commons about his American holdings. Lord Simon was putting the most generous possible gloss on his dissimulation when he described it as "an error of judgement." A less generous but more candid memorialist would have recorded the fact—surprisingly ignored then and since—that Isaacs made money out of the *Titanic* disaster; and he bought his shares while the lists of the dead and survivors were still coming through. It is thus difficult to regard his purchase as an ordinary, run-of-the-mill investment.

If this view seems overly censorious, let us imagine what

would have happened at the *Titanic* inquiry if Isaacs had made known then the facts that came out nine months later. In his opening address, Isaacs had struck a high note: "My lord," he said, "this terrible disaster in mid-ocean, both because in mere magnitude it exceeds any calamity in the history of the mercantile marine and also because of its many harrowing incidents, has in a profound and marked degree touched the heart of the nation." He went on to speak of "heroic sacrifices." Later, when Marconi took the stand, in a packed hall, it was Sir Rufus who put the first question: "Mr Marconi, are you the inventor of wireless telegraphy?" His answer: "Yes."

Suppose the attorney general had then turned to Lord Mersey and said:

My lord, before proceeding further with this witness, may I say that I feel obliged as a point of honor to make a brief statement, lest my position should be misunderstood later. I think it right, as a law officer of the crown, that my interest should be publicly known.

As you may be aware, my brother Godfrey is joint managing director of the British Marconi company. He went to New York with Mr. Marconi last month to extend the activities of the American Marconi company. Capital was needed to finance these activities, and a new share issue was successfully floated, with the British company taking up a large fraction and my brother Godfrey another large block. Godfrey sold 86,000 of his shares to our brother Harry on April 9. I was urged to take some myself, but declined. Two days after the *Titanic* sank, however, I bought in the evening 10,000 shares from my brother Harry at £2 a share. The price was favorable, because dealings had not yet formally opened on the London Stock Exchange.

On the same day, April 17, I transferred 1,000 shares to

the chancellor of the exchequer and another 1,000 to the chief whip of my party. I was in charge then and subsequently of all their dealings in these shares.

At that time, following the tremendous publicity given to Mr. Marconi's invention, and the proof offered by this terrible disaster of the efficacy of his apparatus, and the likelihood that its use would rapidly spread on land and sea—possibly as a result of government regulation—the prospects for the shares appeared bright.

So it has proved. My brother Godfrey and Mr. Marconi were in the United States to arrange for the American Marconi company to buy out a rival company, United Wireless, that had gone bankrupt. The news of this deal was publicly announced on the day that the *Carpathia* reached New York, the day after I bought my 10,000 shares. It was also announced that the American Marconi company had done a second deal, this time with the Western Union Cable Company, to build long-range stations in the United States and outside. I had known about this announcement before I bought my shares.

Now the news of this expansion certainly helped the shares. But it does not account for the exceptional sharpness of their rise that started before and continued after the announcement. Before the *Titanic* sank, nobody had contemplated for a moment that they would rise so fast. Formal dealings in the American shares opened on the London Stock Exchange on April 19. The shares I had bought for £2 opened at £3.5s. During the day, I sold nearly half my holding at an average price of £3.6s.6d. and thus recouped much of my total cash liability, leaving me with a very good paper profit—made in the two days after the disaster—on my original investment.

I should add that I engaged in further dealings in these shares on May 3, the day after this inquiry opened. The position today is that I still hold 4,430 American Marconi company shares, for which in effect I paid £1.5s.3d. each, but which now stand substantially higher. Their prospects, I believe, remain bright—particularly since it is now extremely likely that as a result of this inquiry the governments of Britain and the United States will in future require all sizable ships to carry wireless.

Now, with your permission, my lord, I shall resume my examination of Mr. Marconi.

Would Lord Mersey have allowed Sir Rufus to continue? There were striking contrasts between the way the Americans and the British handled Marconi. The senators took the position that wireless telegraphy was a boon, but the disaster had revealed grave defects in the system, as it certainly had. They questioned Marconi closely about his relations with *The New York Times,* the reasons why the Marconi operators aboard the *Carpathia* had not answered Marconigrams, the hours and low pay of Marconi employees, the interference of wireless amateurs with official communications, and the extent of Marconi's business interests and their possible tendency toward monopoly. At times, the Americans' treatment of the great inventor was overtly hostile. The British inquiry, on the other hand, treated Marconi as a purely technical witness. It confined itself to the priorities given to different types of messages, working hours, the diagrams issued to operators to advise them when shore stations and other ships would or should be within call, and the replacement of the CQD by the SOS distress signal. Many questions aimed to establish the *Californian*'s degree of blame for her failure to pick up the *Titanic*'s desperate calls. The difference between the two inquiries was summed up at the end of Marconi's London appearance when Lord Mersey turned to the silent Sir

Robert Finlay, counsel for the White Star Line, and said, "Do you want to ask anything, Sir Robert?"; and Finlay replied, "I only want to say we are very glad to have had the honour of seeing Mr. Marconi."

When over a year later in May 1913 the House of Commons select committee into the Marconi affair questioned Sir Rufus about his Marconi shares, nobody noticed that he had bought them immediately after the *Titanic* sank and was dealing in them after the British inquiry had begun. The chairman of the committee, Sir Albert Spicer, asked Isaacs, "What did you understand from your brother [Harry] was the reason of the great advance in the American prices?" Sir Rufus replied, "The purchases in America." He was referring to the purchase of United Wireless. He did not mention the huge boost given to the Marconi system by the *Titanic* disaster; nor that it was after the disaster that he took the opportunity, on his brother's advice, to get in on the ground floor.

Whether, but for the attorney general's shareholding, Marconi would have been more closely examined at the British inquiry, as he was in the United States, about the evident defects of his system is a matter for conjecture.

10

THE *TITANIC* REDISCOVERED

During the years that followed the Mersey report, no doubt because a greater disaster supervened, interest in the *Titanic* as a historical event slowly faded away in Britain and the rest of Europe. The name of the ship settled deeply into the general consciousness as a metaphor of calamity, but the accident itself was half-forgotten, recalled briefly in a local newspaper when a survivor died or a features edi tor remembered an anniversary. Things might have been the same in the United States had not the Grand Theater on Main Street, Indian Orchard, Massachusetts, shown the film *Titanic,* starring Clifton Webb and Barbara Stanwyck, in the fall of 1953. From this seed we may date the birth, in an improbable spot, of modern *Titanic* scholarship.

The theater was owned by a Polish-American, Henry Kamuda, who had inherited it from his father. One of Henry's children, Edward, then aged fourteen, is the man who now knows more about the *Titanic* and her fate than anyone else—certainly much more than was known to those who went down in her, or to any of the survivors. In 1953 he was working around his father's theater, putting up posters in the town, doing odd jobs. He saw the film and was enthralled. It was the beginning of an obsession. He read about the *Titanic* in encyclopedias; he asked an old bookstore to look out for *Titanic* books; he made contact with another enthusiast, who had spent a year and a half building a model of the ship and had corresponded with Harland & Wolff and with J. G. Boxhall, one of the surviving officers.

Then came what Kamuda calls "my big break." In 1958 the J. Arthur Rank Organization made the film *A Night to Remember,* loosely based on Walter Lord's book of the same name. The script was by Eric Ambler; Kenneth More starred as Lightoller, and Alec McCowen played Cottam, the *Carpathia*'s radio operator. The lifeboat scenes were shot in the Ruislip reservoir, near Pinewood Studios, and the engine room scenes at Cricklewood Pumping Station.

The film, advertised as "an incredible spellbinding story of six hours unlike any other six hours the world has ever known," was well received. In the United States, to drum up trade, the Exploitation Department of Rank Film Distributors in New York sent local theater owners "business builders," or ideas for local promotions—fashion tie-ins, questions for quiz shows, radio "spots." One of the "spots" went as follows:

> At night the sounds on board a luxury liner at sea are varied . . . Bits of honeymoon conversation filter through the Edwardian mahogany panel . . . somewhere two lovers whisper in muffled tones . . . a door closes softly . . . the "Blue Danube" drifts from the first-class salon down to second-class ears . . . Then quite suddenly you notice it . . . the smooth hum of the great engines has died . . . and the *Titanic* is dying, too . . . "She can't sink! . . . she's unsinkable . . . she can't float . . . how long will she last? . . . another hour and a half" . . . For you, one of the few in the tiny lifeboats, it is indeed A NIGHT TO

REMEMBER ... *The New York Times* calls it "tense, exciting,
and supremely awesome drama on the screen" . . . Never
before seen on screen or television . . . Walter Lord's thrilling best-seller, A NIGHT TO REMEMBER.

All of these items came to Indian Orchard and were exciting enough, but the one that particularly stirred Edward
Kamuda, now eighteen, was a list of *Titanic* survivors. The
idea was that if any of them happened to live in the district
where the film was shown, they could be exhibited along
with the film. Kamuda wrote to every single survivor, and
to his surprise many of them wrote back. Next, a hobbies
magazine featured him in a series about people interested in
obscure subjects. Thus he made contact with others similarly obsessed, until in 1963 he and his new friends, though
scattered across the United States, decided to form a society,
to which they gave the not wholly happy title of the Titanic
Enthusiasts of America. Next, with Kamuda as editor in
chief, the enthusiasts started a journal, *The Marconigram.*
The headline on the first story read, "BRISTOL [i.e., Bristol,
England] HAS *TITANIC* LIFEBOAT." The story turned out to
be false, which made Kamuda determined to tighten up his
standards of scholarship. There was another setback when
the Marconi company in London objected to the title, as
it associated them more closely than they would have liked
with the *Titanic.* The enthusiasts accordingly changed the
name to *The Titanic Commutator.* A commutator is a device
used in electric motors and dynamos, but Quartermaster
Hichens incorrectly used the expression instead of the
term inclinometer, which measures a ship's list. The journal's name perpetuates the error. Since few people know
the word the journal is often called *The Titanic Commu-
nicator.* At the start, Kamuda had only forty-five subscribers, only fifteen of whom paid the annual subscription of

$5. He himself was far from rich; and his first issues were crudely produced on a mimeograph machine owned by the National Volunteers, of which he was a member, with Kamuda himself meeting the cost of paper and postage.

But gradually the membership grew and more subscribers paid their subscriptions, and the society began to acquire *Titanic* relics, usually from survivors. One of the events that shocked Kamuda into starting the society was his discovery, after a survivor died in New York, that his collection of memorabilia had been thrown out, dumped in the city garbage. The society's greatest coup was to secure the lifebelt worn by the pregnant Mrs. Astor when she was rescued. The story goes, according to Mr. Kamuda, that when she was being hoisted out of the lifeboat by one of the *Carpathia*'s crew she promised him $5,000 for helping her. Either the promise was never made or it slipped Mrs. Astor's mind after she climbed aboard and was welcomed in the captain's cabin with other rich, first-class female passengers. In any event, all her rescuer got was the lifebelt, which he took home to Michigan and stowed in a closet. Sixty-seven years later, in New York, his son learned about the Enthusiasts on the radio and, after some negotiations, gave the lifebelt to them. These days it can be studied at close quarters in a glass case at the Philadelphia Maritime Museum, where it forms part of a permanent *Titanic* exhibit.

The fact that this exhibit is in Philadelphia, five hours from Indian Orchard, is proof of the magnanimity of Mr. Kamuda and the other officers of what is now, following a prudent change of name, the Titanic Historical Society. A few years ago they began to consider the idea that rather than keeping their *Titanic* collection in their own widely scattered homes, they ought to turn it over to a properly equipped museum for safekeeping. Their choice for this honor was the relatively new Philadelphia Maritime

Museum, which had been set up through the enthusiastic
support of a well-connected Philadelphia lawyer, Welles
Henderson. He had acquired an old building in the his-
toric heart of Philadelphia, next to the site of Benjamin
Franklin's house, and with civic help equipped it with the
most up-to-date filing and storage systems, as well as tight
security and controlled temperatures. Here now is by far
the best collection anywhere of *Titanic* books, audio tapes,
films, videos, photographs, cassettes, letters, and objects.*

The objects are not numerous, but few visitors to the
museum fail to be affected by them. Mrs. Astor's lifebelt, the
label reads, was "presented by Dr. Gottlieb Rencher, senior
attendant-in-charge to the surgeon of the *Carpathia*. The
imprint of the manufacturer, 'Fosbery, London,' is faintly
visible over the cloth covering over the cork blocks." The
cloth is a rusty brown. The lifebelt rests on a wooden deck
chair with a broken straw back; this was not a first-class deck
chair, since the first-class chairs had wooden slats at the back,
but it might be second-class—although some evidence suggests that second-class deck chairs had slats also. Nearby is
an English silver flask in an alligator leather case given to R.
Norris Williams, the tennis player, by his father. After the
collision, the father felt sure he would not survive and passed
on the flask to his son, advising him to have it filled up. The
barman refused to serve the young Williams on the grounds
that the time was well after midnight and the bar was closed;
so Williams put the flask in his pocket, where he found it
after his father perished and he was rescued.

Other objects turned over to the museum by the society
include a nine-inch piece of wood from a *Titanic* lifeboat seat;
a straight razor once the property of dining-saloon steward

*The fate of the much larger collection of artifacts held by RMS Titanic Inc. is uncer-
tain as of early 2012. Many exhibitions of these and other objects have been held around
the world since Michael Davie's time.—DG

Frederick Ray of Bristol; a bracelet worn by Lillian Black, damaged when she dropped and trod on it in a lifeboat; the discharge book of the lookout who saw the iceberg, Fred Fleet, which, in the column headed "Description of Voyage" says "Intended New York," and elsewhere describes Fleet as five feet eight inches tall, with gray eyes, brown hair, and "dark Indian spots on both hands"; a White Star button from the coat of steward C. W. Fitzpatrick of Southampton; an oblong bread board "believed" to have come from the *Titanic;* a wooden sliver of ship's rail; a menu; writing paper; and a strip of green carpet that a steward squirreled away to take home to show his wife. Most remarkable of all are the relics of Selina Rogers Cook, an Englishwoman who was twenty-two at the time and who died in 1964. She was on her way to visit her sister in the United States, and she not only saved but cherished for the rest of her life two champagne corks, one comb, one coin purse, one wedding ring box from London, one third-class return railway ticket (from Southfields, near Wimbledon, to Walham Green, Hammersmith), the pale blue veil she tied around her head to keep her hat on when she entered the lifeboat, and a tooth that she had had extracted but kept.

Mr. Kamuda has been seeking out and collecting every morsel of *Titanic* information for thirty years, but his appetite is undiminished, stemming, he thinks, principally from the stories of heroism and from the beauty of the doomed ship. His place of work is a museum in itself. When television spoiled the movie-theater business in the 1960s, his father sold the cinema and opened Henry's Jewelry Store directly across the street, in a single-story building shaped like a shoebox, with a dark green side wall and a retractable awning. This is where, since his father's demise, Edward Kamuda spends his time. Inside, among the merchandise—watches, jewelry, greeting cards, photographs of the Pope,

Catholic devotional objects, wineglasses engraved "Bride" and "Groom"—are signs of Mr. Kamuda's passion: cinema posters of every *Titanic* film; postcards of a *Titanic* model at Falls River, Connecticut (with the incorrect inscription "*Titanic,* Southampton" instead of "*Titanic,* Liverpool" painted on its stern), and a photograph of the *Olympic* on its way to the breaker's yard. Prominent also are portraits of Mr. Kamuda's father and mother. His office at the back of the shop is a happy clutter of watch and jewelry repair tools, a Virgin Mary thermometer, a souvenir of the Empire State Building, a color picture of the *Titanic,* a clock with a *Titanic* face, and a penholder attached to a miniature brass ship's wheel, circa 1930.

Mr. Kamuda's society had 2,000 members before the wreck was found in September 1985, and 2,700 soon afterward. Most members live in the United States, but there are at least a hundred in the United Kingdom, forty in Australasia, and others in Germany, France, Holland, Belgium, Norway, and Malaysia. The society has held three conventions: thirty-five people attended the first, and in 1982 six hundred attended the third, held in Philadelphia, where the participants met six of the dwindling band of survivors, listened to speeches, attended a memorial service, and sat down to a banquet featuring Caprice of Fruit Southampton; Poached Breast of Capon White Star with Carpathian Baby Carrots, or Baked Filet of Sole Queenstown with Cape Race Parsley Potatoes; followed by Chocolate Mousse Titanic. The oldest person present was one of the survivors, Edwina Mackenzie, from Hermosa Beach, California, aged ninety-seven. (She died in 1984, aged one hundred, having lived to receive birthday greetings from President and Mrs. Reagan and, via Western Union, Queen Elizabeth; at her funeral the priest referred to her part in the reform of maritime safety laws.)

When Kamuda started writing to *Titanic* survivors—
"our survivors," he sometimes calls them—he did so tentatively, fearing that he might be disturbing memories
which they had tried to forget. Not all of them wished to
be made honorary members of the society, but many were
pleased and grateful. He had a particularly ready response
from the United Kingdom. "They valued the human feelings a little bit more," he said.

One point that had struck me, talking to the descendants of survivors, was that the American children and
grandchildren of the *Titanic* immigrants all seemed to have
moved up in the world—one of them worked for a bank
on the one hundred and eleventh floor of the World Trade
Center in New York—whereas the British descendants of
the crew seemed to have remained in the lowly social stra-
tum occupied by their fathers or grandfathers in 1912. The
point had struck Mr. Kamuda also. In retrospect, Senator Smith's rhetoric about the *Titanic* steerage passengers
who had abandoned the old world for the new because
they no longer regarded endurance as a virtue seemed fully
justified.

I asked Mr. Kamuda, as we sat in his store, what he
felt about the dramatic discovery of the *Titanic* wreck. He
was less enthusiastic than I had expected. Ten years earlier, Kamuda thought that they would never find it; two
years before they did find it, he changed his mind. Now
that his obsession had been located, scrutinized, and photographed, his feelings are mixed. He is afraid that the
Titanic's mystique—the mystery and veneration that have
always surrounded the ship—will somehow be dissipated,
although he is sure that the heroism shown and the beauty
of the ship itself could never be tarnished. His passion, I
felt, was shifting toward the *Titanic*'s sister ship, the *Olympic;* "she was a ship that did her job, yet man broke her up

instead of saving her." There was at least no danger of the *Olympic,* her dignity in tatters, ending up at Disneyland.

It would be unfair to give the impression that Kamuda and his fellow members are merely eccentrics sunk in nostalgia. Nobody could be more up-to-date than the scientist who discovered the *Titanic* wreck, Dr. Robert Ballard, and he was encouraged and given help by Titanic Historical Society members. The American-French expedition he led was based at Woods Hole, Massachusetts, on the southern tip of Cape Cod, which is not far from Indian Orchard.

I arrived there, as it happened, at a time full of depressing echoes for anyone interested in the *Titanic.* Three days earlier the liquid-fuel rockets carrying *Challenger* aloft had exploded in flames off Florida, killing all of the astronauts; it was by far the worst accident in the history of the American space program. It had struck Kamuda, as it must have struck everyone familiar with the *Titanic* story, that there were disturbing parallels between the two disasters. Suddenly in 1986, as in 1912, people felt that man had been taking far too much for granted, putting exaggerated faith in his own powers and believing his technology to be infallible. Some of the leading articles, with the change of a word or two, could have been lamenting not *Challenger* but the *Titanic.* A senior official of the National Aeronautics and Space Administration, which was responsible for the launch, expressed incredulity at what had happened; he had thought such a thing "impossible." P. A. S. Franklin, head of the White Star Line in New York, said much the same thing when he learned that the *Titanic* had sunk. Even the proximate cause of both accidents—cold weather—was the same.

At Woods Hole, I found that Dr. Ballard and the team that had discovered the *Titanic* were "on standby" in case they were needed to search for the remains of *Challenger* in the Atlantic. So was the underwater vehicle used in the

Titanic hunt, the *Argo,* named after the mythological vessel that carried Jason on his quest for the Golden Fleece.

Among the *Titanic, Challenger,* and *Argo* there was a direct link. All three vehicles had to do with "frontier" technology: the conquest of the Atlantic, the conquest of space, the conquest of the ocean floor. Ballard has compared the conquest of the ocean floor to the conquest of space, calling it the "last frontier," and has described another of Woods Hole's underwater vehicles, the *Alvin*—essentially a large shiny silver ball that carries three people—as an undersea space capsule. The word "conquest," in retrospect, seemed misplaced.

While I was wandering around Woods Hole, I detected a further link—a public-relations ingredient common to all three. The size of the *Titanic* was a public-relations exercise in itself, to attract publicity and bookings. NASA had put a woman schoolteacher aboard *Challenger* solely in order to stimulate public interest in the manned space program, and thus to attract public support and funds. Public relations was an element too in the discovery of the *Titanic.* Nothing could have been better calculated to draw attention to the work of Woods Hole and to encourage the funding, both public and private, on which it depends. Most people had never heard of Woods Hole or Dr. Ballard before the discovery of the *Titanic.*

There is yet another link. All three of these technical wonders had a military side. The British government had looked favorably on the building of the *Olympic* and the *Titanic,* as it did on the crack Cunarders, because they would be invaluable assets in the event of war. The space program had explicit military implications. And so did the search for the *Titanic.* Ballard is an ex-Navy man. Woods Hole is partly funded by the Navy. The Woods Hole research vessels and underwater vehicles belong to the Navy; and the Navy gave permission for them to be used to look for the *Titanic* as a good test of underwater technology that the Navy is interested in for reasons entirely unconnected with nostalgia.

Ballard's prime concern is not with the *Titanic,* either. His real interest is in the Mid-Ocean Ridge, the almost entirely unexplored chain of mountains that circles the globe under water like the stitching on a baseball. Unknown before the 1960s, this immense range is said to be 45,000 miles long and to cover no less than 23 percent of the world's surface. Not all of it is under water. It comes out of the Pacific in California, for instance, where it turns into the San Andreas Fault. All of the world's earthquakes are believed to be related to this ridge, and one of the things that concerned Ballard when he was planning the *Titanic* search was the thought that the ship might have been buried by the tumultuous underwater earthquake that severed submarine cables in the area in 1928.

It was not his interest in the Mid-Ocean Ridge, however, but his discovery of the *Titanic* that made Ballard a national, even an international figure. After Piccard and Cousteau, Ballard is the third underwater explorer that the man in the street has heard of. He looks the part: tall, good-looking, and athletic. He is also intrepid, and he easily holds the record for underwater dives. He has made three hundred descents in *Alvin,* sometimes to 13,000 feet—two and a half miles—which is the depth of the *Titanic* wreck. He was born in Kansas in 1942; studied chemistry and geology at the University of California; and went to two graduate schools of oceanography, at the University of Hawaii and the University of Southern California. After that, he spent five years in the armed services, first in Army intelligence and then in the Navy, and later picked up a Ph.D. in marine geology and geophysics at the University of Rhode Island. It was as a naval liaison officer that he first came in contact with Woods Hole.

After the Scripps Institute of Oceanography in California, Woods Hole is the second-largest oceanographic institution in the United States. The staff numbers some nine hundred scientists, several of whom have won the Nobel Prize. Yet, as Woods Hole is no more than a village and the scientific buildings are tucked away, it is rather inconspicuous. Few of the thousands of vacationers who take the Woods Hole ferries in the summer to visit the fashionable offshore islands of Martha's Vineyard and Nantucket—some of them on their way to gaze at the bridge at Chappaquiddick where Senator Edward Kennedy had his accident—realize that they are a quarter of a mile from a scientific powerhouse. In the winter, Woods Hole has a more serious feel, evoking images of Herman Melville and the old whaling stations nearby at Bedford or the islands, and the square clapboard houses at Edgartown, on the Vineyard, where the whaling captains used to live.

The Oceanographic Institute is private, founded in 1930 with three million Rockefeller dollars. It acquired its military connections and expanded greatly during World War II, when among other things it developed anti-fouling paint for ships' bottoms and worked on determining the winds and tides before the Normandy landings. It now carries out every sort of research, from the effect of carbon dioxide buildup in the oceans to aquaculture, plankton distribution, ocean sediments, natural petroleum seeps, salmon ranching, or the use of underwater acoustics. It is organized like a university, with some scientists having tenure, and a board of trustees. Of its $50 million-a-year operating budget, $20 to $25 million comes from the National Science Foundation, $10 million from the Office of Naval Research, and the rest from business.

Dr. Ballard is a senior scientist in the Ocean Engineering Department and head of the Deep Submergence Laboratory, whose mission is to explore the deep-sea floor—less than one tenth of one percent of which has ever been seen by the human eye. Since 1984 Ballard has also been a consultant to the deputy chief of naval operations for submarine warfare. He first became interested in finding the *Titanic* in the early 1970s, purely as a technical challenge, but could find nobody to put up the money. The reason he thought of the *Titanic* was because of a technological advance: *Alvin,* the little three-person submarine, had originally had a steel hull and could dive to 6,000 feet; but then she was given a titanium hull, which enabled her to go down to 13,000 feet—as deep as the presumed site of the *Titanic.* Pursuing his researches into where the ship might be, Ballard came across one of the Titanic Historical Society fanatics, William H. Tantum IV, who persuaded him that the *Titanic* was more than just another wreck. Still, Ballard failed to get backing, as did Tantum, who formed an organization in 1978 called Seaonics International expressly to find and film whatever might be down there.

Tantum died in 1980, and Ballard, while continuing his work on the Mid-Ocean Ridge, had to sit in frustration on the sidelines while a Texas oilman named Jack Grimm mounted three expeditions in search of the *Titanic,* in 1980, 1981, and 1983. Grimm engaged scientists from the Scripps Institute of Oceanography and used an ultrasophisticated research vessel, with first-rate sonar housed in a "fish" towed along the ocean floor. All three expeditions ended in failure (at one point, Grimm was sure he had found the *Titanic*'s propeller, but it was only a rock) and made the whole idea of finding the wreck seem still more outlandish.

Ballard's reaction to Grimm's failures was to conclude that the keys to success for any future expedition must be to spend much more time in the area and to be ready to cover some 150 square miles in case the ship was not where she was supposed to be. To do this would require two months, in Ballard's estimation, and as the appropriate Woods Hole research vessel would be available for only one month a year, he asked the French to collaborate with him—in particular an engineer named Jean-Louis Michel, whom he had come to respect during a joint Franco-American exploration of the mid-Atlantic ridge by submersible in 1973–74. Apart from the Americans, the Russians, the French and the Japanese are most advanced in underwater technology, and Michel worked for the Institut Français de Recherche pour l'Exploitation de la Mer, a French government organization based in Toulon. With Michel working with him, Ballard would have a French research vessel at his disposal to do the preparatory exploration of the targeted area in the search for the *Titanic*.

This time, the U.S. Navy agreed to Ballard's request for aid—his third—because the technology that Ballard proposed to use was new and untried and, if successful, could have valuable military applications. One reason why the Navy is interested in the inventions of Ballard's team is obvious, considering the list of maritime nuclear accidents. The nuclear submarine USS *Thresher* was lost off Cape Cod in 1963; she was found and photographed at some 8,000 feet, scattered in pieces. In 1968 a Russian submarine armed with nuclear weapons exploded and sank 750 miles northwest of Hawaii, at a depth of three miles. A month later another nuclear submarine, the USS *Scorpion,* sank near the Azores. The Russians failed to find their submarine, but the Americans found her, surreptitiously, and raised her a reported 5,000 feet before she snapped and dropped back to the ocean floor. Bits of the *Scorpion* were photographed at 10,000 feet. A more alarming event occurred in January 1966, when as a result of a midair collision over Spain several H-bombs fell on land and one into the Mediterranean.

The bombs on land were soon found; to find the one in the sea the U.S. Navy called in Woods Hole and *Alvin*. After a month's search *Alvin* was successful, using a "deep submersible"—the Reynolds Aluminum Company's *Aluminaut,* designed to operate at 15,000 feet—to retrieve it. "That was when people started taking *Alvin* seriously," says the Woods Hole information manager, Shelly Lauzon.

Like the building of the *Titanic,* the space program, and the military underwater program, the program to recover the *Titanic* was not so much an example of man inventing machines in order to accomplish a necessary task as an example of an undertaking entered into by man as a way of finding something useful for his new machines to do. The French were eager to join in the search for the *Titanic* because they too had new equipment to test: a revolutionary sonar system.

On July 11, 1985, with Ballard aboard, a French research vessel started work, sweeping back and forth across the 150-square-mile search area, plotted by Michel, as if "mowing a lawn" (this became a favorite phrase to describe how the ship was found). The French carried out an "acoustical search," trailing one underwater vehicle able to take soundings in several directions at once, followed by a magnetometer reporting whether objects found by the first vehicle were made of metal or not. Because both vehicles were attached to the parent ship by cable, strong surface currents made their control difficult; and the ship ran into a gale. On August 7, the French search ended; they had found nothing but had "mown" 80 percent of the big square.

In mid-August the Woods Hole (but U.S. Navy-owned) research vessel *Knorr* took over. She is 2,000 tons and 245 feet long, with a satellite navigation system and "cycloidal" propellers that allow her to be driven sideways as well as forward and backward. On board were twenty-six crew and twenty-three scientists, including three Frenchmen led by Jean-Louis Michel. Also on hand was a naval officer from a military establishment in San Diego that operates miniature submarines.

The French search had been acoustical; the American search was visual. The *Knorr's* most important piece of equipment was *Argo,* newly developed by Woods Hole with millions of the U.S. Navy's dollars. The *Argo* is an unmanned search and survey vessel, the size of a small car, which is equipped with high-quality sensors, three cameras in the front, and powerful strobe lights in the back to light up the ocean floor, which at 13,000 feet is in total darkness. It trails behind its parent surface vessel on a cable and has no driving power of its own. The novelty of *Argo* is that unlike previous search vehicles, whether manned or unmanned, it can stay submerged for days—a dramatic improvement.

The terrain that the *Argo* had to inspect was partly canyons, partly mud, and the *Knorr* crew watched with increasing boredom as it sent its pictures back up the cable. There was a monitor screen in the ship's library where the captain of the *Knorr* used to relax when he was not "driving." "I'd watch this camera go along the bottom," Captain Bowen said later, "and look at mud and more mud and sand dunes and a few rocks. Every time we saw something dark come up we'd say, 'Gee, is this it?' This went on for days." The captain was "amazed" that although they were near one of the junction points on the great circle routes that, until a few years ago, ships used to follow religiously (now they use "weather routing"), "there wasn't a lot of junk on the bottom. Seventy-five years of cargo ships dumping hundreds of beer bottles overboard, and passenger liners. It shows how big the ocean is, I suppose. I never saw anything . . . not even a bottle."

Finally, at 1:40 a.m. on the night of September 1 the

dispirited screen-watchers in the control room suddenly saw a shape they thought must be one of the *Titanic*'s gigantic boilers. Someone was sent to wake Ballard. He came rushing into the control room, jumpsuit over his pyjamas, took one look at the screen, and cried, "That's it!" He said later, "It was incredible. All those years and all those efforts and days and days with the French and days and days before and *bang*. There it was." Ballard has a sense of occasion. He led a group to the stern, where he held a short memorial service in memory of the *Titanic*'s 1,496 dead; then he raised a Harland & Wolff flag.

For the next four days Ballard and his associates scarcely slept. The weather window was closing. They "flew" the *Argo* as close to the wreck as they dared, working from the bow toward the stern to avoid the rigging, and then sent down a smaller vehicle to take 35mm color photographs. In four days the cameras shot more than 20,000 frames of film.

The hull of the great ship was more or less upright. With increasing wonder, the crew of the *Knorr* saw strange white objects that they eventually realized must be porcelain dishes; a chamber pot; a tray possibly of silver; wine bottles identified later by their shape as Madeira, port, Bordeaux, and Riesling; a set of bedsprings; a first-class smoking-room tile; lumps of coal; a generator; and a second-class smoking-room window. Ballard said he felt like an archaeologist opening a pharaoh's tomb.

Of the ship's structure, they saw a giant hole left by the forward funnel when it crashed into the sea and nearly killed Lightoller; the bridge; the side of the bridge where Captain Smith had been photographed leaving Queenstown; anchor chains; the forward cranes still in position; bollards that still seemed to be shiny; and empty davits. Captain Bowen found most moving of all the pictures of the crow's nest, with what appeared to be a telephone line dangling out of it, the line down which Fred Lee shouted "Iceberg right ahead!" and got the reply, "Thank you."

When Ballard tried to approach the stern, he was surprised not to be able to find it. On the way back to Woods Hole, examining the film images, he realized that he had seen it after all, but in pieces.★ It was strewn in a "debris field" stretching more than a mile behind the wreck. Going home, after Woods Hole had told the world of the find, the *Knorr*'s radio operator handled a hundred commercial radio calls, forty radio telegraph messages (the radio telegraph, a radio signal sent in Morse code, was still used extensively), eighty-one ham radio calls, and numerous calls from coast stations. Portishead Radio in England called to say they were holding hundreds of calls for the *Knorr*. Ballard was interviewed on radio by ABC, NBC, CBS, and *The New York Times*. At Woods Hole, helicopters whirring overhead, the ship was given a hero's welcome.

What did the discovery reveal? Ed Kamuda surveyed the arguments of seventy-three years. Some had maintained that the liner would have leveled off at 1,000 feet, turned on her side like a falling leaf, and hit the floor at a moderate speed, her masts and funnels snapping off. Others thought she had broken in two and would have hit the bottom at 100 miles per hour, smashing herself to pieces. Still others believed that she would have nose-dived deep into mud, leaving two-thirds of her sticking out almost upright. "Only a few guessed that the ship landed on an even keel, gently, and would be found in pristine condition," Kamuda said in conclusion. The word "pristine," however, turned out to be over-optimistic. Those who said the boilers had smashed down through the ship and

★Ballard was mistaken. The badly damaged stern remains in one piece, about 600 meters from the bow. At least 20 meters of the hull between the two parts disintegrated entirely, creating a debris field linking the two.—DG possibly crashed through the hull were proved right; they had been scoffed at over the years on the grounds that the *Titanic*'s hull was too strong for that.*

Ballard said that he had found the wreck some ten miles farther east than it was supposed to be. He would not reveal the precise location but stated flatly that the position given by the *Titanic* in her distress signals was incorrect. Her navigator thought she was going faster than she was. The indications were, said Ballard, that "a southeasterly current was slowing *Titanic* and putting her off her track."

Why then had Rostron of the *Carpathia* congratulated the *Titanic* navigator on a "splendid" position that enabled him, coming from the southeast, to set a course straight to the lifeboats? Rostron assumed the boats had moved more or less east, whereas in fact they had moved more or less south.

Ballard and his French colleagues concluded, after they found the wreck, that the *Californian* must have been much closer than Captain Lord had claimed. He said eighteen or nineteen miles; Ballard thought the true answer was well under ten miles, and perhaps as little as five. To that, the Lordites instantly replied: if the *Californian* was so close, why—on such a clear night—did not people in the *Titanic* see an unmistakable blaze of lights, and vice versa?

The principal result of the discovery, though, was to raise questions about the *Titanic*'s future, not its past. Could she be salvaged? Grimm, the oilman, had at one time seemed confident that the job could be done; but then he had also seemed confident that expeditions financed by him could find a hole in the North Pole, Noah's Ark in Turkey, the Abominable Snowman in Tibet, and the Loch Ness monster in Scotland. Had Grimm found the *Titanic* on one

---

*Later exploration showed that only five small boilers in the vicinity of the break were dislodged. The remaining twenty-four boilers are in place.—DG

of his three expeditions, he intended to employ robots equipped with blowtorches to cut a hole in the hull and extract any valuables they might come across inside; he would then consider presenting these items to the Smithsonian Institution in Washington, D.C.

Another person who got into the papers by talking about salvaging was an Englishman, Douglas Woolley, who boasted experience as a farmhand, railway signalman, male nurse, and porter in a Ford motor factory. He claimed to be the *Titanic*'s owner, having secured title to the last unliquidated stock share in White Star and a disclaimer from its successor, Cunard. At one time or another he had set up four companies—Seawise and Titanic Salvage Ltd., Titanic Salvage Co., Seawise Salvage Co., and Deftpoint Ltd.—and, with two Hungarian scientists, Ambros Balas and Laszlo Szaskoe, planned to use a bathysphere with mechanical arms to wrap hundreds of plastic containers around the *Titanic*'s hull. They would next pass an electric current through the water inside the containers to break up the water into gases that would lift the ship gently to the surface. Then she would be towed back to Liverpool, refitted, and housed in a dry dock as a maritime museum. To date, Mr. Woolley's plans remain theoretical.

More recently, a salvage engineer in Stamford, Connecticut, proposed packing 180,000 tons of petroleum jelly into polyester bags stowed inside the hull; he has said that the jelly would harden and cause the *Titanic* to become buoyant. John Pierce, a British enthusiast who helped to recover artifacts from the *Lusitania,* spoke of a "giant iceberg" scheme whereby the *Titanic* would be wrapped in a wire net, liquid nitrogen would be pumped through the net, the nitrogen would turn into an iceberg, and the entire package would float to the surface. Pierce also spoke of a simpler-sounding plan of raising the ship by means of giant air bags filled with compressed air—as used to salvage the sabotaged Greenpeace boat, *Rainbow Warrior,* from Auckland harbor in 1985.

In either case, it would be Pierce's intention to take the ship back to Harland & Wolff, restore her to her full 1912 glory, and sail her on another maiden voyage, hoping for better luck next time.

In the view of professional salvage experts, none of these plans would work, nor—at a depth of two and a half miles—would any of the techniques actually employed to raise sunken vessels in the past, such as pontoons, compressed air, or injected polyurethane foam. In any case Dr. Ballard (who is in the exceptional position of knowing where it is) says bluntly, "To raise the *Titanic* is foolish." Lord Grade, after he financed a disastrous film, *Raise the Titanic,* said, "It would have been cheaper to have lowered the Atlantic"; and many people who have considered the costs say much the same about a real-life attempt. William Summers, writing to the London *Times* soon after the discovery of the wreck, put the cost at over £100 million. Summers, a member of the steel-making family of the same name and the person responsible for jacklifting the *Mary Rose* out of the Solent in 1982, pointed out that steel was in its "early manhood" in 1910, and the evidence was that the ship had suffered serious damage in her descent. "This would make complete support of the structure necessary, very much as the *Mary Rose*—but for an 852-foot, 46,329-ton item!" An armada of recovery vessels would be needed to put in place a system of controlling the ascent of such a huge, fragile shell; and the armada would surely run the risk of storm, or indeed icebergs, either during the lift or the laborious tow to shore. Even if the ship could be recovered and put on show, any conceivable revenue would be mopped up by the costs of preventing corrosion.

Scrap steel, he concluded, fetches only £35 to £40 a ton. Captain Bowen has said, "Salvage would be impossible. It would be like trying to lift an old Cape Cod barn with a crane. It would just crumble into a thousand pieces."

Dr. Ballard and all those who helped to find the *Titanic* said as soon as they came ashore that she should be allowed to rest in peace, and so, shortly afterward, did all the survivors and the descendants of survivors whose views were canvassed. But Ballard was not confident that Summers's realism would necessarily deter some of those whose eyes were fixed on the wreck. Even if it became plain to everyone that a salvage operation was a fantasy, greedy treasure-hunters might easily send down instruments to trawl through the wreck and inflict great damage. Nobody, it turned out, not even Mr. Woolley, owned the *Titanic,* and there was no law that could stop anybody from meddling with her.

For these reasons, urged on by Dr. Ballard and survivors, the House of Representatives Merchant Marine and Fisheries Committee approved a bill in November 1985 to "recognize the sanctity of the shipwreck *Titanic* as a maritime memorial," bar Americans from indiscriminate salvage operations, and seek an agreement with other nations, including Great Britain, France, and Canada, "to protect the wreck's scientific, historical, and cultural significance." The Reagan administration supported the bill.

But the discovery of the *Titanic* provoked much wider questions than the future of one old ship. For the first time, the world at large was suddenly made aware of the extraordinary new capabilities of underwater technology. If it was possible not only to find the wreck at a depth of two and a half miles—a feat described by someone at Woods Hole as like dangling a needle into a soda bottle from the top of

the Empire State Building—but to photograph a bottle of
Titanic port as well, what else might be done down there?

Dr. Ballard was on hand to explain, using a new word
to describe the next advance in his science, which is to
establish man's "telepresence" on the ocean floor. He
told the House Merchant Marine and Fisheries Committee that the technology used in finding the *Titanic* was in
the vanguard of the technology that man would soon be
using to project his eyes, ears, and eventually his hands
to the ocean floor. Going to the movies, watching television, using a telephone were all crude forms of "telepresence." Exploration of the ocean floor was not driving the
technology but was benefiting from it. The driving forces
were the space program, with its robots on Mars and Venus;
the commercial world, with its developing television and
cinema techniques; and the military, with "their desire to
remove humans from the risks of combat."

Deep-sea exploration indeed seems to be following the
example of the exploration of space, replacing expen-
sive and not particularly efficient manned vehicles by the
equivalent of unmanned space probes. Ballard's Deep Submergence Laboratory has been developing an unmanned
vehicle named *Jason* that can do everything and more that
has been done over the past fifteen years by their manned
workhorse *Alvin.*

When fully developed, the system will work as follows.
The research vessel will position itself to within a few yards
of where it wants to be by using satellites in "geostation-
ary orbit" 22,000 miles in space. The Global Positioning
System will be plugged into *Argo,* so that it too will know
exactly where it is. *Argo* will conduct a general survey of
the terrain. Then it will be kept still at a height of some
100 meters above the floor. *Jason* then leaves *Argo,* though

still tethered to it, and, equipped with stereo color television and robot arms, zooms in for a close look, picking up samples if required and taking them back for *Argo* to store. Both vehicles can keep up this work for days at a stretch.

Up top, the operator can see what *Jason* sees through its stereo eyes. Simultaneously, he can watch *Jason* through the eyes of *Argo* poised overhead. This is what Ballard means by man being able before long to establish a "telepresence" on the ocean floor.

At great depths, wrecks are preserved as in a giant refrigerator; down there, freezing temperatures and darkness inhibit, where they do not prevent, the biological activity that consumes wood and metal in shallower waters. Around the world, hundreds and hundreds of well-preserved wrecks are "awaiting mankind," Ballard has said. After his *Titanic* triumph, he began to wonder about the chances of finding the most spectacular wrecks of all: the four hundred Roman vessels sunk by a storm after their victory over the Carthaginians in the Second Punic War of 225 B.C.

Ballard is an adviser to the Walt Disney World Company as well as to the U.S. Navy. He is in the strange position of being able to interest them both in the same technology. He imagines that tourists in Orlando, Florida, will one day be able to sit in a capsule and watch direct telecasts relayed via satellite from *Argo* and *Jason* on the ocean floor. At the same time, the technology has implications for hiding submarines carrying nuclear missiles.

Soon after his discovery of the *Titanic,* Ballard took *Argo* on its first scientific expedition. Off the coast of Mexico, he surveyed parts of the East Pacific Rise, looking at recent volcanic activity and hydrothermal vent fields (underwater geysers). Thanks to *Argo,* he saw more of the world's underwater mountain range in a few days than all scientists together had seen of it in the previous decade.

Then, in the summer of 1986, he led another Woods Hole expedition to look at the *Titanic,* and this time descended in person, aboard *Alvin,* to inspect the wreck with his own eyes. "It was like landing on the moon," he said. He and his two fellow explorers took with them a junior version of *Jason,* essentially a two-foot-long robot camera, powered by jets and attached to *Alvin* by cable. Using a remote-control joystick, the *Alvin*'s crew maneuvered the camera down the layers of tangled metal that had once been the grand staircase and then into a room where it photographed an elaborate light fixture suspended from the ceiling. The hull of the liner was coal black on the outside, but inside it had been turned into a brilliant rusty panorama of red, orange, and yellow. In the "debris field" astern of the wreck, the crew saw, among other objects, a lavatory bowl, three safes, and a chair. As on his first expedition, Ballard made an appropriate gesture, leaving on the liner's deck a plaque in memory of those who died.

Back in Woods Hole, he reported his principal finding: that he had seen no evidence of any gash in the starboard side. He had, on the other hand, seen very clear evidence of where the plates had "popped," leading him to think that the fatal damage was really caused by separation of the plates. This discovery was unexpected. It did not invalidate any of the conclusions about the reasons why the ship sank, but it certainly raised further doubts about the efficiency of her construction. Once again, the *Titanic* had lived up to expectations as a source of wonder and surprise, and once again it had confounded the experts.★†

★Since this chapter was written, the wreck has been extensively explored by French and Russian expeditions. Individuals may visit the wreck in Russian submersibles, albeit at great expense. Several thousand artifacts have been recovered, including a large section of the hull plating.—DG

†For up-to-date information on Woods Hole, visit http://www.whoi.edu.—DG

11

THE GRAVEYARD OF A LEGEND

For those seeking to recapture the feel of the far-off days when the *Titanic* went down, certain places are especially evocative: the central square in Southampton with its memorial to the engineers; the cracked and empty concrete of the Belfast slipway; the park in New York on the site of the old Straus family farm. But the most evocative place of all is Halifax, Nova Scotia. It is barely mentioned in the voluminous *Titanic* literature. Perhaps what happened there in the aftermath of the sinking is too grisly to have found a ready slot in what has otherwise become a not unenjoyable legend.

Unlike other substantial towns or cities washed by the Atlantic on the northeast American coast, Halifax at once makes the visitor aware of its strong connection with the British Isles. It is named after an earl of Halifax, not the Yorkshire town; and over the years there has been much marrying of Halifax girls by British soldiers and sailors. One of the town clocks, still going, was erected by Queen Victoria's father, the duke of Kent, who was a stickler for punctuality. The city's chief maritime distinction is that it gave birth to the transatlantic shipping business, as the most successful Haligonian of all was Samuel Cunard. The great shipping line shut its office here in the 1960s, defeated by jet aircraft, but the dark green tankers of the S. Cunard Company—an oil and gas firm started by one of Samuel's sons—are still to be seen filling up the central heating tanks of Halifax citizens. In addition, there is an imposing pair of gates that survives from an old Cunard residence; a Cunard Street; and, at the Holiday Inn, a Cunard Room for functions.

Although Halifax today, with a population of 290,000, is four times as big as it was in 1912 and has the usual quota of high-rise office blocks, it has not changed beyond recognition. It is an architectural historian's hunting ground of styles and fusions of different cultures—British, French, American. Government House is a magnificent Georgian mansion; so is the parliament building. Some of the Georgian houses during the nineteenth century were crowned with French mansard roofs. There are many New England–style white clapboard houses and a profusion of churches, including an old Protestant church in midtown, St. Paul's, built in the best New England manner, which is the only church in the world, it is safe to say, to contain a stained-glass window that commemorates a clergyman who was blown through a church window. He was one of those killed in the great and terrible Halifax explosion of 1917, when two ships, one of them carrying TNT, collided, causing 2,000 deaths and 8,000 injured—the largest manmade explosion, according to local historians, before the atomic bomb.

Historically, the importance of Halifax as a frontier post and fortress, and later as a commercial and military city, arose from its harbor, which is long, narrow, and safe, and one of the best harbors in the world. As elsewhere these days, from Liverpool to Baltimore to Melbourne, the old port, its warehouses made unnecessary by containers, is being tastefully refurbished with harborside hotels, seafood restaurants, museums, restored shops, and boutiques. But the waterfront is still busy and still a naval base; and it is not difficult, with the help of the maps and small displays of *Titanic* relics in the museums and public archives, to think oneself back to 1912, when Halifax witnessed the last and saddest scenes in the *Titanic* drama. More Haligonians knew the North Atlantic in those days than they do now: a thousand fishing vessels then operated out of Halifax. They were the inheritors of a tradition that stretched back to the seventeenth century, when the French fished the Newfoundland Banks for cod, using hand-held lines, each man protected against the wind by an individual canvas windshield.

Halifax was part of the *Titanic* story from the beginning, as it was the site of a shore wireless station that relayed messages from ships at or near the scene of the disaster. At one moment a wild rumor circulated that the *Titanic* had not sunk but was being towed in the direction of Halifax and would be beached on Sable Island nearby, where she would disembark her passengers before being towed on to Halifax harbor.

It was to Halifax that the White Star company turned to collect the Titanic corpses. For hours after the sinking, it was hoped against hope that some ship or ships other than the *Carpathia* had picked up survivors; but gradually a dreadful fact had to be faced: some 1,500 men, women, and children were still out in the Atlantic. The fact was all the grimmer because survivors' accounts agreed that although there had been a shortage of lifeboats, there had been no shortage of lifebelts; the overwhelming majority of passengers and crew had been wearing them. The corpses would be still floating.

White Star chartered a cable ship, the *Mackay-Bennett,* to recover as many bodies as she could. She sailed on April 17 (the day Sir Rufus Isaacs bought his Marconi shares), loaded with a hundred coffins, embalming fluid, the leading local undertaker, John Snow of Snow & Co., and the Reverend Canon Kenneth Hind of All Saints Cathedral. Fog and squalls made her task difficult, but at dawn on the third day bodies were sighted and, although heavy seas were running, boats were lowered. Fifty one bodies were recovered that day, and, after a service by Canon Hind, twenty-four buried at sea, because they were badly decomposed. During the day, it was later reported, the ship's company sighted a woman's red skirt tied to an oar. A photograph shows one of the *Mackay-Bennett*'s boats, with four men at the oars, in the act of hauling a body aboard.

As each corpse reached the parent ship, the purser filled in a careful list: male or female, appearance, estimated age, clothing, effects. Each body was tagged with a number, and the effects, if any, were put into separate canvas bags. Bodies not buried at sea were embalmed and laid out in coffins or canvas shrouds on deck. By Thursday, April 25, White Star had sent another ship, the *Minia,* to relieve the *Mackay-Bennett,* and the next day, following a joint search, the *Mackay-Bennett* set course for home, "having as many on board as we could look after," as the captain later explained. He and his crew had recovered 306 bodies and had buried at sea 116 of them. The *Minia* stayed on until May 3, in bad weather; she recovered 17 bodies and buried 2 at sea. One of those brought back by the *Minia* was Charles M. Hays, president of the Canadian Grand Trunk Railroad, whose last known conversation was with his fellow Canadian, Major Peuchen, when he told him, after the collision, that "this boat is good for eight hours." Two other ships sent to join the search found only five more bodies.

In Halifax, arrangements for the return of the *Mackay-Bennett* were drawn up with care and reverence. The authorities were aware of the turmoil that had accompanied the *Carpathia*'s arrival in New York. It was accordingly decided that the ship would dock at a jetty protected on the landward side by a ten-foot brick wall with only two gates. Twelve extra police were brought in from Ottawa to man the gates; the usual guards were doubled. Press and photographers were to be strictly controlled. Up the hill, in the middle of the city, the Mayflower Curling Rink was converted into a temporary mortuary and heavily draped in black. The city's flags flew at half-mast.

The *Mackay-Bennett* sailed slowly into the Halifax approaches on the overcast morning of April 30, after almost two weeks at sea. Thousands lined the shore in silence, the men with their heads bared. The crowd could see bodies laid out on the foredeck and coffins piled high in the stern. Naturally, the big international wire services had sent squads of reporters and technicians to get the first news about which bodies had been recovered; they had erected their own wireless mast. However, a Halifax *Chronicle* reporter, Jim Hickey, had had the foresight before the *Mackay-Bennett* sailed to make a private arrangement with Canon Hind. As the ship approached, the cooperative clergyman tossed a list of names down to Hickey, who had come alongside in a hired tug. Back ashore, the reporter ran two blocks up the street to the *Chronicle* office; the local man's enterprise is still remembered in Halifax as the *Chronicle*'s one world scoop.

After the ship was secured, one of the first people up the gangway was Captain Roberts, the captain of Colonel J. J. Astor's yacht.

The bodies were carried down the gangway in canvas stretchers by the ship's crew and handed to the undertakers, whose horse-drawn hearses stood on the jetty. Snow & Co. had brought in forty extra undertakers and embalmers from all over the Maritime Provinces. Bodies not in coffins were put in coffins; then the hearses set off slowly to the curling rink. A reporter noted with surprise that only about a hundred people had assembled on the jetty and that onlookers were few on the streets between the jetty and curling rink.

At the rink, friends, relatives, and agents identified and claimed the dead. A young Widener from Philadelphia thought at first that he had found his father, but it was his father's valet wearing his father's coat; the *Chronicle* added that the underclothing was "not of the texture" worn by Widener senior. Upstairs at the rink there was a temporary coroner's office. Certificates of death and burial permits were issued for each body, but formalities were reduced to a minimum. The railroads made special arrangements for the transport of coffins; they could be sent by express on the payment of two first-class fares.

The purser's lists needed remarkably little revision. The lists were quickly printed; and one of them, divided into two parts, on folio sheets with a crumbling brown-paper cover, survives in the possession of Russ Lownds, whose father was the chief accountant on the staff of the White Star agents in Halifax.

These lists make poignant reading, especially in the presence of a man who says, "They came from my dad." I found that I first searched instinctively for J. J. Astor, as no doubt many others, for similarly vulgar motives, had searched seventy-odd years before. I wanted to see if it was true, as the legend tells, that his body was identified by the amount of money he carried. There it was: No. 124.

MALE; ESTIMATED AGE, 50; LIGHT HAIR AND MOUSTACHE.
CLOTHING—Blue serge suit; blue handkerchief with
"A.V."; belt with gold buckle; brown boots with red rubber
soles; brown flannel shirt; "J.J.A." on back of collar.
EFFECTS—Gold watch; cuff links, gold with diamond;
diamond ring with three stones; £225 in English notes;
$2,440 in notes; £5 in gold; 7s. in silver; 5 ten-franc pieces;
gold pencil; pocketbook.
FIRST CLASS.   NAME—J. J. ASTOR.

So he was identified not by his money but by the initials
on the back of his collar, a humdrum clue to identity. The
diamond ring was a surprise; would a rich Englishman of
the time have worn anything similar? Who was "A.V."?
Colonel Astor's body was one of the first to leave Halifax. His young son and heir, Vincent; his lawyer, Nicholas
Biddle; and the captain of his yacht had all come up from
New York in a private railway car named *Oceanic.*★
Next on the list I read "FEMALE; ESTIMATED AGE, 22; DARK
BLACK HAIR. CLOTHING—Blue dress and blouse; black shoes.
EFFECTS—Purse with miniature photo; key; few coins;
photo locket. No marks on body or clothing. Probably
third class."
And probably Irish, I thought. I remembered that Law-
rence Beesley, compiling a list of third-class survivors
aboard the *Carpathia,* noticed that whereas all the Swed-

★In his will, Colonel Astor left the two children from his first marriage, Vincent and
Alice, $87 million and $5 million, respectively. He left his second wife, Madeleine,
$1,695,000, and his unborn son, who became John Jacob Astor VI, a trust fund of
$3 million, with $5 million when he came of age. Madeleine Astor was married again,
in 1919, to a stockbroker named William Dick; and for a third time, in 1931, to an Italian boxer named Enzo Fiermonte. Six years later she committed suicide. John Jacob
Astor VI married three times; when his half-brother Vincent died in 1960, leaving $129
million divided between the Vincent Astor Foundation and Brooke Astor, his third wife,
"Jack" Astor contested the will, but without success.

ish immigrants had brought money away from the *Titanic,* none of the Irish girls had a penny.

Another entry, obviously an aspiring immigrant: Leslie Gelinski. His estimated age was thirty, and he had been carrying when he drowned a primer of the English language.

Almost every entry prompted speculation. "E. Gilbert Dambon: gold watch and chain; opal and ruby ring; bracelet; lady's watch and chain; solitaire diamond ring; check for $1,315.79, Security Bank, Sioux City, Iowa. Jewel case. $266 in notes. $30.00 in gold."

Was E. Gilbert Dambon a real name?★ It sounded invented. He was carrying a lot of money for someone in steerage. Since the third class return rate to Europe in the *Titanic* was advertised by White Star as $36.25, E. Gilbert Dambon had enough cash on him for sixteen crossings. If he had been a migrant, despite the unlikely name, he would scarcely have been carrying a check for more than a thousand dollars drawn on a bank in Sioux City. He must have been an American.

Another entry was bleak: Estimated age, 30; blue suit; no marks; brown hair and moustache; no effects.

Another immigrant: Female, about 25; hair fair. Sum of 150 Finnish marks sewn into clothing.

The saddest of all was No. 328. Four foot six inches. Age about 14. Hair golden brown. Marks: very dark skin, refined features. Lace-trimmed red-and-black overdress, black underdress, green-striped undershirt, black woollen shawl and felt slippers. Probably third-class passenger.

But there was one mystery that puzzled Halifax citizens then and continues to puzzle the public archivists now.

★Ernst Gilbert Danbom (not Dambon) was genuine. He was lost with his wife and son. He had ample money because he was an American agent for White Star and was paid for persuading Swedish emigrants to travel on its ships.

There were two people with Halifax connections aboard the *Titanic*. One, a Miss Slayter, survived (she complained about the number of crew who had been saved in comparison with the number of passengers who had been drowned). The other was George Wright, a very prominent local figure, rich and exceptionally well-traveled. He was a big man, who wore a moustache with waxed tips. He had made a fortune as a developer; there is a street in Halifax named after him. He was a leading local yachtsman, the owner of a fifty-seven-foot boat, a winner of yachting cups, at home on the sea. He was also mildly eccentric: he objected to what he regarded as the growing vulgarity and lewdness of language and campaigned against Puccini's opera *The Girl of the Golden West,* thinking it improper. He was a local benefactor, a pioneer of trade directories and amateur photography—all in all, the sort of man that strangers noticed. He liked to travel in the latest and best and he took the *Titanic;* at least, his name is on the first-class passenger list. Yet none of the survivors mentioned meeting or seeing him, and he was not among those brought back to Halifax. A friend of his said he could only think that, as a heavy sleeper, he had never woken up.

Besides this list of the drowned, Halifax possesses a good crop of other Titanic memorials and relics. Captain de Cartaret of the *Minia* salvaged from the floating wreckage the one surviving object, so far as I am aware, that must convince the most skeptical that the interminably repeated assertions about the *Titanic*'s luxuriousness are true. This is a piece of wood, two and three-quarters feet long and one foot wide, elaborately carved in baroque Grinling Gibbons style with motifs of seeds, berries, leaves, and birds. It is not veneer but carved in one piece. "You would need to be an expert to be confident that this wasn't seventeenth-century but early twentieth-century," said the archivist who showed it to me. Any amateur would certainly assume he was holding a decorative fragment of a Wren church altarpiece or organ casing. Where it fitted into the *Titanic* the archivists do not know, despite intensive study of contemporary photographs. They think it might have been part of the main stairway.

The Maritime Museum owns a *Titanic* steamer (or deck) chair: slatted, heavy, well-made. A vandal has stolen the brass frame on the back that once held a passenger's visiting card. Some people in Nova Scotia own another *Titanic* steamer chair that they use in summer on the lawn. The Maritime Museum chair is definitely authentic. Yet the surprise is that so few *Titanic* items survive. Among the most moving of them are the letters in the Halifax archives from relatives of the drowned. One of them is a letter of July 1912 from Mr. C. Jupe of 74 Buller Road, Southampton, barely literate, stamped "Received Jul 20 Provincial Secretary's Office":

Dear Sir I have been inform by Mr. F Blake Superintendent Engineer of the White Star Line Trafalgar Chambers on the 10th that the Body of my Beloved Son Herbert Jupe which was Electrical Engineer No. 3 on the Ill-Fatted Titanic has been recovered and Burried at Sea by the Cable Steamer "Mackey-Bennett" and that his Silver Watch and Handkerchief marked H.J. is in your Possesion. He bought him half a doz of the same when he was at Belfast with the R.M.S. Olympic to have a new blade put to one of her Perpellors we are extremely oblidged for all your Kindness to my Precious Boy. He was not married and was the Love of our Hearts and he loved his Home But God gave and God has taken Him Blessed be the Name of the Lord. He has Left an Aceing Void in our Home which cannot be filled.

Please Send along the Watch and Handkerchief marked
H.J.
> Yours Truly C. Jupe.
> His Mother is 72 Last april 4th.
> His Father is 68 Last Feb 9th.

Russ Lownds possesses a framed receipt from the provincial secretary's office that he inherited from his father.
Dated April 30, 1912, it confirms that the provincial secretary has received from Mr. Lownds, agent of the White
Star Line, 245 canvas bags "alleged to contain valuables
belonging to persons drowned off the Titanic." Herbert
Jupe's watch and handkerchief would have been returned.
But what happened to the unclaimed canvas bags and their
contents? The public archivists think they may still exist,
mislaid in some government vault.

The unclaimed bodies, 150 in all, were buried in Halifax: 121 in the Protestant cemetery, Fairview Lawn; 19 in
the Catholic cemetery, Mount Olivet; and 10 in the Jewish cemetery, the Baron von Hirsch. An unseemly dispute
broke out between Christians and Jews about the proper
destination of some of the bodies; 4 bodies removed to the
Jewish cemetery were discovered to be Roman Catholics.

Fairview Lawn Cemetery lies in a suburb on a slight
wooded slope some two and a half miles or so from the
jetty where the *Mackay-Bennett* docked, and almost within
sight of it, on the seaward side of one of the arms that open
out into the harbor approaches. Extensive railway yards are
visible nearby. The *Titanic* graves are arranged in straight
rows, mostly small low gravestones with the surnames,
where known, in bold plain letters across the beveled tops.

In this sad, anonymous place, I reflected again on the
nature of the *Titanic* story and its extraordinary pertinacity.

Why was it that interest in the *Titanic* survived, while a no less destructive event, the Halifax disaster of 1917, was all but forgotten? George Bernard Shaw, in his dispute with Arthur Conan Doyle in the correspondence columns of the *Daily News and Leader* during May 1912, was the first person to dare to express exasperation at the public reaction to the catastrophe. Why had it cast the British into "an explosion of outrageous romantic lying"? Shaw thought that the nation, led by the press, had misconstrued the real events. The captain had been turned into a superhero. The officers had been portrayed as "calm, proud, steady, unmoved in the intervals of shooting terrified foreigners." The passengers—at least, the Anglo-Saxon passengers—had been praised for facing death without a tremor. Yet the truth was, Shaw wrote, that the captain was reckless, and the officers had not only been so afraid of a panic among the passengers that they had not dared to reveal that the ship was sinking until it was too late, but they also had failed to ensure that the boats that were not full went back to the rescue of those struggling and dying in the water. "Here is a calamity which might well make the proudest man humble, and the wildest joker serious. It makes us vainglorious, insolent and mendacious. . . . The effect on me was one of profound disgust, almost of national dishonour."

Conan Doyle replied by accusing Shaw of deliberate misrepresentation and perversity. Captain Smith had made a terrible mistake but had given his life in reparation. There was no evidence that the officers had failed in their duty. "As to the general accusation that the occasion has been used for the glorification of British qualities, we should indeed be a lost people if we did not honour courage and discipline when we see it in its highest form. That our sympathies extend beyond ourselves is shown by the fact that the conduct of the American male passengers, and very particularly of the much abused American millionaires, has been as warmly eulogized as any single feature in the whole wonderful epic."

Both Shaw and Conan Doyle were right. To be sure, the event was outrageously romanticized. Yet, for whatever reason, many passengers and members of the crew, perhaps most, behaved with dignity—in some instances, no doubt, because they did not fully realize their danger; and some of those aboard showed a heroic sense of duty— for instance, the engineers. It was true, in the most direct way, that these men laid down their lives that others might live. The same could probably be said of others, if we only knew. Besides those of the engineers, the reputations of the members of the orchestra, of Phillips the Marconi operator, and of Astor, the Strauses, Gracie, Andrews, Lightoller, Father Byles, and Captain Rostron survive wholly intact, as undamaged after seven decades as the chandelier discovered by Dr. Ballard.

Perhaps the explanation of the story's power is that a series of extraordinary and precise visual images—the men in evening dress, the band playing ragtime, the ice on deck, the vertical sinking leviathan, the shrieking people in life-jackets—are not matched by equally precise information about how the bulk of the *Titanic*'s complement of 2,000 people behaved when the crisis struck. Thus room is left for individual imaginations to go to work. How, we wonder, would we ourselves have behaved during those dire hours? As Shaw asked, "Who of us at home . . . feel sure that we should have been any braver or cooler?"

In a graveyard, no explanations are offered. Some of the inscriptions at Fairview Lawn are brief. One of them says, "John Law Hume, Died, April 15, 1912." He was the violinist in the *Titanic*'s orchestra. J. Fred Clarke, the bass player, is buried in the Roman Catholic cemetery.

Two gravestones in the Fairview cemetery have longer inscriptions than the others. One says: "In Memoriam Ernest Edward Samuel Freeman, last surviving son of Capt. S. W. Kearney Freeman, R. N., Husband of Laura Mary Jane Freeman Lost in the 'Titanic' disaster April 15, 1912. He remained at his post of duty, seeking to save others, regardless of his own life and went down with the ship. Erected by Mr. J. Bruce Ismay to commemorate a long and faithful service." One wonders whether Ismay wrote this inscription himself. The last few words have become obscured, but Russ Lownds one day in his garage pulled out a box packed with old glass photographic plates belonging to his father, and one of them was of the Freeman stone; it showed the complete wording.

Another inscription, commemorating a trimmer, reads: "Sacred to the memory of Everett Edward Elliott of the heroic crew S.S. 'Titanic' died on duty April 15, 1912. Aged 24 years.

> Each man stood at his post
> While all the weaker ones
> Went by, and showed once
> More to all the world
> How Englishmen should die."

There is also a special gravestone, taller than the rest, "erected to the memory of an unknown child whose remains were recovered after the disaster to the Titanic April 15th, 1912." The child, who was two years old, with fair hair, was tentatively identified as one of four children named Paulson who joined the *Titanic* at Southampton with their mother. In 2007, DNA evidence identified the child as Sidney Leslie Goodwin, born on September 9, 1910. He was one of a large family that traveled in third class, none of whom survived.

There is nothing else to see. At the entrance to the cemetery, written on a white wooden board in need of paint, is the one word in capital letters: TITANIC.

BIBLIOGRAPHY

SELECTED SOURCES

Wreck Commissioner's Court. Formal Investigation into the Loss of the SS Titanic. Evidence, Appendices, and Index. London: HMSO, 1912.

Shipping Casualties (Loss of the Steamship Titanic). Report of a Formal Investigation into the circumstances attending the foundering on 15th April, 1912, of the British Steamship Titanic of Liverpool, after striking ice in or near Latitude 41° 46' N. Longitude 50° 14' W., North Atlantic, whereby loss of life ensued (Cd. 6352). London: HMSO, 1912.

U.S. Congress, Senate, Hearings of a Subcommittee of the Senate Commerce Committee pursuant to S. Res. 283, to Investigate the Causes leading to the Wreck of the White Star liner Titanic, 62d Cong., 2d sess., 1912, S. Doc. 463 (6179). Washington, D.C.: Government Printing Office.

U.S. Congress, Senate, Report of the Senate Committee on Commerce pursuant to S. Res. 283, Directing the Committee to Investigate the Causes of the sinking of the Titanic, with speeches by William Alden Smith and Isidor Rayner, 62d Cong., 2d sess., 28 May 1912, S. Rept. 806 (6127). Washington, D.C.: Government Printing Office.

These are the four indispensable sources of information about the *Titanic*.

Young, Filson. *Titanic*. London: Grant Richards, 1912. Useful guide to contemporary attitudes.

Gibbs, Philip. *The Deathless Story of the Titanic*. London: Lloyds Weekly News, 1912. Contains early lists of the crew, those saved, and those drowned.

Beesley, Lawrence. *The Loss of the SS Titanic: Its Story and Its Lessons*. London: Heinemann, 1912. One of the basic texts, written with an earnest desire to be fair and accurate.

Bullock, Shan F. *A Titanic Hero: Thomas Andrews, Shipbuilder*. Dublin and London: Maunsel, 1912.

Gracie, Archibald. *The Truth about the Titanic*. New York: Mitchell, Kennerley, 1913. The best of the contemporary accounts.

Lightoller, C. H. *Titanic and Other Ships*. London: Nicholson and Watson, 1935. Primary source, both for the disaster and for an honest man's attitude to pre-*Titanic* navigational practices.

Mersey, Viscount. *A Picture of Life, 1872–1940*. London: John Murray, 1941. Contains a valuable account of the background and character of the first Lord Mersey.

Lord, Walter. *A Night to Remember*. New York: Holt, Rinehart, & Winston, 1955. Racy and dramatic account of the disaster itself, and much criticized by the supporters of Captain Lord.

Oldham, W. J. *The Ismay Line*. Liverpool: Journal of Commerce, 1961. Primary source on Ismay father and son; it includes letters written by J. Bruce Ismay not available elsewhere.

Padfield, Peter. *The Titanic and the Californian*. London: Hodder, 1965. Impassioned defense of Captain Lord, showing that the story was more complicated than either the Senate or the British inquiries supposed.

Mercantile Marine Service Association. *The Californian Incident; text of second petition addressed to the President of the Board of Trade*.

Liverpool, 1968. Contains Beesley's statutory declaration of February 1963.

Marcus, Geoffrey. *The Maiden Voyage.* London: George Allen and Unwin, 1969. Particularly useful on wireless operations; fiercely critical of the Board of Trade inquiry's "whitewash." Marcus has no doubt about Lord's culpability.

Wade, Wyn Craig. *The Titanic: End of a Dream.* New York: Rawson, Wade, 1979. Corrective, written by a Michigan psychologist, to the view that the American inquiry was, in Lightoller's words, "a complete farce."

Stenson, Patrick. *"Lights": The Odyssey of C. H. Lightoller.* London: The Bodley Head, 1984. Careful account of an adventurous life, which helps to explain the attitudes of the *Titanic*'s officers.

Watson, Arnold, and Betty Watson. *Roster of Valor: The Titanic-Halifax Legacy.* Riverside, Conn.: 7 C's Press, 1984. Contains a revised alphabetical list of the *Titanic*'s crew, addresses, and jobs.

Lord, Walter. *The Night Lives On.* New York: William Morrow, 1986. A series of essays by the leading student in the field in which he tackles some of the questions that have puzzled him since he wrote *A Night to Remember* in 1955. Of particular interest are his researches into the tune played by the band and the fate of the steerage passengers.

The Titanic Commutator, published quarterly by the Titanic Historical Society, Inc., P.O. Box 53, Indian Orchard, Massachusetts 01151-0053, is the essential modern source of *Titanic* information. The spring 1983 issue contains the results of research in Halifax, Nova Scotia, by John P. Eaton and Charles Haas; the fall 1985 issue describes the discovery of the *Titanic* and includes detailed interviews by Karen Childs with Dr. Ballard and Captain Bowen of the research vessel *Knorr.*

Oceanus, the journal of the Woods Hole Oceanographic Institution, vol. 28, no. 4, contains accounts and pictures of the discovery of the *Titanic,* and includes Dr. Ballard's statement before the House Merchant Marine and Fisheries Committee of October 29, 1985.

The National Geographic Magazine of December 1985 contains a firsthand account of the search for the *Titanic* written by Dr. Ballard and Jean-Louis Michel.

Readers interested in more recent books on the *Titanic,* may also want to read the following.

Beveridge, Bruce, et al. *Titanic: The Ship Magnificent.* Stroud, UK: The History Press, 2010.

Biel, Steven. *Down with the Old Canoe.* New York: W. W. Norton & Company, 1996.

Caren, Eric, and Steve Goldman. *Extra-Titanic.* Chartwell Books, 1998.

Gittins, Dave. *Titanic: Monument and Warning.* Available as an eBook at http://titanicebook.com/index.html.

Halpern, Sam, et al. *Report into the Loss of the SS Titanic: A Centennial Reappraisal,* Stroud, UK: The History Press, 2012.

Hyslop, Donald, Alastair Forsyth, and Sheila Jemina. *Titanic Voices: Memories from the Fateful Voyage.* New York: St. Martin's Press, 1999.

Lord, Walter. *The Night Lives On.* New York: William Morrow and Co., 1986.

McCaughan, Michael. *The Birth of the Titanic.* Montreal: McGill-Queen's University Press, 1999.

O'Donnell, E. E. *Father Browne's Titanic Album.* Dublin: Wolfhound Press, 1997.

Reade, Leslie. *The Ship That Stood Still.* New York. W. W. Norton & Company, 1993.

—Dave Gittins

APPENDIX
THE POSITION OF THE WRECK

As can be seen in Chapter 10 of this book, early information about the wreckage was misleading. When it came to rest, *Titanic* did not retain two funnels, nor was its stern totally in pieces. These errors might be put down to the difficulty of observing the wreck using the limited lighting available to Ballard. His refusal to release the exact position of the wreck was deliberate. Ballard at first said only that the wreck lay about ten miles to the east of the distress position. Secrecy could not last, as too many were aware of the real position, and soon the exact coordinates were revealed.

We now know that the wreck is in two major pieces in the midst of a large debris field. Satellite navigation gives the position of the bow as 41°43'57"N, 49°56'49"W. The stern lies in 41°43'35"N, 49°56'54"W. The position of the stern is considered to mark the place at which *Titanic* sank, as its lack of hydrodynamic form caused it to sink practically vertically. The bow was relatively intact and traveled some distance forward during its sinking. At least 60 feet of the hull between the two sections was totally destroyed.

The wreck lies about 13 nautical miles from the distress position.

Facts since discovered from the wreck cast new light on two main topics, namely, the navigation of *Titanic* and nearby ships as well as the process of the ship's sinking.

NAVIGATIONAL IMPLICATIONS

The Wreck Position

Titanic's distress signals gave her position after striking the iceberg as 41°46'N, 50°14'W. For many years this was generally accepted as correct, partly because of its endorsement by Captain Rostron of *Carpathia,* which had steamed to the wreck scene with apparently unerring accuracy. Evidence for its inaccuracy came from Captain James Moore of *Mount Temple* and Captain Stanley Lord of *Californian,* but both were overlooked in the general adulation of Captain Rostron. Captain Moore had reached the vicinity of the distress position on the morning of April 15, 1912, and found nothing. To his eastward lay a field of ice, beyond which *Carpathia* could be seen picking up *Titanic*'s lifeboats. A longitude observation showed *Mount Temple* lay in about 50°10'W, somewhat east of the longitude of the distress position. *Carpathia* was even farther east and the distress position was obviously wrong. Captain Lord reached the wreck site on the morning of the sinking and later placed the floating wreckage in 50°1'W.

Writers dismissed these anomalies, with the creditable exception of Peter Padfield, in *The Titanic and the Californian* of 1965. However, Padfield lacked the key needed to fully solve the puzzle. This we now have.

An obvious implication of the wreck position is that *Titanic*'s accident occurred only a few miles south of the normal track for New York. Allowing for some south-erly drift on the Labrador Current during the sinking, an inquiry conducted by Britain's Marine Accident Investigation Branch in 1992 determined that *Titanic* stopped in about 41°47'N, 49°55'W. Given the small inaccuracies inherent in the navigation of 1912, this position may be accepted as satisfactory for all practical purposes. It is certainly sufficient to show Captain Smith made no particular effort to avoid the known ice region. Contrary to some accounts, he had followed the usual track within the limits of practical navigation. This was realized by Lord Mersey and his assessors in 1912. In his report, Mersey wrote, "The alteration of the course at 5·50 p m was so insignificant that it cannot be attributed to any intention to avoid ice."

The often repeated claim that *Titanic* was steaming ten miles south of the usual track stems from unreliable testimony from Third Officer Herbert Pitman and Fourth Officer Joseph Boxhall. It was seized on by both plaintiffs and defendant in the British civil claims court. The plaintiffs said it proved Captain Smith was aware of ice. The defense said it proved he did something about it.

The Incorrect Distress Position

With the inaccuracy of *Titanic's* distress position known, the question of how it was arrived at can be considered. Several possible explanations, none of them authoritative, have been proposed.

The position was determined by Joseph Boxhall, acting alone. He allowed a speed of 22 knots "over the ground," which was in line with *Titanic's* known speed during the previous day. He took as his starting point a position obtained by multiple star sights at 7:30 p.m. and calculated the distance run since the sights.

His next task was to convert the distance run to degrees and minutes of longitude and determine the new longitude. The present author has proposed three ways in which he may have gone astray. Using a marine table known as a Traverse Table, he may have taken out figures for a latitude of 48° instead of for 42°, which appears on the same page. He may have made the calculation using spherical trigonometry and logarithms, as taught for the Board of Trade examinations. In this case, using the logarithm of a sine instead of the logarithm of a cosine would produce a similar error. Thirdly, he may have taken as his starting point the customary dead reckoning position made for 8:00 p.m., instead of the more accurate 7:30 p.m. position.

An American researcher, Sam Halpern, has proposed a novel theory. He suggests the 7:30 p.m. position was itself incorrect because an error of one minute was made in the timing of all the evening longitude sights. The present author has checked this idea with a modern master mariner and he agreed it was possible, though officers were aware such an error could be made.

All these possible mistakes would produce an error approximating to the distance proven by the wreck position. However, the truth will never be known. Boxhall may have merely written down an incorrect figure at some point.

Carpathia's Rescue Mission

With the wreck position known, *Carpathia*'s rescue mission can be reassessed. The present author was probably the first to do this, publishing his findings online in 1998.*

From Captain Rostron's evidence, it can be calculated

*For more detail, see http://www.titanicebook.com/carpathia.html.

that he believed he started from 41°10'N, 49°12'W, a point 58 miles from the distress position, and steamed to it on a course of 308° True. This course misses the wreck site by about seven miles, passing well southwest of it.

The answer to this anomaly lies in evidence from Captain Rostron and others. After *Titanic* sank, Joseph Boxhall, in emergency boat 2, periodically fired green hand flares, with the intention of keeping the lifeboats together and attracting a rescuer. Toward the end of his passage, Rostron sighted one of these flares a little off *Carpathia*'s port bow. Had he been on the course he thought he was steering, the flare would have been sighted off his starboard bow, if at all. Furthermore, the flare must have been no more than ten miles away, as can be shown from nautical tables. Rostron thought he was much farther away, as by his reckoning he had only been steaming toward the wreck for slightly more than two hours. It has been shown that he was mistaken in his timing and the sighting was made after about two and a half hours.* *Carpathia* covered about 38–40 miles in that time at a realistic speed of 15 knots. She covered the last ten miles in about forty-five minutes, occasionally slowing and changing course to avoid icebergs. *Carpathia* had started from a point farther east than Rostron calculated and no more than 50 miles from *Titanic*.

Californian and *Titanic*

No *Titanic* topic raises more controversy, hot tempers, and outright rudeness than the question of what the captain and crew of the Leyland Line's freighter *Californian* did or did not do during the night of April 14, 1912.†

---

*See evidence from *Carpathia* passenger Howard Chapin, radio records, and *Titanic* survivor, Mahala Douglas.
†See Chapter 5.

When *Titanic*'s wreck was discovered, some hailed it as a vindication of Captain Stanley Lord. It was about 22 miles from his claimed overnight position. He had claimed the distance was about 19 miles. Therefore the ship seen from *Californian* could not have been *Titanic*. There is another side to the argument and it is not helpful to Captain Lord and his apologists.

In a statement written on board *Californian* at Captain Lord's request, his second officer, Herbert Stone, said he had observed a stationary ship bearing SSE from the stationary *Californian*. If *Californian* was anywhere near the place claimed by Captain Lord, this is the bearing of *Titanic*'s wreck. Moreover, it was on the same side of the ice field that halted *Californian*. The distress position was to the SSW of *Californian* and it was in this direction that Lord steamed on the morning of April 15.

The wreck position does not improve our knowledge of the distance between *Californian* and *Titanic*. It does greatly increase the likelihood that the ship seen from *Californian* was *Titanic*.

THE SINKING REVISED

The American and British inquiries agreed *Titanic* sank intact. This was in spite of rather contradictory reports of the hull breaking in the last stages of the process. There may have been an element of class distinction in this decision. The evidence of officers Charles Lightoller and Herbert Pitman was preferred to that of seamen and passengers. In Britain one of *Titanic*'s designers, Edward Wilding, testified that the hull was strong enough to have withstood the stresses of sinking.

The discovery of the wreck has settled the argument over the breakup, but a good deal of controversy remains, with a few crank theories to boot. There is now broad agreement on a few matters.

At the point when the hull failed, *Titanic* was on the verge of sinking, purely through the weight of water in her forward compartments. This was determined by naval architects C. Hackett and J. G. Bedford and published in the journal of the Royal Institution of Naval Architects in 1996. The fracture of the hull did little to accelerate the sinking.

The hull probably first began to fail at the double bottom, this being in compression. This occurred when the hull was inclined at ten to fifteen degrees, with the propellers clear of the sea. Failure of the sides and upper decks quickly followed and the section immediately forward of the reciprocating engines disintegrated. Five small boilers fell from this area but the twenty-four remaining boilers stayed in place, contrary to the accounts of 1912 and later books. The extreme violence of the event is demonstrated by the separation of the two foremost cylinders from the engines.

The two main parts of the hull fell to the seafloor at a considerable speed. The bow was driven some fifty feet into the mud, decelerating at a rate that left many interior items in place. The stern also dug deep, bending the propeller shafts to the level of G deck, though the rudder remained intact. Much of the stern section was reduced to a tangle of steel plate, probably because compartments imploded under pressure during the descent.

Since 1985 the wreck has been extensively examined. Details are beyond the scope of this book, but a few points are worth mentioning, in view of the amount of misinformation floating about.

In 1996, Paul Mathias of Polaris Imaging used ground-penetrating sonar to obtain images of the damage to the starboard side of *Titanic*'s hull. The results show intermittent narrow gaps in the plating, rather than the legendary three-hundred-foot gash. The images obtained agree fairly well with eyewitness testimony, especially the long gap extending along most of boiler room 6 and into boiler room 5. The total area of the gaps agrees well with calculations made by Harland and Wolff's Edward Wilding in 1912.

Parts of the hull have been recovered, enabling the steel plating to be tested. Much was made of test results published in 1992 which showed that when cooled to around the freezing point the steel was readily fractured by a sharp blow, in what is termed a Charpy V-notch test. "Brittle steel" was for a time a popular hobbyhorse. Less publicity was given to tests performed in 1999 that showed that when bent at a moderate rate the cold steel simply bent, as can be seen on the wreck.

Attention turned to the rivets recovered from the wreck site. Some of these failed because their points failed. (The ends hammered or pressed down by the builders are called points.) Metallurgists discovered that the proportion of slag in the wrought iron rivets, hammered in manually, was higher than would have been ideal. This may have contributed to the iceberg damage, but it should be noted that steel rivets pressed hydraulically also failed.

Argument over details seems likely to continue forever, but the essentials of the sinking appear settled. A hull built to withstand the normal rigors of the North Atlantic failed when confronted by the abnormal.

INDEX